Yiddish Folktales

PANTHEON BOOKS

NEW YORK

PUBLISHED IN COOPERATION WITH

YIVO INSTITUTE

FOR JEWISH RESEARCH

Yiddish Folktales

EDITED BY
BEATRICE SILVERMAN WEINREICH

TRANSLATED BY
LEONARD WOLF

Copyright © 1988 by YIVO Institute for Jewish Research

All rights reserved under International and Pan-American Copyright
Conventions. Published in the United States by Pantheon Books, a division of
Random House, Inc., New York, and simultaneously in Canada by
Random House of Canada Limited, Toronto. Originally published in hardcover
by Pantheon Books, a division of Random House, Inc., in 1988.

All photographs are from the archives of the
YIVO Institute for Jewish Research, New York.

Library of Congress Cataloging-in-Publication Data

Yiddish folktales.
(Pantheon fairy tale and folklore library)
Bibliography: p.
1. Jews—Europe, Eastern—Folklore.   2. Folk literature, Yiddish—
Translations into English.   3. Folk literature, English—Translations from
Yiddish.   4. Folk literature, Yiddish—Europe, Eastern.   I. Weinreich,
Beatrice.   II. Wolf, Leonard.   III. Series: Pantheon fairy tale
& folklore library.
GR98.Y52   1988   398.2'089924047   88-42594
ISBN 0-394-54618-0
ISBN 0-679-73097-4 (pbk.)

Book design by Chris Welch
Manufactured in the United States of America
3456789

For
Nina and Nienke
Stephanie Shifra and Don
Alex and Barbara

Acknowledgments

It is with a wish to honor the memory of the tellers and collectors of the stories and with a sense of privilege that I share these folktales, which managed miraculously to survive the destruction of the community in which they were told.

It is also with a wish to honor the memory of my mentors, Uriel and Max Weinreich, who I felt were constantly looking over my shoulder these past years.

Many colleagues, friends, and family members have helped me along the way. First and foremost, I feel extremely fortunate in having Leonard Wolf as translator-collaborator on this volume. It has been a pleasure to work with him. Many times he would call simply to share his enjoyment and excitement in a group of tales I had sent along for translation. Many times I would call only to express how delighted I was with his marvelous translations.

I am deeply grateful to Samuel Norich, director of the YIVO Institute for Jewish Research, for freeing me from other duties so that I could concentrate on this project, and for his continued support during difficult moments. For their constant and warm words of encouragement and their good advice, I owe a debt of gratitude to my folklorist colleagues Dov Noy, Barbara Kirshenblatt-Gimblett, and Eleanor Gordon Mlotek.

I also want to take this opportunity to thank Sara Bershtel of Pantheon Books for initiating this project and for involving YIVO in it. She and her assistant, Julia Bogardus, together with copyeditors Mary Barnett and Ed Cohen efficiently smoothed out rough edges in the manuscript. And special praise for the fine illustrations goes to the art department at Pantheon.

The library, archival and research staff at YIVO generously gave their assistance whenever called upon. I thank them one and all. My YIVO colleagues David Rogow, Lucjan Dobroszycki, and Zachary Baker earn special mention for helping me put order in the Polish· and Russian spellings of place names. I am also grateful to Sheyndl Fogelman for the skill with which she handled the typing of the Yiddish manuscript, to Shari Davis and Lorin Sklamberg for their technical assistance, and most particularly to Jeff Shandler, who in the last weeks, when time pressures threatened ominously, came to the rescue with research and editorial assistance, always cheerfully given.

And what would I have done without the readiness of good friends like Ulrike Abelson, Rosaline Schwartz, and Kate Resek, who lent a friendly ear whenever I needed to test an idea. Sydney Weinberg, Marcia Vevier, Sylvia McKean, and Eleanor Gordon Mlotek, in addition, were there whenever I asked them to cast a critical eye over a rough draft, and I am particularly grateful to them for this.

I also wish to thank Don, Stephanie, and Barbara Weinreich for their encouragement, patience, and good advice during various steps along the way. Don gets special thanks for all the time he spent teaching me how to use his computer, and for getting two otherwise incompatible computers—Don's and Leonard Wolf's—to "talk" to each other.

And finally, this book would not have been possible without a generous grant to the YIVO Institute from the New York State Council on the Arts.

Beatrice Silverman Weinreich

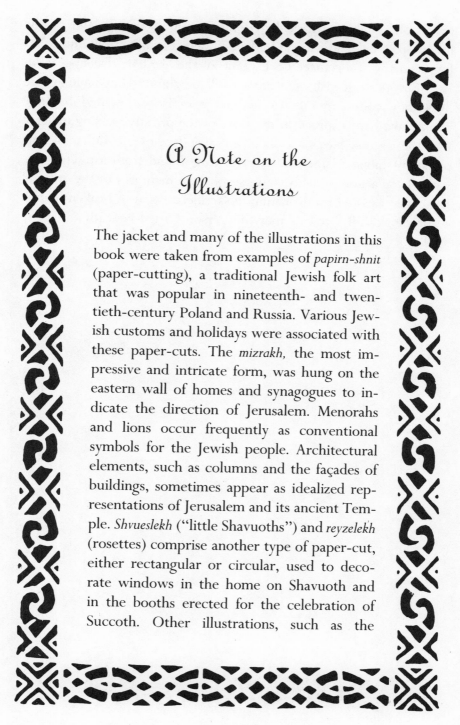

A Note on the Illustrations

The jacket and many of the illustrations in this book were taken from examples of *papirn-shnit* (paper-cutting), a traditional Jewish folk art that was popular in nineteenth- and twentieth-century Poland and Russia. Various Jewish customs and holidays were associated with these paper-cuts. The *mizrakh,* the most impressive and intricate form, was hung on the eastern wall of homes and synagogues to indicate the direction of Jerusalem. Menorahs and lions occur frequently as conventional symbols for the Jewish people. Architectural elements, such as columns and the façades of buildings, sometimes appear as idealized representations of Jerusalem and its ancient Temple. *Shvueslekh* ("little Shavuoths") and *reyzelekh* (rosettes) comprise another type of paper-cut, either rectangular or circular, used to decorate windows in the home on Shavuoth and in the booths erected for the celebration of Succoth. Other illustrations, such as the gravestone rubbings made by Monika Krajewska in Poland or the lithographs by Yudovin and Malkin, depict similar folk motifs as found in the stonecutter's art. Some of the symbols that appear on East European Jewish tombstones tell us about the people whose lives they commemorate. A learned man is represented by holy books; two hands spread in the form of the priestly blessing indicate that the deceased was a Kohen, a descendant of the Kohanim (the priests of biblical Israel); a hand pouring liquid from a pitcher is a symbol for a Levite, whose ancestors were members of the tribe of Levi, who assisted the Kohanim in sacrificial ritual. A broken branch or broken candles tell us that the person buried beneath the stone died at a young age.

Contents

PART TWO

A Rooster and a Hen, Let the Story Begin: Children's Tales

PART THREE

Magic Rings, Feathers of Gold, Mountains of Glass: Wonder Tales

PART FOUR

Justice, Faith, and Everyday Morals:
Pious Tales

PART FIVE

Nitwits, Wits, and Pranksters: Humorous Tales

PART SIX

Sages, Tsadikim, and Villains: Legends

PART SEVEN

Elves and Dibbuks, Ghosts and Golems: Supernatural Tales

Introduction

Some of them began in the age-old, reassuring way, *Amol iz geven,* "Once upon a time." Others began, *S'iz an emese mayse,* "This is a true story." And they were told on all sorts of occasions. Comic and sentimental tales were told at weddings by the entertainers known as *badkhonim.* In the synagogue, grandfathers told stories about the Patriarchs and Elijah the Prophet to their grandsons during the intervals between early and late-evening prayers. Mothers and grandmothers told tales of wonder and magic around the stove in winter. *Kheyder*-students told scary ghost and demon tales when their teacher left for evening prayers. Teachers told stories of God's wonders; preachers and rabbis told homely parables to illuminate the great truths, and the disciples of Hasidic rebbes told tales about their leaders that showed how wise and holy they were. Seamstresses and tailors, market-vendors and wagon drivers spun yarns to while away the hours as they worked.

Amol iz geven. Once upon a time.

This volume presents a selection from the wealth of Yiddish folk-tales and legends told in the Yiddish-speaking world of Eastern Europe during the nineteenth and twentieth centuries. Many of the tales in their present versions have never been printed before in any language and most of them appear here in English for the first time. Together they offer us a privileged entry into a vibrant and vital community. The Jews of Eastern Europe—some seven million people by 1939—lived throughout a vast territory, from Poland in the west to Russia in the east, from Latvia in the north to Rumania in the south. Jewish communities ranged in size from *derfer* (villages) of a few families to *shtetlekh* (towns) to cities of hundreds of thousands. The ideological spectrum of these Jews was equally diverse. Numerous Hasidic groups, as well as their opponents, the *misnagdim* (rabbinic traditionalists), followed a variety of observance. During the nineteenth century a secularized Jewish population also emerged, and by the beginning of the twentieth, there were more than a dozen major Jewish political movements in Eastern Europe, ranging from the Jewish Labor Bund to the various Zionist parties.

Yet diverse and decentralized as this population was, the vast majority of East European Jewry were united by their *mame-loshn* (mother tongue), Yiddish. Hebrew and Aramaic were the languages of sacred texts and prayer; Russian, Polish, Lithuanian, Hungarian, and a half-dozen other languages were used for communicating with non-Jewish neighbors and government bureaucracy. But the vernacular was Yiddish, the language of daily life, the language, too, in which an extensive oral and written literature, religious as well as secular, was created.

The Yiddish tales included in this volume were drawn largely from the documentary efforts of folklorists and amateur collectors who, in the decades before and between the two world wars, wrote down thousands of legends, fables, jokes, and stories as they heard them from hundreds of gifted tellers. Though collected in this century, these stories embody a far older heritage of Jewish narrative art.

Throughout Jewish history there has been a continuous reciprocal relationship between stories communicated by word of mouth and stories in writing. An example of this is "The Trustees," one of the pious tales in this collection. This tale, recorded in 1926 in Poland, is a variant of a tale that appears in a book of moral literature published in 1707 in Yiddish *(Simkhes hanefesh)*; and an even earlier version of this tale is found in a Hebrew book published in Salonica in 1521 *(Yalkut shimeoni).*[1] Other tales in this collection can be traced back to *agodes,* stories and legends from the Jewish oral tradition that were written down some fifteen hundred years ago in Babylonia and Judea by the sages of the Talmud. The Talmud, in fact, is our earliest evidence of the fundamental role of storytelling in Jewish life. Over the centuries, in Eastern Europe as well as in other Jewish communities, stories from the Talmud and other rabbinic works re-entered the oral tradition in a variety of ways: preachers used them in their sermons, teachers read them to their pupils, parents told them to their children.

With the advent of print, Jewish publishers issued not only sacred Hebrew texts for prayer and study, but also a large variety of books in Yiddish, which could be read widely. Perhaps the most popular of these collections was the *Mayse-bukh* (Book of Tales), compiled some time in the sixteenth century.² The publishers of the *Mayse-bukh* sought to provide Jewish men and women with a wholesome alternative to the current "ungodly" worldly literature by presenting them with over two hundred edifying tales and legends drawn from a variety of oral and literary sources. Some of the stories in the present collection are related to tales found in the *Mayse-bukh,* some of which are themselves variants of Talmudic *agodes.* Thus the rich sample of twentieth-century Yiddish tales printed here in English translation comprises one more link in the extensive interaction between the spoken and the written in Jewish culture.

If the compilers of works such as the *Mayse-bukh* saw Jewish tales as a means of reinforcing the traditional pious life, the collectors of the tales presented in this book were inspired by quite different motives. These modern folklorists saw their work as part of the neo-Romantic, nationalistic movement popular among Jewish cultural activists at the turn of the century. Like other nationalists of the time, these folklorists and amateur collectors gathered lore from those who preserved the greatest number of distinctive folk traditions so that these traditions could serve as the basis of a modern national culture. Classic Yiddish writer Y.-L. Peretz, for example, reworked Yiddish folktales into stories for the modern Jewish reader. Our "Seven Good Years" is one such story, a variant of a Talmudic legend which is the basis for one of Peretz's *Folkstimlekhe geshikhtes* (Folktale-like Stories).

The most famous enterprise to gather the folklore of East European Jews was certainly the ethnographic expedition organized in

Avrom Rekhtman, a member of the An-ski expedition, 1912–1914, recording a legend in Brailov, in the Ukraine. (YIVO Photographic Archive)

1912 by writer-folklorist Sh. An-ski (pen name of Shloyme Zanvl Rappaport). An-ski and his colleagues set out with the ambitious goal of finding and preserving all genres of Yiddish folkways, including oral tales and legends, throughout Jewish communities in the Ukraine. Over the next three years, the expedition, which was cut short by the outbreak of World War I, gathered some 1,800 tales and legends, among other folklore materials, from sixty-six villages and towns in Volhynia and Podolia.[3] An-ski later drew on some of this lore when writing his famous play, *The Dibbuk*.

The most enduring effort to collect and publish Yiddish folklore —one which continues to this day—came with the establishment of the *Yidisher Visnshaftlekher Institut*—YIVO (the Institute for Jewish Research) in 1925 in Vilna. YIVO was committed to the scholarly study of East European Jewish culture in Yiddish. Folklore and ethnography were seen as central to the task, and soon after its founding, YIVO established an Ethnographic Commission, whose major responsibility was to collect and publish Yiddish folklore. YIVO's scholars and students were conversant with the latest international theories in the study of folklore, and these had direct implications for what they set out to collect and the methods they used.

At first YIVO's efforts to record Yiddish folktales were largely carried out by amateur *zamlers* (collectors) from all walks of life. Tailors, shopkeepers, artisans, school teachers, rabbis—all responded to YIVO's appeal to "listen attentively to the stories people tell each other in traditional Jewish homes, in Jewish neighborhoods, in cities, as well as in isolated little towns."[4] Collectors' circles were established in cities and towns throughout Eastern Europe, and by 1929 such societies were sending local folklore to YIVO. Yiddish folklore was being collected on an unprecedented scale. According to one account, in 1938, after little more than a decade of concentrated

Shmuel Lehman, folklorist, recording a story from an old woman in Warsaw, in 1931, while her family watches. Lehman is known for his unique collections of folktales about Elijah the Prophet, of cante fables, and of underworld lore. (YIVO Photographic Archive)

collection, YIVO's folklore archive contained over 100,000 items: 32,442 proverbs, 4,989 folk beliefs, 4,673 children's tales, 4,311 folksongs, 3,807 anecdotes, 2,340 folktales, 1,009 customs, 630 nigunim (songs without words), 79 Purim plays, etc.[5]

In an effort to promote effective and uniform collecting, the Ethnographic Commission issued a series of informal anketes (questionnaires) and a guide to novice zamlers entitled Vos azoyns iz yidishe etnografye ("Just What Is Jewish Ethnography?"). A good picture of who the best storytellers were likely to be is found in one of the early anketes:

> They are the merchants who travel to fairs and meet all kinds of people and get to hear a variety of tales and bring these home together with their hard-earned groshn. Then there are the village artisans and craftsmen, who travel with their tools from village to village; klezmorim [musicians]; badkhonim, specializing in humorous and sentimental semi-improvised rhymes, who go from one wedding to another in neighboring towns and villages; shadkhonim [marriage brokers]; mendicants; blind musicians; street singers. There are also the Hasidim, who go on visits to their rebbe, or stay a while at his hoyf [court], where they hear many tales about Hasidic rebbes and about pious, saintly men.[6]

The ankete goes on to warn the folklore collector:

> People tend to be shy (in today's world of newspapers and sophisticated books!) about telling such bobe-mayses [old wives' tales], current among children and old-timers. People may think you want to make fun of them. Therefore, it is important first to gain the complete confidence of the person from whom you wish to write down a tale, and to explain, if necessary and if it seems appropriate, that these tales are not as silly as they themselves may feel they are in today's world. Also tell them that many of these folktales, in all their charming simplicity, and with their wealth of colorful fantasy, may, in fact, surpass stories that get printed in books.

The YIVO publication also lists the most common Yiddish folktale motifs and heroes, which the commission felt would help the collector to prod the memory of storytellers:

> Everywhere mothers still tell wondrous tales to their children about *gute yidn* [Hasidic rebbes; literally, "good Jews"] who help poor people in hard times. Grandmothers still like to tell about the days of yore; or about the *shretelekh* [elf-like creatures], who bring good fortune to the home; about evil men who invent libelous stories about Jews; about the Prophet Elijah, who does not forget the poor man. And in the small houses of worship and study where ordinary folk gather to pore over sacred works or huddle near the stove, stories are told, with equal fervor and enthusiasm, about miracles performed by Hasidic rebbes . . . and about the hidden *tsadek* [saintly man] who wanders over cities and small towns, disguised as a water carrier or a poor tailor or sexton, and who brings with him consolation and redemption.

The *ankete* closed by urging the collectors: "Please do not make the stories prettier while writing them down. Set them down exactly as the teller tells them, including all asides and aphorisms."

In 1930 a group of young collectors at YIVO in Vilna received some formal training from Y.-L. Cahan,[7] head of YIVO's Ethnographic Commission and editor of its folklore publications. After his visit to Vilna in 1930, Cahan, who by then was living in New York, continued his instruction of the young folklorists via a lively correspondence. Shmuel Zanvl Pipe, represented in this volume by some legends about Napoleon, was one of Y.-L. Cahan's students and correspondents. In early letters to his brother we learn of this young tailor's infatuation with Yiddish folklore. While the impoverished Pipe was serving in the army, he wrote that he had received some money, but instead of spending it on himself, he used it to buy stamps to mail folklore materials to YIVO. "I guess you could call me a passionate *zamler*," he observed.[8]

As the YIVO guide suggested, eloquent storytellers were to be found in all parts of Jewish society. Thanks to the efforts of some of the collectors, we know a little bit about the life and art of individual storytellers. One early collector, A. Litwin, who went on to become a Yiddish journalist in America, offered the following description of a particularly good teller of tales, the woman who told him "In Heaven and Hell" and "A *Balshem* Drives Out a Dibbuk."

> In the province of Mohilev there lives an amazing old woman known as the town's *khakhome* [wise woman], whom I met by accident. Her name is Sonye Naymark. She is eighty years old, takes good care of herself, looks healthy, and is so lively and cheerful that it's a pleasure to spend time with her. I spent several hours with her. It wasn't easy for me to get that much of her time. She comes from a family of status, and considers herself well-born. At first it was hard for me to approach her; later she began to trust me. She started to feel at home in my presence and spoke freely. And then the proverbs and stories began to flow. She tells her stories like an artist. Her language is unusually rich and color-ful, and her style is sharp and peppery. She makes use of a rhyme, a Biblical verse, even a Talmudic proverb. It was from her that I learned that there were once women *badkhentes*. Such a *badkhente,* she said, once paid her three rubles for a story that she taught her and which the *badkhente* then used at a wedding. Sonye, however, is anything but a *badkhente*. She is a very proud woman and com-mands everyone's respect. Old and young are happy to spend time with her and enjoy her stories and proverbs.[9]

Whereas "Sonye the Wise" had a fixed place in her *shtetl,* another prized storyteller, Sholem Troyanovski, traveled extensively in his life and held numerous different jobs. His varied experiences may well have enhanced his repertoire:

> Sholem Troyanovski is sixty-two years old. He is a shoemaker in Yevpatoriye, Crimea, and a former longshoreman and member of a collective farm in Peretsfeld. He came over to the Crimea in 1930 from Skvir, near Kiev. He is not highly literate, and uses a great many Russian words in his daily life. Troyanovski tells tales well. He has a rich repertoire of around fifty folktales. There was

Storyteller Sonye Naymark, called "Sonye di Khakhome" (Sonye the Wise), circa 1915. (YIVO Photographic Archive)

a time, he says, when people trailed after him, begging, "Sholem, tell us a story." [10]

Troyanovski's wonder-tale "Forty Hares and a Princess" appears in this volume.

Not all great Yiddish storytellers lived in small towns or on remote farms, like Naymark and Troyanovski. The larger cities contained whole enclaves of Jews who had recently migrated from *shtetlekh* and villages, and were still a rich source of small-town and rural folkways. In addition, there was a folklore of the city, of the "beardless," the "modern," the "enlightened" Jews; even tales of the Jewish underworld.

Finding gifted storytellers was not the *zamler*'s only challenge, however. Documenting the art of the storyteller was limited by the

Zusman Kisselhof on the An-ski ethnographic expedition, 1912–1914, to Volhynia and Podolia. Here he is seen making sound recordings of Yiddish folksongs. (YIVO Photographic Archive)

pen-and-paper technology of the time. Though some Yiddish folk songs have been recorded on wax cylinders, no Yiddish tales seem to have been preserved in the same manner.

Some *zamlers* were quite ingenious in their efforts to render the authentic performances of the tellers. S. Verite, for example, invented an original way of noting speech patterns. In order to convey what words or phrases were stressed by the teller, he devised a system of dots and dashes to indicate emphases and pauses. Still, collectors remained poignantly aware of the difficulties of "writing everything down exactly as the teller told it, not adding or subtracting an iota," as Litwin put it. For him, the written form of the storyteller's art was "but a weak echo of what I heard from her mouth. What's missing is the pose she strikes as she narrates, her gestures, her alertness, the naïve enthusiasm with which she spins her yarns, the sound of her voice, her uncontrived yet artistic manner, which cannot be conveyed in words."[11]

Most of the stories in this volume were deposited in the archives of the YIVO Institute in Vilna between 1926 and 1940.[12] They are part of the hundreds of thousands of books, documents, and other artifacts miraculously recovered following World War II—something of a wonder-tale itself. In 1941, when Vilna was occupied by the Germans, YIVO's extensive collections were expropriated; some materials were destroyed, others designated for transfer to the Nazis' Institute for Research on the Jewish Question in Frankfurt am Main. These were discovered after the war by Allied officers, and, with the help of the U.S. State Department, some 50,000 bound volumes and 30,000 archival folders were shipped to YIVO's headquarters in New York City.

As a student at YIVO in the autumn of 1948 I witnessed the dramatic arrival of the huge wooden crates. I remember hoping to work with these precious materials some day; and in preparing this book, I began my research by combing through the historic files. I never knew just what I would come across in a folder. Paper was a precious commodity in interwar Eastern Europe, and whatever snippet was available at the moment had to suffice. Some folders contained typed

Crates of archival materials and books from the Vilna YIVO as they arrived in the New York building in 1948. (YIVO Photographic Archive)

manuscripts; others, tales scribbled in schoolboy's notebooks. Many of the various handwritings were quite difficult to decipher; on the other hand, there were a few collectors who wrote like calligraphers, with elaborate *perldike shrift* (pearl-like script).

The materials in these files were not organized by genre. Instead, jokes, wonder-tales, pious tales, and legends might all be found in a single file. There was no way to predict which genres would be well represented and which not. This complicated considerably the process of selecting the tales for this volume. I wanted to include stories representing all of the Yiddish folk narrative genres, as well as stories told by men and women of different age groups, professions, and religious backgrounds. Thus the tales in our collection include samples from the repertoire of a young *kheyder*-student in Vilna ("Little Bean"), an artist from Zhitomir ("The Luck That Snored"), a Hasid of the Stoliner Rebbe ("Yisroel, the Child Rebbe"), a night watchman

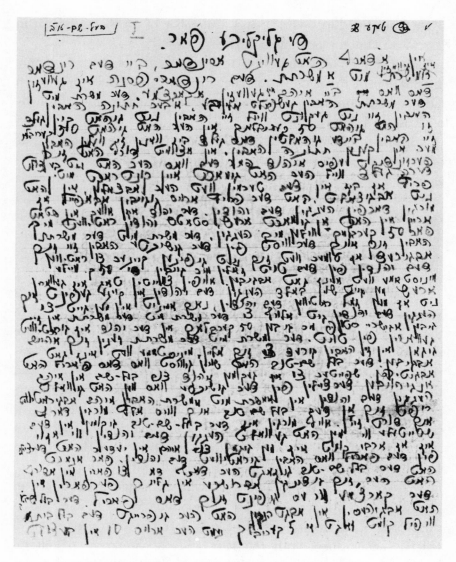

Manuscript of "The Happy Pair and the Baal Shem Tov." (YIVO Archive)

in Kiev ("The Beggar King and the *Melamed*"), a tailor from Rovne ("Stones and Bones Rattle in My Belly"), a Rumanian carpet salesman

("The Naughty Littly Girl"), and a member of a collective farm in the Soviet Union ("Sowing Salt").

I also wanted this collection to give a sense of the geographic distribution of the Yiddish folktale, so I have included stories from farming communities and villages, *shtetlekh* and major cities throughout Eastern Europe.

A hallmark of oral tradition is the coexistence of multiple variants of a single tale. When selecting among variants I have given preference to a never published version from the archival sources over a published one. Where there were several unpublished variants, I chose the most skillfully told, the one that preserved the greatest number of features of local color and oral tradition: rhymed introductions and endings, narrator's asides, idiomatic language, and rhetorical questions.

Finally, there was the question, What constitutes a "Jewish tale"? Some scholars insist that the only tales that are truly "Jewish" are those with a *muser haskl,* i.e., a moral message, and that all others are ultimately foreign. They therefore limit themselves to fables, allegories, parables, and pious tales. Other folklorists, like Y.-L. Cahan, thought the only true Jewish folktales were the secular, non-moralistic wonder-tales. My own view, as reflected in this collection, is that whatever stories East European Jews told one another in Yiddish are "Yiddish folktales," regardless of whether or not they contain Jewish cultural markers or impart traditional moral values.

The Yiddish folktale provides us with a unique opportunity to glimpse the rich inner-life of East European Jews in the art and in the words of its storytellers. Each folk narrator, each generation of tellers, shapes anew both the tales and the literary and cultural heritage that they embody. And there is an invitation implied in this process of creation. An invitation best expressed in the style of nineteenth-century Yiddish chapbooks: *Un itst, tayere leyeners, iz ayer rey ibertsudertseyln di mayses in ayere eygene verter*—"And now, dear readers, it is your turn to retell these tales in your own words."

Amol iz geven. Once upon a time.

PART ONE

Naked Truths

and

Resplendent

Parables:

Allegorical

Tales

In the *besmedresh**—the House of Study—between afternoon and evening prayers one could often hear an itinerant
preacher deliver a sermon embroidered with beautiful *mesholim,* parables. Even women used to come then: in summer
they filled the women's section, and in winter, wrapped in
many shawls, they used to stand along the walls or fill the
anteroom of the *besmedresh.* Some older pious women would
boldly enter the *besmedresh* itself and stand by the oven and
listen from there.

— Memoir from Tishevits, Poland, ca. 1930

$\mathcal{T}$he Yiddish folktale, no matter
how pleasing, is often busy giving its readers moral or spiritual
instruction. The favorite form such instruction takes is the *moshl,* a
tale that employs examples or analogies to make its point. Broadly
conceived, the *moshl* (*mesholim* is the plural) is a simple parable in
which the deeds of ancient heroes or even ordinary folk serve to
illustrate a moral. It can also be a fable in which animals who act like
people provide a commentary on human affairs; or it can be a
formally patterned allegory in which abstract concepts like "wisdom"
or "truth" or "luck" become characters whose actions illuminate
moral issues.

* See the glossary on p. 369 for definitions of Yiddish terms and a guide to their
pronunciation.

· 3 ·

Often, *mesholim* originated with religious teachers who were also master storytellers like Yankev Krants (1741–1804), called the *dubner maged,* the Preacher of Dubno, whose "Naked Truth and Resplendent Parable" and "A Bit of Herring, a Pinch of Salt, and a Morsel of Bread" are included here. In his sermons, the *dubner maged* made use of folkloric materials, and his own parables, in turn, passed into folklore. Parables have been attributed to other rabbis and Hasidic rebbes as well.* In fact it is common to begin or end such tales by citing a prestigious source: "This was told by the Rebbe of Alexander when . . ." But ordinary folk, too, could tell parables, and a common opening is: *Dos folk zogt a moshl* (people tell a parable . . .).

Mesholim are frequently presented as tales within tales. First, there is the framing tale, the *nimshl,* as in "Letting In the Light" when the Rebbe of Apt asks the Rebbe of Pshiskhe a question. Then follows the fictional situation, the *moshl* which takes the form of the Rebbe of Pshiskhe's oblique, anecdotal answer. Sometimes the moral of the tale is explicitly drawn. For example, in "Things Can Always Get Worse," the beggar who complains to God about his situation is given a humped back and another mouth to feed, and the tale concludes: "Never say that things are bad. They can always get worse."

In the second type of *moshl,* the fable, animals talk and act like the humans they represent. "Why Dogs Chase Cats and Cats Chase Mice" demonstrates a hard fact of political life. "A Fable of a Bird and Her Chicks," which has a history in Yiddish going back at least to the seventeenth century, is an astringent commentary on the commandment "Honor thy father and thy mother."

The third type of tale in this section is the allegory in its most traditional form. Such tales provide the starkest picture of the life

---

* *Reb* is the traditional title prefixed to a man's first name, like "Mister" in English. A *rebbe* (literally, "my master") is a Hasidic spiritual leader, who may or may not also be a rabbi (or *rov*), an ordained graduate of a rabbinical academy, who is qualified to serve as the legal and ritual authority of a Jewish community.

from which Yiddish folklore emerged. It is a world of grinding poverty, in which hard work brings few results. In "Poverty Grows and Grows," the naked stranger ensconced in the poor man's house grows fatter and fatter—too fat for the suit the man has made in order to get rid of him. Among the hundreds of "lucks" in a faraway field described in "The Luck That Snored," a poor man's luck is particularly sleepy, scabby, and surly. In "Wisdom or Luck?" luck accomplishes in a minute what wisdom failed to do in years. What is amazing in these tales as they address misfortune is a playfulness of tone in which there glows an optimism that is subtly defiant of the very meanness of the life that they describe so well.

1

Naked Truth and Resplendent Parable

The great scholar known as the Vilna Gaon once asked the Preacher of Dubno, "Help me to understand. What makes a parable so influential? If I recite Torah, there's a small audience, but let me tell a parable and the synagogue is full. Why is that?"

The *dubner maged* replied, "I'll explain it to you by means of a parable.

"Once upon a time Truth went about the streets as naked as the day he was born. As a result, no one would let him into their homes. Whenever people caught sight of him, they turned away or fled. One day when Truth was sadly wandering about, he came upon Parable. Now, Parable was dressed in splendid clothes of beautiful colors. And Parable, seeing Truth, said, 'Tell me, neighbor, what makes you look so sad?' Truth replied bitterly, 'Ah, brother, things are bad. Very bad. I'm old, very old, and no one wants to acknowledge me. No one wants anything to do with me.'

"Hearing that, Parable said, 'People don't run away from you because you're old. I too am old. Very old. But the older I get, the better people like me. I'll tell you a secret: Everyone likes things to be disguised and prettied up a bit. Let me lend you some splendid clothes like mine, and you'll see that the very people who pushed you aside will invite you into their homes and be glad of your company.'

"Truth took Parable's advice and put on the borrowed clothes. And from that time on, Truth and Parable have gone hand in hand together and everyone loves them. They make a happy pair."

2
A Bit of Herring, a Pinch of Salt, and a Morsel of Bread

The *dubner maged* once heard a scholar get up on the *bime*, the platform of the synagogue, and deliver a learned discourse, citing Biblical verses, Talmudic and rabbinic commentaries, and who knows what else. In the course of his talk, he managed to heap scorn upon the folk preacher who had spoken before him.

When the learned man was done, the *dubner maged* said to him, "Let me tell you a parable that may prove useful."

In a certain town there once lived a great merchant, a very clever man. A very, very clever man. He observed that there were many rich and powerful people in his town, so he opened a jewelry store and had many customers. But some while later, he moved to a smaller town whose inhabitants, sad to say, were poor and threadbare.

Seeing that, the clever merchant opened a store—no, not a store, a little shop, in which he sold herring, salt, kerosene, and other ordinary things. And with the same hands that had once handled diamonds, he now served up herrings and kerosene. And just as the merchant had been satisfied with the jewelry store, so now he was pleased with his poor little shop. No—he was actually more pleased with it; everything he did delighted him.

Things went on like this until one day a friend from the larger town came to visit him and said, "I don't understand. How is it fitting for a man who once sold diamonds and gems to be selling herring and salt and other such stuff?"

The good and clever merchant replied, "I'm sorry to say that you don't get the point. Let me tell you something: The people who live in the large city are rich. They own many jewels and they are great connoisseurs of jewelry. But in this little town, the people are poor. They work with their hands and struggle to make ends meet. They don't need diamonds, nor do they understand them. Indeed, what they need . . . yes!—they need a bit of herring, a pinch of salt, and a morsel of bread."

3
Things Can Always Get Worse

Once there was a poor man who thought it was too bad that he had to go about begging for bread, and he complained about it to God. With that, a hump grew on his back, and in addition to the hump, a man grew there too, and the man had a mouth as well, and each time the beggar tried to eat a morsel of bread, the man on his back snatched it from him.

Then the beggar prayed, "Neither erase, O Lord, nor write. Let things be the way they were."

And this is why one must never say that things are bad. They can always get worse.

4

The Luck That Snored

Once upon a time there were two brothers, one rich and the other poor. The poor brother was a servant in his rich brother's house. One day as he was standing guard at the gate, there came a tiny man wearing a golden cap and carrying a sack of gold on his shoulders.

"Who are you?" the poor brother asked.

"I'm your brother's luck."

The poor brother was amazed. "Perhaps you can tell me where I can find *my* luck?" he said.

"Of course I can, but it won't do you any good," said the tiny man. "Because he's lying in a deserted field that's hard to find. And your luck is mangy and run down and asleep."

But the poor brother begged and pleaded and wept, until finally the man took pity on him. "All right then, I'll tell you," he said. "Go off that way for a long, long time till you come to a field. Go past it for a long time till you come to another field, where you'll see thousands of lucks lying asleep. Don't wake them. Go on until you see thousands of other lucks who have just woken up. They will be sitting around yawning and scratching themselves, but don't let that bother you. Keep going, keep searching until you find a luck who's sleeping sounder than the others, and snoring louder. That one is your luck."

And when the little man with the gold cap had finished speaking, he disappeared.

Early the next morning the poor brother started off in search of his luck. He walked on and on until he came to a barren field, just as the little man had said. He didn't stop but went on until he came to another field that was equally barren. He looked about and saw a great many lucks sleeping and snoring, but he did not disturb them. He saw others who sat around yawning and scratching themselves, but he paid no attention.

He went on and on, searching and searching, until he saw a luck that was sleeping more deeply than the others. He went up and tried to wake him: "Luck, my luck, wake up. Why do you sleep so hard?" His luck never stirred, just slept and snored. Again he tried to wake him, but nothing helped. Finally the poor man wept. "Luck, ah my luck, get up. You've slept enough, you've slept enough."

Then slowly, slowly, his luck opened his eyes and yawned. The poor man was delighted. "Luck, ah my luck," he pleaded, "don't sleep anymore. Pay attention. My wife and children are hungry. Help me. Give me something."

His luck said nothing. But he put a scabby hand into his breast pocket, took out a silver gulden, and handed it to the poor man.

"What good will this do?" the man asked.

"Some good, some good," grumbled his luck. "Go to the marketplace and buy the first thing that comes your way."

The poor man went to the marketplace, where he met a peasant with a hen to sell. So he bought the hen and took it home. He went to sleep, and the hen flew up to a shelf and went to sleep too.

When the poor man woke in the morning, he saw something gleaming on the shelf. He got out of bed and found that the hen had laid a golden egg. He woke his wife and children and showed them the golden egg, and they all danced and leaped for joy. Then the poor man took the egg and sold it for a great deal of money. And from that time on, he grew richer and richer.

Things are well for them
And for us, even better.

5

The Fever and the Flea

Once upon a time a Fever and a Flea, meeting each other on the road, got into an argument. "You're a nobody," the Flea said to the Fever. "Why, you're so unimportant that you're invisible."

The poor Fever, hearing this, was terribly upset. It was more than he could bear to be talked to this way by a flea. "You," he said angrily, "what makes you think you're anybody? Just because you can be seen, just because you can leap about, that doesn't make you better than me."

"Yes it does," declared the Flea. "I lead a better life than you do. I wouldn't trade mine for yours for anything."

The Fever, red with rage, said, "You lead a better life? You? Ha! Invisible though I am, I wouldn't trade places with you in a million years."

The quarrel grew more and more heated until it seemed that the two were about to leap at each other and scratch each other's eyes out. But finally the Fever calmed down and said, "What's the point of arguing like this? Why don't we try an experiment to prove beyond question which of us leads a better life?"

"All right," said the Flea, "I'm willing. What did you have in mind?"

Said the Fever, "Each of us will go off and find a victim to infest for three days. At the end of that time we'll meet and compare results. Then we'll be able to decide which of us has the better life."

"Very well," said the Flea, and they shook hands and went their ways.

Three days later they met again. The Fever, seeing the Flea, said, "What's the matter? You look unhappy."

"Ah," said the Flea, "I've had a hard time. A very hard time."

"What happened?"

Heaving a deep sigh, the Flea said, "After we parted, I made my way inside a palace. Ah, it was wonderful there, a veritable paradise. I spent the night in a bed that would have pleased the most demanding public official. What a bed! I wish I could describe it to you. But it's impossible; after all, I'm a flea and not a poet.

"At midnight just as I was sleeping most sweetly, I felt someone getting into bed with me. Ugh. Whoever it was gave off a terrible smell of brandy. I tried to ignore it, but he started tossing and turning in the bed so I couldn't get back to sleep. 'Well,' thought I, 'if that's what you're up to, let me show you a trick or two.'

"Well, you know me. I'm a flea. I went after him tooth and nail. In no time I gave him a good reason to toss and turn. He was thrashing so hard I had to laugh.

"All at once he uttered a roar that brought everyone in the palace running. 'A flea!' someone cried, and then every last one of them went after me. They hunted me up and down, forward and backward. It was all I could do to escape with my life.

"And now I've spent the last three days just wandering, hungry and restless. Can't seem to settle down."

"How sad," said the Fever. "You've had a really hard time."

"Yes," groaned the Flea. "But what about you? How did you make out?"

The Fever stuck his stomach out like a gentleman and said expansively, "Ah, me. I told you I lead a good life. No sooner had I left you than I met a peasant and jumped right into him. Feeling my presence, he ran off to his house and cried to his wife, 'Woman, I think I've got a fever. Get my bed ready.'

"Well, I looked around. It was plain to see that I was in a poor man's house, but no matter. Once the peasant was in bed, I began to do my business.

"The man's wife brought him a large bowl of hot soup and some black bread, so I fed nicely on that. Then, to warm us up, she covered us with some pelts and old coats.

"Well, you can imagine how my peasant tossed and turned. Whenever I got a little bored, I would stroll about inside him. Seeing how feverish he was, his wife kept putting good things into his mouth, and of course I got my share. Mmm, mmm, it was tasty. If I hadn't finally taken pity on him, and if we hadn't agreed to meet in three days, I'd still be there.

"Well, what do you think?" said the Fever. "Which of us leads the better life?"

"You do," the Flea admitted, and slunk away.

6
___

Why Dogs Chase Cats and Cats Chase Mice

Once upon a time the dogs applied to the king for a decree that would forbid people to bother dogs. The king signed the decree and gave it to them, but then the dogs couldn't think of a place to put it. Finally they passed it to the cats for safekeeping, because cats are able to creep into all sorts of snug nooks and crannies. The cats took the paper and hid it in the eaves of a house.

Sometime later, dogcatchers started rounding up dogs. "Hey," cried the dogs, "wait a minute. We've got a decree from the king that says you can't bother us."

"If that's true," said the dogcatchers, "where is it?"

So the dogs ran to the cats and said, "We need the king's decree that forbids anyone to bother us. Where is it?"

"Wait a minute. We'll go and look," said the cats, and off they went to the eaves. The document was there all right, but the mice had gnawed it to shreds and tatters. When the dogs heard this, they were furious and chased the cats; and when the cats were chased, they were furious and chased the mice.

And that's how it's been ever since.

7
Wisdom or Luck?

Wisdom, meeting Luck one day, got into an argument about which of them was more powerful.

Wisdom said that nothing can be accomplished in the world without wisdom, whereas everything is possible with it. Luck, on the other hand, said, "What good is wisdom without luck? An ounce of luck is worth more than a pound of wisdom." But Wisdom insisted that only wisdom is necessary to accomplish anything.

As they stood quarreling, it happened that somewhere in the world a boy was born. Wisdom and Luck agreed that one of them should enter into him, and then they would see what he could achieve.

So Wisdom entered into the boy, who was born to a very poor woman who was unable to provide him with any sort of education. But when he was fourteen or fifteen, a goldsmith took pity on him and made him an apprentice. The boy was so clever that it was not long before he became more skillful than the goldsmith. Seeing that there was nothing more he could learn, the boy told his master that he wanted to leave and go to a larger city. His master was sad to be losing such a good worker, but the boy was eager to make his way in the world.

He traveled for a while until he came to the capital city, where the king lived. There he met the town's finest tailor, who sewed for the royal family. "Let me be your apprentice," said the boy, and the tailor agreed. Before long his master saw with astonishment that the boy was a remarkable tailor. He was continually inventing such wonderful new designs that the king wondered why his new clothes were so much better than the ones he had before. "Who is making these clothes?" the king asked the tailor.

"I am," replied the tailor. "I spend a lot of time thinking and thinking up new and more beautiful robes for you." The king, hearing this, rewarded the tailor richly.

Now, the king's only daughter was so brilliant that no one had been able to find her a husband as clever as she. "I don't care what rank in life he has. If he can make me talk, I'll marry him. But let every man who wants to marry me take warning: if he's not clever enough, it's off with his head." Her father had no choice but to abide by her terms.

Naturally every eligible young man wanted to marry her. For in addition to brilliance and birth, she had extraordinary beauty. So the first of her suitors were well-educated, important young men who thought themselves her equal. But one and all were unsuccessful. She listened to what they had to say and made no reply. The suitors, one and all, had their heads chopped off.

Hearing about the princess, the tailor's apprentice decided that he would seek to win her hand. "I'll find a way to make her talk," he said. "Anyhow what do I have to lose, sad and poor as I am?"

He went to the king's palace and asked to be admitted. "I've come to talk with the princess," he said, "and get her to talk to me."

He was led into the room where the princess sat, but he acted as if he had not seen her. Instead, he looked around the room and, catching sight of a candelabrum, addressed it: "Good morning, Candelabrum. I have something to tell you, and I'd like your opinion about it when I'm done." With that he launched into a tale.

"Once upon a time, dear Candelabrum, there were three men who lived in a village: a woodcarver, a tailor, and a teacher. But there was not enough work in their village, so they decided to take their tools and go out into the wide world to look for employment.

"They traveled on and on until they came to a forest, where night soon fell. They had to sleep where they were, but because they were afraid of wild animals, they agreed that each of them would stand guard for two hours.

"The first watch was taken by the woodcarver. It was not long before he looked about for something to while away the time. He examined the pieces of wood lying around and found a fine log, which he carved into the form of a woman. He finished the statue just as his two hours were up, so he woke the tailor and went to sleep.

"The tailor, like the woodworker, looked about for something to do. His eye fell on the statue of the naked woman, so he took his scissors and needles and several yards of cloth and sat down to sew a dress. When it was finished, he clothed the statue in it. Just then his two hours were up, so he woke the teacher and went to sleep.

"The teacher too looked about for something to do. Suddenly he saw a lovely woman in a beautiful dress, but when he spoke to her, she remained still and silent. It seemed too bad that so splendid a woman should be unable to talk. So he sat down beside her and undertook to teach her to speak. And he was so skillful and patient that she began to learn.

"Meanwhile the dawn came and his companions awoke and saw him in conversation with a beautiful, well-dressed woman. When each of them recognized his handiwork, he wanted her for himself. So of course all three men quarreled. The woodcarver said, 'I carved her out of wood, so she belongs to me.' The tailor said, 'What? She was nothing but a naked piece of wood when I found her. I clothed her, so she belongs to me.' The teacher said, 'What good is a beautifully clothed dummy? I taught her to speak, so she belongs to me.' And they went round and round. Now, dear Candelabrum, what do you think? To whom does she belong?"

The princess, who had naturally listened to the whole story and admired the boy's cleverness, spoke up: "Of course she belongs to the man who made her talk."

The youth, however, was cleverer than he was lucky. Servants had been posted in the room to report whether the boy made the princess talk and they simply didn't hear her when she spoke. So they concluded that the boy had failed like all the others. Nor were they surprised, since he was after all so poor. And without delay they led him off to the executioner.

Just as the sword was raised to behead the boy, Luck turned to Wisdom and said, "Well, see what you've accomplished with your wisdom. You did your best, but when it comes right down to it, without me you can do nothing. So let's trade places; in a few minutes I'll get more done than you've accomplished in the boy's whole lifetime."

No sooner had Luck entered into him than the princess chanced to walk out onto her balcony. Seeing that the clever boy was being led to execution, she halted the procession and sent word to the king. This, she informed him, was the young man who had provoked a reply from her, and this was the one she would marry.

The king commanded that the servants who had been about to behead the youth should themselves be executed. And the princess married the tailor's apprentice and they lived happily ever after.

And that was how Luck proved that he was stronger than Wisdom.

8

Pleasing All the World

An old man and his ten-year-old son were leading a camel through the desert. Their way was long, the sun was hot, and they were tired. They met a man who looked at them amazed. "How foolish that you both go on foot," he said, "when the camel was created to carry people."

Heeding the stranger's words, the old man mounted the camel and his son followed on foot. A while later they met a second traveler, who said, "Have you no pity on your son? He's still a child with tender feet; look at them, cut to ribbons. How can a father allow his own child to suffer like that?"

The father, ashamed, dismounted and set his son upon the camel. But a while later they met a third traveler, who cried, "For shame

—and in the heat of the day, too! A child has no right to ride while his old father walks."

So the old man hit on another idea: He and his son both mounted the camel, making themselves comfortable while the camel went on. But then they met a fourth traveler who threw up his hands in horror. "Abusing a dumb creature! Making him carry a double load! Have you no pity in your hearts?"

The father and son quickly dismounted. The father said, "Well, there's no help for it, we'll just have to carry the camel ourselves. Though someone will probably come along and say that it's stupid. No matter what we do, we can't please all the world."

9

Poverty Grows and Grows

Once upon a time a poor man noticed that there was a naked stranger in his house. "Hey," he shouted, "you get out of my house, do you hear?"

"Dear sir," said the stranger, "just look at me. How can you bring yourself to drive a naked man into the street?"

"You're right," said the poor man, "that would be a sin. But tell me, who are you?"

"You don't recognize me? Well, to tell the truth, my name is Poverty."

When the poor man realized that he had Poverty living in his house, he was deeply distressed. He racked his brains for a way to get rid of him. Finally he went to a tailor's shop, described Poverty, and ordered a suit to fit. The tailor wrote down Poverty's measurements and went to work.

To pay for the suit the tailor was making, the poor man had to sell everything he owned. But he gritted his teeth and bore it, because anything was better than having Poverty as a permanent guest.

Finally the tailor delivered the suit, and Poverty put it on. "Sorry." Poverty smiled. "It doesn't fit."

The poor man turned on the tailor and cried, "How could you do this to me? I paid you good money, how come you made the suit too small?"

"Don't scold the tailor," said Poverty, "it's not his fault. It's just that while you were spending the last of your money, I grew bigger."

10
The Sacrifice of Isaac and the Caretaker of Brisk

The story is told that the leading men of the community were unsatisfied with the work of the caretaker of Rabbi Yoshe-Ber's rabbinical court in Brisk. They held a meeting and decided to fire the caretaker. Then they gave the task of dismissing him to Rabbi Yoshe-Ber, but he refused.

"Why not, Rabbi?" the community leaders asked. "You're the rabbi and he's your employee."

"I'll tell you," Rabbi Yoshe-Ber replied. "Since you read and know the story of the sacrifice of Isaac, you know that when the Blessed Name commanded Abraham to sacrifice Isaac, we find that it is written that He Himself spoke as follows: 'Take now thy son, thine only son . . .' But when He commanded Abraham to spare Isaac, God sent an angel, as it is written, 'And the angel called unto Abraham . . .'

"This poses a question. Why was it that the Blessed Name did not send an angel at the beginning? The answer is that He knew very well that no angel would have accepted the assignment. Each of them would have said, 'If You want to command death, You had better do it Yourself.' "

11

The Treasure at Home

The Rebbe of Aleksander used to say, "Many people think that when they come to the rebbe, they will be helped." And he liked to tell this tale to young people who came to see him for the first time.

One night, Ayzik, the son of Reb Yekl, dreamed that there was a treasure hidden under the Praga side of the Warsaw bridge. So he traveled to Warsaw. At the bridge he tried to reach the spot, but a soldier was standing guard there. So he paced back and forth as he waited for the soldier to go away. The soldier meanwhile became aware of someone on the bridge, so he went up to Ayzik and asked what he wanted. Ayzik told him the truth: that he had dreamed about a treasure buried under the bridge. The soldier said, "Aw, go on. Just because I dreamed about a treasure in the oven at the home of Ayzik, Reb Yekl's son in Cracow, doesn't mean I have to go there."

Ayzik turned around and went home, where he took his oven apart and found a treasure that made him a very rich man.

12

A Fable of a Bird and Her Chicks

Once upon a time a mother bird who had three chicks wanted to cross a river. She put the first one under her wing and started flying across. As she flew she said, "Tell me, child, when I'm old, will you carry me under your wing the way I'm carrying you now?"

"Of course," replied the chick. "What a question!"

"Ah," said the mother bird, "you're lying." With that she let the chick slip, and it fell into the river and drowned.

The mother went back for the second chick, which she took under her wing. Once more as she was flying across the river, she said, "Tell me, child, when I'm old, will you carry me under your wing the way I'm carrying you now?"

"Of course," replied the chick. "What a question!"

"Ah," said the mother bird, "you're lying." With that she let the second chick slip, and it also drowned.

Then the mother went back for the third chick, which she took under her wing. Once more she asked in mid-flight, "Tell me, child, when I am old, will you carry me under your wing the way I'm carrying you now?"

"No, mother," replied the third chick. "How could I? By then I'll have chicks of my own to carry."

"Ah, my dearest child," said the mother bird, "you're the one who tells the truth." With that she carried the third chick to the other bank of the river.

1 3

Letting In the Light

The Rebbe of Apt once asked the Rebbe of Pshiskhe why he did not watch his disciples to make sure that they obeyed all the precepts and prayed piously. The Rebbe of Pshiskhe replied, "Let me tell you a tale."

Once three men were confined in a pitch-dark prison. Two of the men were intelligent, but one of them was a simpleton who knew nothing at all: he couldn't put his clothes on, he didn't know how to eat; nothing. One of the intelligent men worked hard to teach the simpleton to dress himself, to eat, to hold a spoon, and so on. The other intelligent man did nothing at all. One day the hardworking man asked the indifferent one, "Why don't you make some effort to help teach the simpleton?" The other replied, "In this darkness you'll teach him nothing, no matter how many years you spend. I use my time thinking of ways to break a hole in the wall to let in the light. When that happens, he'll learn on his own what he needs to know."

14
Bad Luck

Once upon a time there were two brothers, one rich, the other poor. The rich brother supported the poor one, but there came a day when the rich man's wife said, "Enough. You've given him enough. No more."

Well, what was the poor brother to do? Then he thought, "It might be a good thing to take my family and move to another town. Who knows? A change of place, a change of luck."

He gathered his household goods, put them and his wife and children into a wagon, and drove off. When he had gone some distance, he remembered that he had forgotten a pot. He stopped the wagon and ran back to his house for it, and inside he found a tall stranger leaning against a pillar.

The stranger seemed very pleased to see him, which frightened the poor man. He snatched up the pot and ran off to the wagon, but looking back, he saw the stranger running after him. "Sir," said the poor man, "what do you want from me?"

"Don't you know who I am?" said the stranger. "I'm your bad luck. Where you go, I go." And he climbed into the wagon.

Well, there was nothing to be done. So the poor man drove on with a heavy heart until they entered a forest. There he had an idea. He took his ax and went up to a huge tree and began to chop away. He swung the ax so hard that it stuck deep in the wood and wouldn't budge.

"See here," he said to the tall man, "it's true you're my bad luck. But that doesn't mean you can't help me out a little. Put your fingers into the crack so I can get my ax out and we can go on our way."

And that's what the tall man did. He put both his hands into the crack, and the poor man pulled out his ax and left the tall man standing there with his hands caught.

The poor man and his wife and children drove off until they came to a city. There he went into business and, with God's help, prospered and became rich and happy.

When the rich brother heard the news that his poor brother was now rich, he thought, "Let's see if I can find out what changed his luck." So he set off on the same road his brother had taken and came to the place where the tall man was still standing with his fingers caught in the tree.

The tall stranger wept and pleaded, "Please, please help me."

"How can I help you?" the rich brother asked. "What do you want me to do?"

The tall man told him the whole story: "I'm your brother's bad luck, and he's run away from me. I beg you, get an ax and drive it into the crack of the tree so I can get my fingers out."

"If I do, will you go back to my brother?" asked the rich man.

"Of course," said the tall man.

When the rich man drove the ax into the crack, the tall man pulled out his hands. Then he leaped and danced for joy and kissed the rich man. "What a good fellow!" he said. "From now on I live with you. You're so rich that I'll be well taken care of, and it was always a hard life with your brother."

And that's what happened: the poor brother was rich, and the rich brother grew poor.

·   ·   ·

PART TWO

A Rooster

and

a Hen,

Let the

Story Begin:

Children's

Tales

I never heard a *maysele* from my grandfather. He was always engrossed in the study of Talmudic law, in pious acts, in prayer, and in the Torah. But my grandmother—it was she who told me a *maysele,* or asked me a riddle. At twilight on *shabes,* as it got dark outside and long evening shadows fell over our ill-constructed little house, my grandmother Khane would sit me on her lap near the large clay oven and tell me a story.

        —Memoir from Pumpyan, Lithuania, ca. 1920

$\mathcal{A}$lmost everyone's experience with folktales begins in childhood. The tales in this section are for young children, and often about them too. They were told throughout the Yiddish-speaking world, and traveled to America as well. I can recall sitting in my grandmother's lap while she combed my hair and related "Stones and Bones Rattle in My Belly" in her Ukrainian-Yiddish dialect. My children in turn remember my mother telling the same tale to them. Their favorite, though, was an adventure story about a very young hero named Bebele, Little Bean, that their grandfather, *zeyde Maks,* told them at bedtime.

Some of these tales are simple and consist of a single incident, while others have a more complex plot. Rhymed verses may be part of a story, as in "Moyshele and Sheyndele," and rhymed endings commonly recur. One favorite is:

A hun un a hon	A rooster and a hen
Dos maysele heybt zikh on.	Now my story's begun.
A kats un a moyz	A cat and a mouse
Dos maysele lozt zikh oys.	Now my story is done.

And another:

A flekl arayn, a flekl aroys	One spot out, one spot in
Dos maysele iz oys.	My little tale is done.

The beginning of these tales is almost always *Amol iz geven . . .* or, "Once upon a time . . ." Many open with "Once upon a time there was a rabbi and his wife . . ." The abundant use of diminutives—the suffix *-ele* ("little") is attached to many of the nouns—is a clear indicator of a tale for little folk. Indeed, the genre itself is called the *maysele* in Yiddish, literally, "little tale"—or *kinder-maysele,* "little tale for children."

There are several categories of *kinder-mayselekh.* Didactic tales such as "The Naughty Little Girl" teach the lesson of obedience to one's parents. In "A Tale of Two Brothers" the lessons to be learned are kindness to animals and respect for nature, while the importance of good manners is dramatized in "Next Time That's What I'll Say." These tales warn of what may happen to a child who is impolite or disobedient.

Tales told from a child's point of view make up another group. Some, like "Clever Khashinke and Foolish Bashinke," tell of parental favoritism, of the consequent rivalry between the goody-goody and the bumbling child, and of justice restored. Others, like "Stones and Bones Rattle in My Belly," evoke common childhood terrors, such as the fear of being left alone. Yet others, like "Moyshele and Sheyn-dele," test the limits of disobedience, sometimes with drastic conse-quences. "Next Time That's What I'll Say," and "Little Bean" are tales told by children.

Finally there are the nonsense tales that form part of the humorous repertoire of and for the very young. They are called *lign-mayselekh,* "little fibbing tales," or tales that are *nisht geshtoygn, nisht gefloygn*—

far-fetched; literally, "that neither ascend nor fly." Their humor lies in a continuous flow of contradictions, nonsequitors, and strange juxtapositions of people and events. They were especially popular at Purim, the holiday that celebrates the defeat of Haman in his plans to destroy the Jews of Persia during the reign of King Ahaseurus. A carnival mood pervades this holiday, and nonsense tales were part of the revelry.

15

The Pain in the Neck: A Nonsense Tale

Once upon a time there was a very rich poor man. He had no children except for nine daughters. His oldest son took it into his head to go to the fair. So he saddled a match, rode up the chimney, and was driven, riding, to the water. Two sieves, one with a bottom, the other without, were floating in the water. He sat down between them and floated. Suddenly he heard someone shout that the synagogue was on fire, so he ran to rescue the bathhouse, but just then remembered that he hadn't yet eaten. So he went to buy something to eat. Someone said, "You're going to eat? Today is such an important fast day. The Russians are beating each other." He went on and was told, "You're going to eat today? On such a holiday? Your wife has given birth to a boy." He remembered that he didn't have any diapers, so he rode to the forest for twigs, but his hands got stuck; so he ran to fetch an ax. As he went, he saw a fly at the tip of the church steeple, and she didn't look well. So he went to the doctor for medicine. Then he ran into the city to get a pain in the neck, because he *was* a pain in the neck.

The Six-Pointed Homentash: A Purim Tale

One day an imp of Ashmodai who lived in a village ran into a dense forest where the trees were a mile apart from each other. He went up to the first tree, where he saw a parrot. He went up to the second tree, where he saw a flea as big as a walnut. Well, if you have a nut, you crack it; and when you crack a nut, thirteen yards of cloth come out. If you have cloth, you become a merchant; and if you are a merchant, you travel to markets. When he got to the market, he saw a peasant woman and bought a turkey from her. He brought the goose home and roasted the chick. He asked his wife to make him an omelet with six eggs, so she made him a six-pointed *homentash,* and she was frightened and died. So he had to sit down to mourn her for seven days. So he sat down at seven and a half kopecks per month and did not have enough, so he added a bit. And if you have a bit, you take it to the synagogue.

Arriving at the synagogue, he saw three men quarreling. He asked, "Why are you quarreling? Why don't you cast lots?"* So they cast lots, which showed the Saturday before Passover as auspicious. On the Saturday before Passover, it's a good deed, a *mitsve,* to put your foot in the oven. If you put your foot in the oven, you get dried out. If you get dried out, you pull on a sock. If you pull on a sock, you have to bite. And so he took bites out of the living and the dead. His dead wife said, "Why are you taking bites out of everyone? Why don't you take a bite out of yourself?" So he began to take bites out of all the food. Food spills, and if it spills, you get the itch. And if

---

* According to one theory, the Jewish holiday of Purim (which literally means "lots") is related to the Babylonian New Year, on which day it was believed that one's fate for the coming year—i.e., one's lot—was sealed. This nonsense tale was told on Purim, hence the reference to "casting lots."

you get the itch, you go to the doctor, who says, "Why should I guess? Let the rabbi guess. Let the rabbi hit on it." So the rabbi struck the windowpane. And if you strike a windowpane, things get mushy. And if they get mushy, you get butter. And if you have butter, you spread it, and if you spread it, you drive off, and so he drove right into a huge mudhole, and if we ever get out of it, we'll go on with this tale.

17
A Tale of Two Brothers

Once upon a time in a small town there lived a father and mother who had two sons. One of them was clever and the other was foolish. When they were children, the foolish son used to sit by the fireplace gnawing away at the carob bread he had in a sack beside him while his clever brother was off studying in *kheyder,* in school. And this is why the father and mother loved the clever brother. He was their pride and joy.

When the two brothers were no longer small, the foolish one still sat beside the fireplace eating his carob bread as if there were nothing better to do. However, his clever brother, looking about him, now understood what a poor man his father was. He mulled the matter over for a while, then said one day to his parents, "Look, I'm almost grown up. What will become of us in our poverty? If you'll let me, I'd like to go out into the wide world and seek my fortune. I'll work hard and bring home a lot of money, so we can rebuild the house and live like proper people."

What he said pleased his parents and they kissed him and hugged him and loaded him down for his journey with the best they had: a great sack of butter, biscuits, apples, pears, and other good things. Then they gave him what money they could spare and sent him on his way.

The boy, feeling cheerful and lively, left the town and was soon in the country. As he walked along, a dog came running toward him. The poor thing was filthy, matted, and hungry, and it said, "Dear boy, I beg you to wash me and comb me and give me something to eat. I'll show you my gratitude one day."

But the boy was, after all, a clever fellow and not about to be fooled, so he said, "Beat it, you dog. My father wouldn't do such a thing and neither would my mother. And I'm not about to, either." And the dog ran away.

The boy went on a bit farther until he came to a well. A green mold floated on the water's surface, and there was mud everywhere. The silver cup hanging beside it was tarnished. The boy was thirsty and would have drunk, but he was repelled by the filthy well. Then the well spoke to him: "Dear boy, I beg you to clean me up. Scour my silver cup and clear away the mud. I'll show you my gratitude one day."

The boy said angrily, "My father wouldn't do such a thing and neither would my mother. And I'm not about to, either." With that he went on his way.

A little farther on, he came to a pear tree whose branches were dry and whose leaves were withered and the earth all around it was hard and parched. The tree said, "Dear boy, I beg you, trim my branches, turn over the earth around my roots, and give me some water. I'll show you my gratitude one day."

The boy said, "My father wouldn't do such a thing and neither would my mother. And I'm not about to, either." And he went on his way.

He went on and on until he came to a city. There he went into an inn and said to the innkeeper, "I want to work for you. I'm not asking for money, I'll leave that to your sense of justice."

"Good," said the innkeeper. "Work for me for a year. I'll give you food and drink, and if you prove to be a good worker, I'll reward you."

The boy worked for a year and the innkeeper was pleased with him. When the boy asked for his wages, the innkeeper said, "I won't give you money, but if you'll go into my stable you'll find horses and wagons, large chests and small chests. Old horses and young ones; new wagons and old. Take whatever your heart desires and go home to your parents in good health."

The boy bade the innkeeper farewell and went into the stable. Looking around, he was overjoyed at what he saw. Since he was a clever fellow, he rolled up his sleeves and went to work gathering the best of everything: the finest horse, which he fitted with the best saddle, and the newest wagon, which he loaded with the finest and largest chests. Then he cracked his whip and off he went.

He was no sooner out of the city than he saw a large pear tree with fine, shapely branches loaded with golden pears. The sun lit up the tree; it was a lovely sight. The boy got off his wagon and ran to it. He pulled down a branch to pluck a pear, but the branch tore itself out of his hand. "Go away, you horrid boy," said the tree. "When I asked you to loosen the soil around my roots, you refused. And now you want to pick my pears! Off with you!"

Embarrassed, the boy went on his way. A little further he saw a bright, clean well with gleaming clear water and a silver cup that glowed. What a delight! Being thirsty, the boy thought, "I'll have a drink," and took down the cup. He bent to scoop up some water, but the cup tore itself out of his hand. "Go away, you horrid boy," said the well. "When I begged you to clean me and scour my silver

cup, you replied, 'I'm not about to.' And now you want to drink my water! Off with you!"

Ashamed again, the boy got back in his wagon and went on his way, on and on. When he was near his home town, he saw a dog running toward him. A lovely, clean dog, a delight to the eye. On its neck it wore a blue ribbon hung with pearls and diamonds. The boy stopped his wagon and called, "Here, dog. Here, dog." And the animal leaped into the wagon. But when the boy tried to take the ribbon off the dog's neck, the dog said, "Bow, wow! So, you want my diamonds and pearls? But you wouldn't wash or comb me, or give me anything to eat. Ugh! You'll get nothing from me. And if you make a move toward me, I'll tear you to bits." The dog jumped out of the wagon and ran away.

Furious, the boy cracked his whip and drove off toward home.

When he got there, it was midnight and everyone was asleep. The shutters of his house were closed, the gate and the doors were locked. All was silent and dark. But the boy began to pound on the door and at the windows, crying, "Father, Mother. Get up. Your son is back, bringing all sorts of good things! Spread out your tablecloths, and I'll unpack my chests for you."

His parents got up, and oh, what gladness there was; what joy! Their son had returned loaded with all sorts of good things.

"Friends, neighbors," they called, "gather round. See what our son has brought."

They lit up the house. They spread tablecloths. Good friends gathered, and everyone waited to see what the clever son had brought back with him.

The fool, poor boy, came from his place beside the fire and watched the parade of good things. But when daylight came, everyone saw that the fine young horse was now an old mare; the splendid new wagon had turned into a rickety open-sided cart, and the new chests were shabby old boxes. The clever son couldn't understand what had happened. Finally he said, "Never mind, open the chests. They're filled with gold and silver."

His parents opened the chests and began to pour out the contents.

And what was it they poured? Rats and mice and mud and dung. The house was a mess. The mother wept; the father scolded the clever boy and beat him. Friends and neighbors laughed and went away.

The clever son just stood there, dismayed. Then the foolish son gave himself a shake and said, "Don't beat him, don't scold him. It's not his fault. Let me go out into the wide world to seek my fortune."

His father laughed. "Just see how well our clever son has fared, and now our fool wants to try his luck."

But the fool insisted on going. "Well," said his mother, "let him try." They gave him a sack full of dry biscuits, a flask of water, and a few kopecks and off he went.

As he was going along, he met a dog, bedraggled and hungry. The dog licked his hand and said, "Dear boy, I beg you, comb my hair. Give me something to eat and let me have a little water. I'll show you my gratitude one day."

The fool untied his sack, fed the dog some of his biscuits, and let him drink from the flask. Then, having washed the dog and combed out its tangled hair, the fool went on his way.

As he walked, he came to a well. He saw that the surface of the water was green with mold. There was mud everywhere, and the silver cup hanging beside the well was tarnished. The well said, "Dear boy, I beg you. Clean me up, please, and scour my tarnished cup. I'll show you my gratitude one day."

The fool rolled up his sleeves and went right to work. He cleaned up the well, scoured the silver cup, and cleared the mud away. Then he resumed his journey.

As he went along he saw a tree with withered branches. Its leaves were dried out, and the soil at its roots was parched and hard. The tree said, "Dear boy, I beg you, cut back my branches. Dig up the soil at my roots and give me some water. I'll show my gratitude one day."

Again the boy rolled up his sleeves. He cut back the branches properly, loosened the soil at the roots, and gave the tree some water. Then he went on his way.

He walked on and on until he arrived at a city—the same one his brother had come to. He took service for a year with the same innkeeper, and when his year was up, he asked for his wages.

The innkeeper said, "I won't give you money. But if you'll go into my stable you'll find horses and wagons, large chests and small. Old horses and young; new wagons and old. Take whatever your heart desires and go back to your home in good health."

The fool bade farewell to the innkeeper and went into the stable. Seeing all that was there, he grew confused. "He was a good master," the fool thought. "He trusts me, so I won't betray him. I'll take the old horse, the old wagon, and a couple of small chests. That'll be enough." Well, since he was a fool, after all, the result was that he picked out the very worst things in the stable and drove off with them.

As he was riding along, he saw a pear tree laden with golden pears. Feeling the urge to eat one, he approached the tree and said, "Pear tree, pear tree, may I pluck a pear from your branches?"

The pear tree, hearing him, rustled its leaves. "Dear boy," it said, "pluck as many pears as you like. It was you yourself who cut back my branches and cleaned me up."

The fool plucked a pear, for which he thanked the pear tree, and drove on.

In a while he saw a well. Since he was thirsty, he approached the well and said, "Dear well, may I drink some of your water?" The moment the well heard him, its waters sparkled and its silver cup leaped into his hand. "Drink, dear boy," said the well, "drink to your heart's content. You yourself cleaned me up. Take the silver cup as a memento."

The fool took the silver cup and thanked the well. Then he drove on with the sun shining brightly. His horse moved at a lively pace and his wagon gleamed.

As he went, he saw a dog running toward him. A lovely dog, so well groomed that it was a delight to the eye. Around its neck it wore a blue ribbon hung with pearls and diamonds. The dog, seeing him, jumped into the wagon and said, "Bow, wow, wow. Dear boy, take the pearls and diamonds from my neck. They're a gift for you, because you washed and combed me. And you fed me and gave me water to drink." The boy took the pearls and diamonds and thanked the dog. Then he drove on.

And thus, loaded with good things, he arrived at his home. It was already midnight and everyone was asleep, so he sat down on the porch and waited for the sun to rise.

In the morning he knocked at the door and cried, "Father, Mother. Open up. Your foolish son has returned. Spread out your tablecloths and bed linen, and I'll empty my chests into them."

His parents got up and let him in. His mother said, "You want me to spread tablecloths out? Sackcloth will be good enough for you." But when the chests were opened and his parents began to pour out the contents, the whole house glowed from the gold and silver, diamonds and pearls and assorted treasures that tumbled out. His mother hugged him and kissed him, and his father cried, "Now which of my sons is the fool and which is the clever one?" With that he began to beat the clever son, but the fool restored peace and the family was happy at last.

They lead a happy life,
Drink honey by the cup.
We lick ours from a knife,
And lick each droplet up.

18

Stones and Bones Rattle in My Belly

Once upon a time there was a rabbi and his wife, and they had many children. One day the rabbi went to the synagogue and his wife went to do some work in the mill. A bear came along and broke down the door of their house and ate all the children up. When the rabbi came home from the synagogue and his wife came home from the mill, they looked everywhere but couldn't find the children.

"Children," they called, "children, children, where are you?"

And the children called back, "Here we are, inside the bear. He came to the house and broke the door. Then he ate us up."

So the parents called, "Bear, bear, come let us pick your lice."

"No," said the bear. "I won't."

"Come," said the parents, "and we'll give you a bowl of cereal with butter."

But again the bear said, "I won't."

"Come," said the parents, "and we'll give you groats with butter."

But again the bear said, "I won't."

"Come," said the parents, "and we'll give you some sweets."

But still the bear said, "I won't."

"Come," said the parents, "and we'll give you some meat."

"For meat," said the bear, "I'll come." And he came. The parents gave him as much meat as he could eat and he ate and ate until he fell asleep. Then they took a huge knife and cut his belly open and took all their children out.

The rabbi and his wife washed and scrubbed each of the children. Then they put one of them on top of the table, one under the table, one in the bed, one under the bed, one on the clay oven, and one beside the clay oven. They fed them all boiled groats with milk.

Then the rabbi and his wife put stones and bones inside the bear's belly and sewed him up. When they were done, they woke the bear, who grabbed at his belly, but there were no children there. Then off he went singing,

> *"Tra, la, tra, la, tri, li.*
> *Oh, I've got bones*
> *And big heavy stones*
> *Rattling in my bell-eeeeee."*

19

Sóre-Kháne at the Tip of the Church Tower

Once upon a time there was a father and mother who went off to the market, leaving their daughter Sóre-Kháne alone in the house.

Sóre-Kháne swept the floor. Then a raven flew down and caught her up in his bill and carried her to the tip of the church tower. When her father and mother came home and saw her at the tip of the church tower, they said, "Sóre, dear. Sóre, dear. Come down from the tower."

But she replied,

> *"No, father, no.*
> *You don't know what I want.*
> *The maidens are all married*
> *And I'm still all alone."*

Then her mother called up to her, "Sóre, dear. Sóre, dear. Come down from the tower."

But she replied,

> "No, mother, no.
> The maidens are all married
> And I'm still all alone."

Then her brother called up to her, "Sóre, dear. Sóre, dear. Come down from the tower."

But she replied,

> "No, brother, no.
> The maidens are all married
> And I'm still all alone."

Now her sister called up to her, "Sóre, dear. Sóre, dear. Come down from the tower."

But she replied,

> "No, sister, no.
> The maidens are all married
> And I'm still all alone."

When night fell, she climbed down from the tip of the church tower and went slowly to her house. She stood outside her father's window and said, "Father, open up."

"No," he said. "You wouldn't come down from the tower when I asked you."

So she went to her mother's window, but she also said no. Then to her brother's—again, no.

So she went to her sister's window, and her sister opened the door and let her in and sat her down on the oven and fed her boiled groats with milk, and Sóre-Kháne ate it all and went to sleep at once.

2 0

Little Bean

Once upon a time there was a couple who did not have children, and they often went to the cemetery,* where they prayed to have a child. One day, as they were praying, an angel flew down from heaven and told them: "God has heard your prayers. Which would you prefer: to have a son who will be no bigger than a bean, or a daughter who, when she is thirteen, will abandon Judaism for another faith?"

"Better," they said, "to have a son no bigger than a bean." A year went by and they had a son who was indeed no bigger than a bean. And he never grew any bigger, which is why he was called Little Bean.

One day when the mother was preparing a meal, she poured what she was cooking into an earthen pot and gave it to Little Bean to take to his father in the marketplace. Little Bean, delighted with the task, put the pot on his head and ran off to his father.

He ran and he ran and he ran until he met an old beggar. The beggar said, "It's three days since any food has passed my lips." Little Bean pitied him and gave him all of his father's meal. The beggar thanked him warmly: "God bless your little bones. May the light of happiness and good fortune shine on you."

When the beggar had done eating, Little Bean put the empty pot

---

* There is a belief that ancestors, particularly deceased parents and grandparents, can intercede on one's behalf in heaven. For this reason, Jews sometimes went to the cemetery to pray that a particular wish be granted.

on his head and started off at a run. He ran and he ran and he ran until he met a gang of thieves.

"Where are you off to so fast?" they said.

"I'm running to tell my father that I've given his supper to a beggar," he said.

"Well, if you're so nice, we'll take you into our gang and you can come stealing with us."

Little Bean wanted to say, "Stealing is forbidden," but he was afraid they would kill him, so he said, "Good. I'll join you."

They went on together until they came to a locked stable. And as the thieves were looking the place over, Little Bean leaped up into the keyhole and disappeared.

The thieves wondered, "Where did the little fellow get to? He was here just a minute ago." They searched everywhere but couldn't find him. In the end they left.

Little Bean looked around and hid in a tub of chopped beets, and so the cow ate him up with the beets. When Little Bean saw how dark it was in the cow's belly, and found that there was no way to get out, he was very angry. "The devil take you!" he shouted at the cow. "I hope the cholera gets you."

In the morning a servant who was milking the cow heard someone shouting. "The devil take you! I hope the cholera gets you." So frightened she was, more dead than alive, she ran out of the stable. "Mistress," she cried, "the cow is cursing!"

"Don't be a fool," said her mistress. "I've never heard of a cursing cow." She went to the stable to milk the cow herself, but as she was milking, she heard someone cry, "The devil take you! I hope the cholera gets you." More dead than alive, the woman ran to the rabbi and told him the whole story. The rabbi said, "Kill the cow and throw the innards into the street."

The next morning the *shoykhet,* the butcher, came and killed the cow. Just as he was cutting the cow's stomach to take out the innards, he heard a voice that cried, "Don't cut from the belly, cut from the side." The *shoykhet* too was frightened, and he began to cut from the side. Little by little he drew out the innards, which he threw into the street.

A hungry beggar passing by saw the fresh innards and thought, "God has sent me a real gift. I'll take these home and cook a fine meal." So he put them into his sack, slung the sack over his shoulder, and went happily on his way.

He walked and he walked and he walked, when suddenly he felt something stabbing his shoulder. Since he couldn't imagine what it was, he ignored it and continued on. But as he walked, something stabbed his shoulder again. "I wonder what that can be," he thought. "I don't have any pins in the sack, nothing there but soft innards. Then what's stabbing me?" Again he tried to ignore it, but the farther he went the sharper the stabs, until finally he couldn't stand them.

He stopped and said to himself, "Shall I throw the innards away? But that would be sinful, and I'd have nothing to eat. But if I keep carrying them, who knows what will happen to my shoulder? It's a bad business."

Then he heard someone call, "Throw them away. Throw them away." Frightened, he threw the innards into the street. As he stood looking, he saw a tiny boy, no larger than a bean, creep out of them. The beggar recognized Little Bean at once. "You're the boy who gave me his father's supper to eat," he said.

"That's me," said Little Bean.

"Then what were you doing in there?" asked the beggar. And Little Bean told him the whole story.

"Tsk, tsk, tsk," said the beggar. "What strange things can happen in this world."

"I was afraid you would eat me for supper," Little Bean said.

"Well, do you want to go home?" asked the beggar.

"Yes," Little Bean said, "I want to go home."

So they went to Little Bean's house, and when his father and mother saw him they cried, "Little Bean! Where were you?" And Little Bean told them the whole story.

A rooster and a hen . . .
Now my story's begun.
A cat and a mouse . . .
Now my story is done.

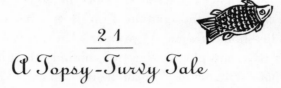

A Topsy-Turvy Tale

Once upon a time, four live dead people were out walking. One of them was blind, the other was mute, the third was lame, and the fourth was naked.

The blind man saw a tree loaded with apples, so he said to the mute, "Tell the lame fellow to climb up into the tree and throw us down some apples." So the lame man climbed into the tree and threw down an apronful of apples for the naked man.

That done, the blind man went on. Then, seeing what he saw, he stopped. It was a crowded marketplace, so crowded that one wagon was a mile away from another. He went up to a peasant woman and said, "I want to buy a goose."

She said, "That will be twenty kopecks for the turkey."

So he bought the duck.

Then he saw a woman who was selling fish—a fish that weighed some twenty pounds, but when he picked it up, nothing was there. So he took it home and said to his wife, "Cook this fish."

"All right," she said, "I'll cook the fish if you'll bring me a pot the size of three thimbles into which I can put three yards of flour."

So he brought her a pot the size of three thimbles which could hold three yards of flour, and she cooked the fish.

Now guess what the sly young rascal did? He took the head of the fish for himself and gave the tail to his wife.

A tail is an end, and an end is a finish, and this is the finish of my tale.

Clever Khashinke and Foolish Bashinke

There was a woman who had two daughters, one clever and the other foolish. The clever one was called Khashinke, and the foolish one was Bashinke. The mother preferred the clever daughter to the foolish one and finally drove the foolish one from the house.

The foolish daughter walked and walked and walked, until she came to a little pear tree. The pear tree said, "Why are you crying?"

Bashinke said, "Because my mother drove me away from home."

The pear tree said, "Shake my branches, then you'll have a measure of pears, and I'll have a measure."

So she did, and took away her measure of pears. She walked on, still crying and crying, until she saw a little cow. The little cow said, "Why are you crying?"

"Because my mother drove me away from home," said Bashinke.

The little cow said, "Well, milk me and then you'll have a quart of milk, and I'll have a quart."

So she did, and went on her way, crying and crying until she saw a kneading trough filled with flour. "Why are you crying?" asked the kneading trough.

"Because my mother drove me away from home," replied Bashinke.

The kneading trough said, "Take my flour. Knead it and bake it. That way you'll have a loaf of bread, and I'll have a loaf."

So she did. And now she had bread and milk and pears, all of which she ate. Then she lay down to sleep.

When she woke the next morning, she walked on, still crying, till she came to a little hut, where she found an old granny. And the old *bobetske* said to her, "Why are you crying, girl?"

"Because my mother drove me away from home," said Bashinke.

"Why did she do that?" asked the *bobetske*.

"Because she says I'm foolish. And I have a sister who's clever, and my mother loves her and hates me. That's why she drove me away from home."

"In that case," said the bobetske, "just wait a minute. I'll fix things so your mother will care for you." The old woman spread out a sheet and threw all sorts of good things on it: candies and cookies, gold and silver. Then she tied the sheet up and said, "Take that home to your mother."

Bashinke carried the good things home with her, stood in front of the house, and cried, "Mother, Mother, open the door."

"The plague take you," came the reply. "Be off!"

Bashinke, seeing that her mother would not open the door, called, "Mother, I've brought you all sorts of good things."

When her mother heard that Bashinke had brought all sorts of good things, she opened the door at once and let her in. And when she untied the sheet, her eyes were dazzled by the brightness of the gold and silver and everything else. "Ah, ah, what wonderful things!" she said. "Where did you get them?"

Bashinke told her about the old bobetske who lived in the little hut. "Ah," thought her mother, "if Bashinke, who is a fool, could bring such wonderful things, just think what my clever Khashinke will bring." And she drove her clever daughter from the house so that she too would come home bearing all sorts of good things.

Khashinke walked and walked until she came to the little hut. She went in, crying. The old bobetske sitting there asked, "Why are you crying?"

Khashinke said, "Because my mother has driven me out of the house so that I too can bring back all sorts of good things."

"Ah," said the old woman, "she drove you from the house so that you can bring her good things? She likes good things, does she? Well, then," she said, "I'll send her good things." With that she spread a sheet out on the floor and oh, the good things she threw on it. Alas and alack: snakes and frogs and mice and cats—and more. Then she tied them all up and gave the bundle to Khashinke, saying, "Here, take these good things home to your mother."

And that's what Khashinke did. When she got home, she called, "Mother, let me in."

Her mother ran eagerly to the door and Khashinke came in. No sooner had she set her bundle down than the snakes and the frogs and the mice and the cats began to leap up into her mother's face. Her mother screamed, "Oh, the devil take you. What have you brought me? Oh, Lord, what will I do? What will I do? Help! People, save me! I feel sick."

A crowd came running into the house and stood around staring at her. Finally the mother gave Khashinke a good beating and drove her away from home.

Foolish Bashinke was now the clever one, while the clever Khashinke went away like a fool and disappeared.

2 3

The Granny Bear

Once upon a time there was a granny bear whose children, all ten of them, loved to eat *farfl* with beans. One day the granny bear cooked up a pot of *farfl* with beans, then went off to the forest to gather wood. As soon as she was gone, her children ate all the *farfl* and beans in the pot. And when they were done, they were afraid that the granny bear would spank them for it.

This is what they did: they took a towel and stuck it full of needles. because they knew that when the granny bear came home, the first thing she always did was to wash and dry her hands.

Then the children all hid. One hid in the closet while another crawled under the closet. One climbed on top of the clock while another crawled under the clock. One got into a chest while another crawled on top of the chest. One got into a cubbyhole while another crawled under the cubbyhole.

When the granny bear came home from the forest, she knocked at the door, but no one answered. "Children, children," she called, "open the door." But the door stayed shut. Again she cried, "Children, children, open the door. I'll give you some piping hot *farfl* and beans."

When the children heard the words *farfl* and beans, they came out of hiding and opened the door for the granny bear. "Granny Bear, Granny Bear," they said, "wash and dry your hands." And the granny bear did. She washed up, and when she wiped her hands on the towel they got so badly stuck by the pins that she couldn't spank the children.

24
Moyshele and Sheyndele

Once upon a time there was a poor woodcutter who had a wife and two small children, a boy and a girl. The boy was called Moyshele, the girl Sheyndele. The woodcutter's wife died and he married a second wife who was a very wicked woman and a cruel stepmother to the children.

One day the woodcutter left the house to chop wood in the forest, and the stepmother got ready to go to market to do the Sabbath shopping. Before she left, she gave the children some food, putting Moyshele's in a pot and Sheyndele's on a plate. She said,

"Moyshele, if you break the pot
I'll chop off your head,
So you'd better not."

She told Sheyndele,

"Sheyndele, Sheyndele, just you wait,
I'll chop off your legs
If you break this plate."

Then she slammed the door and went to market.

The children were afraid to eat lest they break something, but the rooster suddenly flew up on the table and knocked over the pot. It fell to the ground and broke into teeny-tiny pieces. Moyshele, seeing them, was terrified and began to cry. Sheyndele comforted him, saying, "Hush, Moyshele. Don't cry." And she took the shards of the pot and pushed them into a corner of the room.

When the stepmother came home, she couldn't find the pot. "Where is the pot?" she asked Moyshele.

"The rooster broke it," he said.

The stepmother was very angry, but she pretended that nothing was the matter. Later she said to Moyshele, "Come with me and I'll wash your hair." So Moyshele went with her. She took him into another room and cut off his head, after which she cooked it for supper.

When the woodcutter came back from the forest he said, "Where is Moyshele?"

"I don't know," said the stepmother. Then they sat down at the table and ate the soup and the meat. Sheyndele, unaware of what she was eating, sucked the marrow from the bones and threw them out the window.

A little mound of earth covered the bones and when the glad summer came again, a new Moyshele grew up out of it. Moyshele stood there on his little mound until, seeing a tailor pass by, he called, "Tailor, tailor, make me a pair of trousers and I'll sing you a song:

> *Murdered by my mother,*
> *Eaten by my father,*
> *and Sheyndele, when they were done,*
> *Sucked the marrow from my bones*
> *And threw them out the window."*

The tailor, hearing the song, pitied him and made him a pair of trousers. Moyshele put them on, and then a shoemaker went by. Moyshele called, "Shoemaker, shoemaker, make me a pair of boots and I'll sing you a song:

> *Murdered by my mother,*
> *Eaten by my father,*
> *and Sheyndele, when they were done,*
> *Sucked the marrow from my bones*
> *And threw them out the window."*

The shoemaker, hearing the song, pitied him and made him a pair of boots. Moyshele put them on, and then a hatmaker went by. Moyshele called, "Hatmaker, hatmaker, make me a hat and I'll sing you a song:

> *Murdered by my mother,*
> *Eaten by my father,*
> *and Sheyndele, when they were done,*
> *Sucked the marrow from my bones*
> *And threw them out the window."*

The hatmaker, hearing the song, pitied him and made him a hat. And Moyshele put it on and ran off to school.

> *One log there,*
> *One log gone.*
> *As for my tale—*
> *My tale is done.*

2 5
Next Time That's What I'll Say

Once upon a time there was a king who had two sons, one of whom was a fool while the other was clever. One day the king called his sons to him and said, "It's time that you both learned some profession or skill. You can't spend your lives doing nothing. So now, each of you tell me what you would like to learn."

The clever son promptly said, "I want to learn every skill there is."

"And you?" said the king to his foolish son.

"Well," said the fool, "I want to wash clothes in the river."

"Good," said the king. "Washing clothes is also a skill."

The king gave each of them money and the sons went away, the clever one to study and the foolish one to the river.

The fool stood beside the river and washed clothes. He washed and washed and washed. All at once one of the socks he was washing floated away and disappeared. So he crossed over to the other bank to look for it. There he ran about and ran about until he met a postman. "Listen," he said, "have you seen a sock, by chance?"

The irritated postman, unaware that this was the king's son, slapped his cheek so hard that it swelled up like a round loaf. The boy ran crying to the king, "Father, I was washing clothes in the river and a sock floated away. So I asked the postman if he had seen it, and he made my cheek swell like this."

The king thought, "A fool is a source of grief, and yet he must be taught wisdom." So he said, "My son, if it happens again that you meet a postman, take your hat off and say to him, 'Good morning, Mr. Postman, have you perhaps seen my sock?' "

"Good," said the fool. "Next time that's what I'll say."

So he walked and he walked and he walked until he passed a house where a wedding was taking place. He went inside. There, he took his hat off and said to the groom, "Good morning, Mr. Postman. Have you perhaps seen my sock?" The groom and the assembled relatives stared at him as if he was mad. "Postman! Who? Sock? What, where?" So they grabbed him and beat him well, after which they threw him out of the house.

Away he went, crying to the king, "Father, I've been to a wedding where I said, 'Good morning, Mr. Postman, have you perhaps seen my sock?' And oh, how they beat me up!"

The king thought, "A fool is a source of grief, and yet he must be taught wisdom." And so he said, "My son, if you're ever at a wedding again, drop a coin on a plate and dance with everyone."

"Good," said the fool, "that's what I'll do if it happens again." And he went off once more.

He went on and on until he saw a house that was burning—a huge conflagration. He ran into the burning house, threw a coin on a plate, and started to dance. When the firemen saw what he was doing, they burst out laughing and doused him from head to foot with the firehose. He ran to the king crying, "Father, I saw a house burning, and I went in and threw a coin on a plate and began to dance. When the firemen saw me, they doused me with their hose."

Hearing that, the king grew sad. "Now pay attention. If it happens again, don't be a fool. If you see a fire, grab a bucket of water and put it out."

"Good," said the fool, "that's what I'll do." And away he went again.

The morning after his beating, the fool was walking in the street when he saw a woman carrying a basketful of steaming-hot rolls. Thinking that they were on fire, he grabbed up a pail of water and flung it over them. The woman slapped him silly and snatched his hat from his head. Hatless, the fool ran to the king, crying, "Father, I saw a woman carrying rolls that were steaming, so I took a bucket of water and poured it over them. Then she slapped me silly and snatched my hat from my head."

Now the king grew angry and shouted, "You fool. If you see a poor woman carrying rolls, you buy a roll for a kopeck."

"Good," said the fool, "that's what I'll do next time." And away he went.

He went on and on until he saw a soldier scratching about in the dirt. So he said to the soldier, "Sell me a kopeck's worth."

"With the greatest pleasure in the world. Why, for a kopeck, I'll sell you a whole wagonload."

The delighted fool ran home to the king, crying, "Oh Father, what a terrific bargain I've just made." Then he told his father what the soldier had said. Hearing this, the king was now well and truly angry and drove his son out of the house.

The Naughty Little Girl

Once upon a time there was an old crone who lived all alone in a hut in an open field, and she used to take in naughty children who would not obey their parents. One day a mother gave the crone her naughty daughter and said, "Teach her to be obedient." The crone took the little girl with her, and they went off into the forest to gather kindling.

Meanwhile a bear came to the old crone's hut and began to turn around and around. As he was turning around and around, a dog came up and asked him, "Bear, why are you turning like that?"

"What difference does it make?" said the bear. "Why don't you turn too?" Then both of them turned around and around, and as they were turning, along came a stag that said, "Hey, bear, hey, dog, why are you turning like that?"

They said, "What difference does it make? Why don't you turn too?" Then all three of them turned around and around, and as they were turning, along came a rooster and said, "Hey, bear and dog and stag, why are you turning like that?"

They said, "What difference does it make? Why don't you turn too?" Then all four of them turned around and around, and as they were turning, along came a teapot cover and said, "Hey, bear and dog and stag and rooster, why are you turning like that?"

They said, "What difference does it make? Why don't you turn too?" Then all five of them turned around and around, and as they were turning, along came a bit of pitch and a pin and said, "Hey, bear and dog and stag and rooster and teapot cover, why are you turning like that?"

They said, "What difference does it make? Why don't you turn too?" Then all seven of them turned around and around until night fell and it was time for them to go to sleep.

Well, where should they sleep? Inside the old crone's hut. So they went inside and each of them found a place to sleep. The bear lay down in the bed, the dog in the cradle, the stag on the oven, the rooster on a shelf, the teapot cover in the chimney, the bit of pitch inside a box of matches, and the pin, unable to find anyplace else, stuck himself into a towel.

When the crone and the little girl came back from the forest, they wanted to go to sleep. They went to the bed, and the bear kicked out at them and frightened them so that they sprang away. They tried to lie down in the cradle, and the dog bit them. "Ouch, ouch," they cried, "what's going on here?"

Next they tried to lie down on the oven, but the stag threatened them with his horns and made them tremble and turn cold with fear. The crone went to the oven to warm herself, but the teapot cover fell out of the chimney and struck her hand. Frightened, the crone cried out, "Woe is me. What's going on here?" Meaning to light the lamp so that she could see what was happening, she opened the matchbox to take out a match, but the bit of pitch stuck so tightly to her fingers she couldn't shake it off. So she washed her hands to get rid of the pitch. Then she reached for the towel, but the pin pricked her so hard she began to yell. The rooster, hearing her, yelled back, "You don't scare me." When the crone heard that, she was so frightened she dropped dead on the spot.

The little girl, meanwhile, ran from the hut and all the way home to her mother. From then on she was an obedient child and did everything her mother told her to do. And afterward, children everywhere obeyed their mothers.

PART THREE

Magic Rings, Feathers of Gold, Mountains of Glass: Wonder Tales

We children loved it when mother told us wonder tales. She
was always busy helping to earn the family's living, but on
shabes she had time. At dusk, before it was permitted to light
candles and say the prayers that ended the Sabbath and
ushered in the more prosaic week, we used to gather around
her and ask her to tell us a wonder tale. Sometimes she told
us a tale about a snake. Sometimes it was about a forest child
or a princess . . .

—Memoir from a Lithuanian *shtetl*, the turn of
the century

*I*n Yiddish the genre of fairy
tales, or *märchen,* is called *vunder-mayses,* literally "wonder tales." They
are rich with supernatural figures and things: helpers, like *Elyohu
hanovi,* Elijah the Prophet, who stand in for the fairy godmothers of
the folktales of other cultures; hinderers like devils, sorcerers, and
the witch Bobe Ha, who must be a relative of Baba Yaga; magical
objects like enchanted rings, golden feathers, and glass mountains.
The time and place are indefinite ("once upon a time," "in a city");
the heroes and heroines are unnamed ("there was a young girl," "a
rabbi," "a princess"). These tales generally contain a series of episodes
told as a string of events, or, in the more complex tales, as a revolving
stage ("now we leave the heroine and return to the hero"). Wonder
tales clearly don't mean to command our belief, though there is a
Hasidic view that they may veil mystical secrets of the greatest
importance. (According to Reb Nakhman of Bratslav, "The fairy tales

of the world may hold many hidden and exalted things, but they have become distorted because they are deficient and people have become confused and no longer tell them properly."')

The standard introduction *amol iz geven*, "once upon a time . . . ," reminds listeners that the story is a fictitious one. A rhymed ending, recited with tongue in cheek, was also a common device to signal that this was a flight of fancy, a *bobe-mayse*:

> *I too was there*
> *And had a good little glass of brandy.*
> *From my beard it dripped*
> *But none I sipped.*

The vast majority of the wonder tales tell about a young woman or man who leaves home and has many adventures. Such tales frequently end with a lavish celebration of marriage. Just as the *kinder-mayselekh* of the previous section represent the fears and challenges of early childhood, the wonder tales dramatize the problems and perils of young adulthood. In a sense they chart the course to maturity. Typically, fairy tale heroes and heroines must confront a number of adversaries: mean parents, stepparents, or siblings; witches, demons, or sorcerers. More specifically, they must overcome a lack—of money or a profession, of a parent or mate. In "Forty Hares and a Princess" and "The Orphan Boys," the heroes lack status in the community, while in "The Orphan Boy Who Won the Bride," the hero lacks traditional Jewish learning. By the end of the tale the challenges are met, the needs are satisfied, and the heroines and heroes live happily ever after.

A smaller group of wonder tales uses the magical settings of the fairy tale world for more spiritually edifying purposes. These pious, didactic wonder tales combine marvelous transformations with religious motifs drawn from the Cabalistic and Midrashic literature.

Certainly a tale like "The Orphan Boy Who Won the Bride," though on the surface a male Cinderella tale, owes much of its power to the imagery of prophecy and redemption with which it is studded. The story of a Jewish boy raised by a gentile nobleman recalls the early life of Moses. The Jews wandering in the desert after the flight from Egypt, and Moses receiving the Ten Commandments are figured in the episodes of the Congealed Sea and the island where the boy finds stones on which beautiful writing has been inscribed. Finally there is the climactic wedding scene in which a favorite theme of the Cabalists is replayed: the mystical marriage between the masculine and feminine emanations of God, the *eyn sof* and *shkhine*. In the mystical tradition, it is that union that will precede the coming of the Messiah.

But for the most part, the stories in this section have no specific cultural markers except for linguistic and stylistic ones. They were told in Yiddish by East European Jews and share features, such as formulaic beginnings and endings, with other Yiddish tales that are more culturally colored. Some may represent recent adaptations of stories learned from Polish or Russian ethnic neighbors with whom there was a tradition of story swapping. As one Yiddish scholar points out: "There were at least two large areas in which the interaction of the Yiddish and the Slavic speech communities assumed what may be called mass proportions: the Jewish nurseries in the towns, and the huts of the peasants where Jewish artisans would spend the whole week among their customers, to return to their home town on the eve of the Sabbath."[2]

The inclusion of a Yiddish proverb or a citation from the Bible, Talmud, or Book of Prayers was one way of turning a universal story into a Jewish tale. For example, the theme "the king's haughtiness punished" is widely known throughout folktale literature. In the Yiddish variant, "The Beggar King and the *Melamed*," the teller includes a passage from the morning prayer *Ezras Avoseynu* (God topples the haughty), converting the story into a pious wonder-tale that illustrates the passage. One can postulate that only stories that felt culturally "right" in form and content were translated into Yiddish by Jewish storytellers. But in time, and after successive retellings, they began to sound and feel like traditional Yiddish folktales.

Borrowing—selective borrowing, to be sure—went both ways: from Slavs to their Jewish neighbors and from Jews to their Slavic neighbors. The great Romantic poet of Poland, Adam Mickiewicz

(1788–1856), is said to have praised a certain Jewish coachman, with whom he had traveled for two days, as an exquisite storyteller. Coachmen and shoemakers, peddlers and cattle dealers, loggers and beggars, merchants and innkeepers were some of the many Jewish raconteurs who played a significant role in the story-swapping tradition.

27

Hang the Moon on My Palace Roof

Once upon a time there was an old fisherman who lived with his wife in a little hut beside the sea. As he was fishing one day, he caught a duck that swam by and took it home to his wife.

Some time later the duck laid a brass egg. The man took the egg to the *porets,* the local squire, who gave him a kopeck for it. The fisherman was very pleased. A while later the duck laid a silver egg. Again the man took the egg to the squire, who this time gave him two kopecks. Later still, the duck laid a golden egg. The man took the egg to the squire, who said, "Fisherman, sell me the duck; I'll give you a rendl for it."

Now, a rendl was a gold coin worth more than the fisherman could make in a lifetime, but he wasn't sure he necessarily wanted to sell a duck that lays golden eggs. So he said, "Let me talk it over with my wife."

His wife said, "You'd better sell him the duck for a rendl. Otherwise, since he's the squire, he's likely to take it from us." So the man took the duck to the squire, who gave him a rendl for it.

The squire looked the duck over and noticed that there were some blue markings under its right wing. But he couldn't read them, so he sent for the priest, who looked at the blue markings and read aloud: " 'He who eats the liver of this duck will become king. And he who eats the right wing will become the viceroy.' "

So the squire had the duck killed and its liver and right wing put into a pot to cook. And he sat stroking his belly while he waited for the precious meal.

But the squire's two sons, both of them terribly hungry, ran into the kitchen and saw the pot cooking. They lifted the cover, and the older son snatched up the liver and ate it while the younger son ate the wing. Just then the cook came in to dish up the meal. Finding that it had been eaten, he roared, "Who did this?" The children replied, "We did."

The cook hurried to the squire and fell on his knees. "Your two sons ate the dish I was making for you." The squire was furious and sent for the priest to ask his advice.

The priest said, "Order your sons to be killed and eat their livers. That way you'll get to be king." So the squire sent for the cook and said, "I want you to kill my sons and roast their livers." The cook fell on his knees and begged, "Oh Lord, have pity on your own children." But the squire ordered the cook whipped, and finally the cook agreed to do it.

At night when the children were sleeping, the cook went into their room with a huge knife and a sharpening stone. He stood there sharpening the knife, sharpening and sharpening as the tears rolled down his cheeks. The sound of the knife on the stone woke them, and they saw him sharpening and weeping.

"Why are you crying?" they asked.

"Because the squire has commanded me to kill you and cook your livers for him to eat."

The older boy said, "Have pity on us! Why don't you let us go and kill our dogs? Let Father eat their livers."

So the cook killed and buried the dogs and carried their livers to the squire. As for the boys, they jumped out of the window and ran away.

They traveled on and on and on until they came to a large city. There they went from street to street looking for some way to earn their living. As they passed an open window, they saw a tailor. "Little tailor, little tailor," they said, "can you help us earn our clothes and food?"

The tailor replied, "Take needles and thread, scissors and pressing irons. Help me to cut and sew, to baste and press clothes, and then I'll feed and clothe you." So the boys took up needles and thread, scissors and pressing irons, and helped the tailor to cut and sew, to baste hems and press clothes. They became good apprentice tailors.

One day the king died. And the king's daughter announced: "I will marry the strongest and cleverest man in the country." So all the strongest men in the country were sent for, and a great wrestling contest was held. A very strong man from the other side of the *hore khoyshekh,* the Mountains of Darkness, defeated everyone until the two tailor's apprentices came along. Everyone laughed at them, but the older apprentice wrestled with the champion and beat him. Then the younger apprentice wrestled with all the other strong men and defeated them.

To choose between the two winners, the princess ordered fifty candles lighted in a row. She said that whichever apprentice could blow out the candles with a single breath would be her husband. Both brothers, however, blew them out in a single breath. Next the princess said to the older apprentice, "Take the moon out of the sky and hang it from the tip of the palace roof."

He replied, "First braid me a rope of sand so I can use it to hang the moon from the tip of the palace roof."

The princess said to the younger apprentice, "Go up to the sun and bring back one of its coals so I can use it to heat my oven."

He replied, "Harness the wind to your chariot so I can use it to drive up to the sun for a coal to heat your oven."

The princess said to the older apprentice, "Sew me a dress without any seam."

He replied, "Give me a length of silk made of smoke, and I'll sew you a dress without a seam."

The princess said to the younger apprentice, "Sew me a coat without taking my measurements."

He replied, "Give me an endless length of thread and I'll sew you a coat without taking your measurements."

Well, the princess still didn't know which of the two to marry. So they cast lots for her, and the lot fell to the older apprentice. He became the king, and his brother was made the viceroy.

One day the king said to the viceroy, "Let's take a trip back to our old home and see what's going on there."

"A good idea," the viceroy said.

They wore shabby clothing over their royal garments, and stuck needles and threads into their lapels. They took shears and pressing irons with them and rode away to the village of their father, the squire.

They arrived in the evening and asked for a place to sleep. They were told, "You can sleep in the kitchen behind the oven." To which they replied, "Good." Just then the squire sent for them, and the brothers were taken to a room where their father was sitting with the priest and a group of noblemen.

The squire said, "Tailor boys, tell us an interesting tale."

So they began the story of a magic duck and related all that had happened to them from the time when they ate its liver and wing to the time when the older brother became king and the younger one became the viceroy. And when they had finished their tale, they threw off their ragged clothes and stood revealed in their imperial garments. Everyone fell to his knees before them and bowed down.

The squire and the priest were beheaded, while the cook was taken with great honor to the royal palace and made prime minister.

From that day to this
They have lived content
And have never again
Known any want.

The Sorcerer's Apprentice

Once a rich man who had no children went to consult a wonder rebbe. The rebbe said, "You were born with either of two fates: you can be rich, or you can have children. It's up to you. If you have children, you'll have to be poor. Choose."

The man replied, "I prefer to have a child."

The rebbe said, "Go back home. In nine months your wife will give birth to a son." A few months after he returned home, all the man's goods were destroyed in a fire and he became poor. And in nine months, his wife gave birth to a son.

The family struggled for thirteen years to keep their home together. Then, seeing that nothing could be done about their poverty in that town, the father and son decided to beg their way in the wide world. They went from town to town until finally they arrived at the city of Odessa.

In Odessa, they went to the House of Beggars, where all the poor folk seemed to be delighted by something. The father asked them, "What makes you all so happy?"

"Don't you know?" they said. "There's a rich man in town who makes a banquet for poor folk once a week. If you like, you can come too."

So the father and son went to the banquet and had plenty to eat and drink, the best of everything. At one point a coach drawn by four beautiful horses drove up. A sorcerer stepped out and began to astonish the guests by turning himself into a horse, then an elephant, then a lion, then a cat. He kept the company entertained until two o'clock in the morning.

When the father was ready to leave, the son said, "I won't move from this place until you apprentice me to the sorcerer." The father first reasoned with him, then wept, but the son was stubborn. "Apprentice me to the sorcerer," he said.

So the father ran after the sorcerer's coach and lay down in front of the horses. "Sir," he said, "my son won't move from his place unless he can become your apprentice."

And the sorcerer drew up a contract agreeing to teach the boy sorcery for three years. "When the time is up," said the sorcerer, "You can come and get him."

Three years later the father arrived at the sorcerer's house. The path to the door was guarded by wild animals, but he loved his son so much that he walked bravely past them. In the house he found his son sitting with the sorcerer and the sorcerer's daughter.

The sorcerer recognized the father at once. "You've come for your son," he said. "Well, you may have him only after you have passed a test. I will turn my daughter and your son into doves, and if you can tell me which of them is your son, you can have him. If you fail, he stays with me forever."

The father was very angry and ran from the house, ran and ran until he came to a forest where he lay down and wept bitterly. Then he fell into exhausted sleep. He dreamed that somebody was poking him, and he awoke to see a gray old man standing by his side. "Why were you crying, my friend?" the old man asked.

The father told him all that had happened. "I sacrificed everything I owned for a child," he concluded, "and now I'll lose him forever if I fix on the wrong dove."

The old man said, "Leave the forest and you'll come to a field of rye. Pluck several stalks and take them with you to the sorcerer's. Tell him that you're ready for the test, and when he presents the doves to you, throw the kernels of rye in front of them. Watch carefully: The dove that gobbles up the rye is the sorcerer's daughter. The bird who is your son will eat slowly because he is yearning to be with you."

The father did as he had been told, and everything happened as the gray old man said.

After the father had chosen the dove who was his son, the sorcerer said, "Yes, you've picked out your son. But you can't have him unless you sign a contract that he will perform no magic in my lifetime."

The father agreed to the contract, and he and his son went on

their way. Then the son said, "Father, you're very poor. Let me turn myself into a horse so you can take me to market and sell me. You're certain to get a good price. But when you've sold me, be sure to take my bridle off; otherwise I'll be a horse forever. When you've taken off the bridle, I'll turn into a dove and fly after you. And when I spot you, I'll fly down and turn into a human again."

So the son turned himself into a horse and his father led him to market. A great many dealers were interested in the horse. But the sorcerer was also there and saw what was going on. Disguising himself, he went up to the father and asked, "How much do you want for your horse?"

"A thousand rubles," said the father.

"Let me try him out to see if he's worth it," said the sorcerer.

"Go ahead," said the father.

The sorcerer jumped on the horse and said, "You'll see your son about as soon as you can see your own ears. You signed a contract and you've broken it." With that he lashed the horse and rode away.

When the sorcerer arrived home, he kept the animal in his stable. He beat it and watered it, but gave it no food. Then one day the rich man in Odessa sent for him again to perform tricks at another banquet for the poor. Before leaving, the sorcerer told his daughter to give the horse ten lashes and some water every day.

Yet the next morning when the daughter entered the stable, she was moved by the horse's beauty. She caressed his head and removed his bridle. As soon as he was free of the bridle, the horse turned into a human and she recognized him at once. "Give me some water," he said. And when she went to get the water, the boy turned himself into a dove and flew away.

The sorcerer on the way to Odessa saw the dove in flight above him. At once he understood what had happened and he turned himself into a hawk and flew in pursuit, upon which the dove turned himself into a ring and dropped into the sea. The hawk transformed itself into a duck with a copper bill and searched for the ring in the sea. The ring, meanwhile, moved toward the shore, little by little, until it washed up on a beach. There it was spotted by the king's daughter, who had come to bathe. The duck, seeing her put the ring on her finger, flapped his wings and said to himself, "I'll not be able to get him now, but just wait, I'll use all my powers to get him back."

Once she was at home, the king's daughter felt the ring squeezing her finger. So she tugged and tugged at it until it fell to the ground, where it turned into a young man.

"Don't be frightened," he said to her. "I'm human, and I'm a sorcerer. But a more powerful sorcerer is coming who means to kill me. He'll promise you mountains of gold for me, but it's only a trick. When he tries to take me, I'll turn into a ring again. Put the ring on your finger, and if he tries to grab it from you, throw it to the ground and it will turn into a pea. Then he'll become a hen and try to eat me. But if you put your foot on the pea, it will turn into a polecat and wring the hen's neck."

And that's what happened. And they threw the hen's carcass into the street. The boy went back to the sorcerer's daughter and married her, and they are alive and well to this day. Now the boy rides to Odessa instead of the sorcerer and performs tricks for the poor folk.

The boy's father lives with them and is happy and has no need to go begging any more.

29

The Beggar King and the Melamed

In the city of Amsterdam there once lived a king and this king knew several languages, the Jewish sacred tongue, Hebrew, among them. Going to bathe in the river one day, he happened to pass through the Jewish ghetto. There was a small house where a traditional Jewish schoolteacher, a *melamed,* was teaching children the passage, "God topples the mighty to the ground and raises the lowly to the heavens."

Getting out of his coach, the king went into the house and asked the *melamed* what those words meant. The meaning was, the *melamed* replied, that God can turn a king into a beggar and a beggar into a king. Hearing this, the king was very angry. "Prove it to me personally and I'll reward you," he said. "But if you can't, I'll have you beheaded."

The *melamed* said he would indeed prove it, on condition that the king stay away from his house for at least five days. And the king promised.

As it happened, this *melamed* was one of the thirty-six holy men without whom the world could not exist, a *lamed-vov tsadek,* and he sat down and prayed.

Meanwhile the king went on his way to the river and, after turning his clothes over to a servant, jumped into the water. In a minute a demon out of hell assumed the king's shape and emerged from the river. The demon called the servant to bring him his clothes, then dressed himself in the royal garments and rode home to the palace.

When the true king had had a good swim, he came out of the water and called his servant, but there was neither sound nor reply. The king shouted louder and louder and ran about trying to find his clothes and the carriage. Naked, he searched for hours until he was frozen. Finally he went home, still without clothing. The peasants in the street were amazed at the sight of a naked man shouting that he was the king. One even started to strike him with a whip, but an old peasant stopped him and then gave the king a ragged coat to cover himself.

The king went to his palace, but the soldiers guarding the gates drove him away, saying, "We don't allow beggars to approach the king's residence." The peasants pitied the refined-looking beggar, but none of them believed him when he claimed to be king. Everyone knew that the king was exactly where he was supposed to be.

And that was how the king came to be a beggar. When he wanted to sleep, he had to go to the place where all the beggars spent the night. So after two days he left the city and went off to beg in the company of several other poor people like himself.

Little by little, the king got used to his new life traveling from town to town in the company of beggars. One day he was passing through the capital city again and found himself in the street that led to the river. From the house of the *melamed* came the teacher's voice discussing the same passage, and interpreting it to mean that God could turn a king into a beggar and a beggar into a king.

The king went into the house and begged the *melamed*'s forgiveness for having doubted him. And he asked the *melamed* to help him become a king again. The teacher promised that he would. The first thing he did was to trim the king's matted hair and beard. Then he bathed him and ordered a tailor to make him new clothes fit for a king. After that was done, he told him to go to church and wait outside at the time the king usually went to pray. When he saw the false king's coach drive up and the imposter enter the church, then he, the real king, should call his coachman by name.

The king, now dressed like a king, did everything the *melamed* advised him to do. On Sunday he stood outside the church and waited till the imposter drove up. When the false king was inside the church, and after the first prayer was recited, the real king called the coachman, who drove up at once and helped him into the coach. So the king drove home and no one was any the wiser.

When the demon-King discovered the trick, he fled back to his place in hell. Then the real king commanded that the *melamed* be brought to him at the palace. He thanked him for his help and rewarded him royally.

And from then on, and to the end of his days, that king was a friend to the Jews.

30
Of Nettles and Roses

Once upon a time there was a rich man and his wife who had an only child, a very pretty daughter. When the girl was already well grown, the mother was taken ill and died. After a time the father began to worry because there was no woman to take care of his daughter, and so he decided to marry again.

At first his new wife loved her stepdaughter and tended her carefully. But when the stepmother gave birth to an ugly daughter of her own, she resented the beautiful child and began to think of ways to get rid of her.

Now, the rich man, a merchant, traveled frequently on business. Once when he was gone, the stepmother said to the lovely daughter, "Gather up the dirty clothes and wash them in the river outside of town." Hearing this, the girl wept bitterly. No one ever went to that river because it was said to be under a curse. Nevertheless, she gathered up the clothes and obeyed her stepmother.

When she got to the river, tears rolled down her cheeks as she worked. Suddenly three water spirits rose out of the water. "Why are you crying?" the first water spirit asked.

"Because my stepmother has sent me here to get rid of me."

"Don't cry, princess," said the water spirit. "Go back home. And from now on, the rarest roses in the world will spring up in your footsteps."

The second water spirit said, "And when you wash yourself, the water in the basin will turn to gold."

The third water spirit said, "When you speak, your breath will perfume the air and please everyone who hears you."

Then the water spirits washed the clothes for her, and the pretty daughter went home. Sure enough, roses sprang up in her footsteps as she walked. When she got home she put the clothes away and went to wash herself. And sure enough, the water in the basin turned to gold.

Her stepmother, seeing this, asked her how it had happened. When the pretty stepdaughter described the water spirits, her breath perfumed the room.

"Aha," thought the stepmother, "I'll send my daughter on the same errand and the same things will happen to her." But when the ugly daughter came to the river and the water spirits asked her what she wanted, she replied rudely. "You gave my sister gifts. Now give me some, too."

"You want gifts, do you?" said the first water spirit. "Very well, then. When you walk, nettles will spring up in your footsteps."

The second water spirit said, "And when you wash yourself, the basin will fill up with frogs."

"And when you talk," said the third water spirit, "your breath will have such a stink that no one will want to listen to you."

And that's how it was. As she went home, nettles grew in her footsteps. And when she washed herself, frogs appeared in the basin. And when she told her mother what had happened, the house filled with such a dreadful odor that her mother ordered her to stop talking.

Now it happened that in a nearby country there lived a king who had an only son. And this son was looking for a wife, but he had turned down every match that was proposed to him. Somehow he heard of the beautiful girl in whose footsteps roses grew. He discovered where she lived, and the moment he saw her he was enchanted. Not only was she beautiful and well bred, but when she spoke she breathed such a fragrance that talking with her was pure delight. What with one thing and another, they soon arrived at an understanding that she would come to his country and marry him in a month's time. And at the end of the month, the beautiful girl stole away from her stepmother and her country in the dead of night and married the king's son in his own land.

But through consultations with fortune-tellers, the wicked stepmother soon learned of this, and learned that the royal couple lived in great happiness. And later she heard that her stepdaughter had given birth to a child as lovely as she was. Of course, many years had gone by and it all took longer than it takes to tell.

Needless to say, the wicked stepmother was furious at the news. She sent for a sorceress and said, "Name your price. Just find a way to kill that stepdaughter of mine."

"I'll do it," said the sorceress. And off she went to the palace of the stepdaughter. Using her magic, the sorceress found her way inside and to the bedroom where the princess lay sleeping beside her baby. The sorceress took out a long, sharp knife, cut the baby into four parts, and put the bloody instrument into the princess's hand.

Later the prince, wondering why his wife was still sleeping, went into her bedroom and found the murdered baby and the sleeping princess holding the knife. The prince shouted, "What have you done? What have you done?"

The princess, awakened, looked around bewildered. Seeing the corpse of the baby, she cried, "No, no! I didn't do it. I didn't do it."

But nobody would believe her, because, after all, who else could have done it? Besides, no more roses grew in her footsteps, no more water turned to gold when she washed, and her breath did not perfume the air when she spoke. The water spirits' magic had been destroyed by the sorceress's evil deed.

The king commanded that the princess's eyes be put out. Then the mutilated body of her baby was placed in a sack and given to her, and she was driven from the palace.

Weeping bitterly, the blinded princess found her way into a forest. When she sensed that night was falling, she sat under a tree and sang softly to herself like one of the birds in the boughs above. Singing thus, she fell asleep. As she slept, her own mother appeared to her in a dream and said, "My child, you have suffered much and you are destined to suffer more. But soon you will gain some relief. In the morning you will find yourself sitting beside a well. Touch some of the well water to your eyes, then take more water and wash the body of your baby."

In the morning the princess followed her mother's instructions. And when she touched some of the well water to her eyes, her sight returned. And when she washed her baby's body, it came alive again. Happy to be carrying her living baby, she made her way through cities and towns and villages, earning her keep by singing wherever she went.

Eventually the princess tired of wandering. For her growing child's sake she settled in a large city, where she found work with a family of rich people.

Sometimes she sang as she worked, and always her song told the story of her life. Everyone who heard her was deeply moved.

Now it happened that her rich employer, who was a friend of the king, gave a banquet to which he invited the king and his son, the prince. The guests were entertained by singers with all kinds of songs. "These songs are very beautiful, the young prince said, but none tell of lives that are anything like mine. Ah, what I would give if I could hear a song that resembled in some way the story of my life."

At this the hostess said, "There is a young woman working for me who often sings a song that resembles the story of your life."

The prince begged his hostess to send for the young woman. The servant, finely dressed and very beautiful, came in and began to sing, and the prince was transfixed as he heard episode after episode of a song that touched on his own life. Then the singer came to the part that told how she had married the king's son, how he had cast her away, and what had happened to her afterward.

Hearing it all, the prince wept and wept. Then, taking the singer by the hand, he said, "This is she. This is my true and blameless wife, whom I love dearly."

And so they were united once more. And they lived happily ever after.

3 1
The Demon and Sosye

There was a man whose great sorrow was that Sosye, his wife, was a terrible shrew. Though he wanted to get rid of her, he didn't know how. He talked it over with a good friend, who said, "Listen, there are demons in your well. Why don't you throw Sosye in? Let them have her."

And that's what he did. But three days later it occurred to him that it would be only decent to pull his wife's body out and give it a proper burial. So he tied an anchor to a rope and lowered it into the well. When he pulled the rope up, he found a demon clinging to the anchor. He would have thrown the demon back, but it cried, "No, please don't! Three days ago a woman named Sosye fell in, and she's down there driving all of us to distraction."

When it saw that the man was listening, the demon said, "Don't throw me back and I'll make you rich. Here's how. I'll go haunt the houses of the nobility; then you can come and say that you know spells and incantations for exorcising demons. You'll recite some words, I'll disappear, and the nobles will pay you a fat fee. But remember, we can do this only three times. Any more and it won't work."

"Very well," said the man, and he let the demon go.

The demon kept its word and haunted a count's palace so effectively that the household was turned topsy-turvy. Then Sosye's husband showed up and said to the count, "My lord, for a fee, I can recite certain spells and incantations that will drive away the demon who haunts your castle."

"If you can do that," said the count, "I'll reward you well."

With that, Sosye's husband recited spells and incantations and the demon promptly left the castle. As he had promised, the grateful count gave him a rich reward.

Sosye's husband and the demon played this trick on a second nobleman and then on a third. As a result Sosye's husband acquired a considerable reputation as an exorcist and a lot of money besides.

Then one day he was called in to exorcise the demon for a fourth time. But the demon said, "Too bad for you. I warned you the trick would work three times only. Now I'm here to stay for good."

Sosye's husband stood sadly for a while, lost in thought, then he brightened and called in a loud voice, "Sosye, my wife, come back." When the demon heard the name Sosye, it took to its heels and ran off.

And the exorcist was richly rewarded again.

3 2
How Much Do You Love Me?

Once upon a time there was a rabbi and his wife who had three daughters. The rabbi, wanting to know how much his daughters loved him, said to the oldest, "Rokhele dear, how much do you love me?" To which she replied, "As much as gold." He went to his second daughter. "Khavele dear, how much do you love me?" "As much as silver," she replied. Then he said, "Sorele dear, how much do you love me?" And she said, "Father, I love you as much as food that has been properly salted."

When he heard, "as much as food that has been properly salted," he drove her out of his home.

Sorele went weeping. Night overtook her and she had no place to go, but still she walked on. Then she met an old man, who was really Elijah the Prophet.

"Where are you going, my child?" he asked.

So she told him her story. "I see," he said. "Here, take this little stick. Keep on this road until you come to a house where you hear someone making the blessing over wine. Then be sure to say 'Omeyn,' amen. But no matter who asks you into the house, don't go unless it is the rabbi himself. Then, you may go in. When you are inside, go up to the attic and hide the stick there. Then whenever you need anything, take the stick out and say, 'Stick, open!' And whatever you want will appear before you."

When he had done speaking, he disappeared. She went on until she saw the house and heard someone making the *kidesh* over the wine. Three times she responded "*Omeyn.*"

Hearing an *omeyn* from outside, the people in the house were startled. The rabbi's wife went out and invited the girl in, but she refused. It was not until the rabbi came out and repeated the invitation that she entered.

Inside she crouched sadly beside the oven. The rabbi's wife

brought her food, but it did not cheer her. The next morning the rabbi, his wife, and his son dressed up and left the house to attend a wedding. The girl wanted to go too, so she went up to the attic and, taking out her stick, said, "Stick, open!" The stick opened, revealing a basin of water and a bar of golden soap. When the girl had washed, she said again, "Stick, open!" and it opened to present her with a costly set of clothing. The girl dressed in an exquisite gown and put on a pair of golden shoes. Looking absolutely beautiful, she went to the wedding.

There she dazzled the rabbi's son, who did not recognize her as the beggar maiden living in his own house. But though he asked her several times to say who she was, she always turned the conversation to something else.

Finally he said to his mother, "That beautiful girl won't tell me her name, but I have a plan to find out who she is."

He fetched some pitch and used it to smear the doorsill of the house. When it came time for the wedding guests to leave, the beautiful maiden started hastily toward home. But when she crossed the threshhold, one of her shoes stuck in the pitch, and she had to go on wearing a single shoe. The rabbi's son picked up the other one and put it in his pocket.

Meanwhile Sorele went up into the attic, changed into her old clothes, and came back down again.

The rabbi, his wife, and their son returned from the wedding. The son said, "See, I have the beautiful maiden's shoe. I'm off into the wide world to find her." He searched high and low for a maiden who could wear the golden shoe, but he couldn't find one. At last he returned home in despair.

"Let me try the shoe," Sorele said. "Perhaps it will fit me."

"Come on," he said. "As if a shoe like this could fit a beggar girl like you!"

She snatched it from him and slipped it onto her foot, where it settled as snugly as if it had been sewn for her.

Seeing this, the rabbi and his wife and son were very unhappy. How could he marry a beggar?

A few nights later they were sadder still, because each of them had been warned in a dream not to hinder their son's wedding to the poor girl. The troubled parents went for a walk to consider what to do.

Left alone in the house with the rabbi's son, Sorele said, "If you'll come to the attic with me, I'll show you who I really am."

He followed her up the stairs, and the girl said, "Stick, open!" Suddenly all sorts of wonderful clothes appeared. "Some for you," she said, "and some for me."

Each of them put on the finery and went out for a stroll.

Later, the rabbi and his wife, out on their walk, met their splendidly dressed son walking with a beautiful girl as richly garbed as he. This frightened them because of the dream that had warned them not to hinder their son's marriage to Sorele. And here he was walking about with some beautiful and wealthy girl whom they had never seen.

The two young people returned to the house and changed to their ordinary clothes. When the rabbi and his wife came home, the son said to his parents, "Stop worrying. I'm going to marry Sorele. Everything will be all right."

"Well . . . ," said his parents, in some confusion. "If you are determined, then marry her you will." And they sat down to address invitations to all the rabbis in the country.

As the wedding preparations went forward, the girl went to the kitchen and said to the cooks, "Whatever dishes you make, be sure to cook some without salt."

Came the wedding day. Rabbis from cities throughout the land arrived. To the amazement of the groom's parents, the bride, in her fine clothes, looked like a princess.

After the ceremony people sat about enjoying their food. One of the rabbis, however, did not find the menu to his liking. Seeing his unhappiness, the bride went up to him and said, "Dear guest, what's the matter? Everyone but you is eating."

"Ah," he said, "no doubt the food is very good, but the dishes have no salt."

"Father, dear Father," she said, "do you remember that I said I loved you as much as food that has been properly salted? Yet you drove me away from home."

Her father, hearing these words, dropped into a dead faint. When he came to, he told everyone that the bride was his daughter.

And there was carousing and merriment until dawn.

Elijah the Prophet gave the couple a diamond chandelier for a wedding present. And the moment they touched it, they ascended into heaven.

3 3

The Master Thief

Once upon a time there was a king who had three sons, two of whom were clever while one was a fool. The clever ones could not abide the fool and continually ridiculed him. To make matters worse, the fool drifted into bad behavior, such as stealing goods in the marketplace. When the king learned about this, he drove the fool out of the country.

The fool traveled on and on until he came to a forest, where he met a band of thieves. "I'm a thief, too," he said, "so let me join you."

"Very well," they said, and took him into a cave where they gave him food and drink. "Now show us a thievish trick," they said.

"Give me a new shoe; then come with me to the highway outside the forest," said the fool.

On the highway they saw a peasant driving a horse and wagon. The young thief took one of the shoes, slipped it onto the road where the peasant would pass, and hid in the forest.

Seeing a shoe lying in the highway, the peasant thought, "One shoe! What good is a single shoe?" and went on. When he was gone, the fool ran out, grabbed the shoe, and ran through the forest for a mile or so. When he was ahead of the peasant again, he darted onto the road, dropped the shoe, and hid in the forest again.

The peasant, driving by, saw the shoe lying there and said to himself, "Ah, if there are two shoes they might turn out to be useful." So he got down from the wagon and ran back to look for the other shoe. As soon as he was gone, the fool came out of the woods and drove the horse and wagon to the thieves' cave.

Meanwhile the peasant came to the place where he had seen the first shoe. He spent several hours looking for it without success and then went back to his horse and wagon. When he came to the stretch of road where he had left them, he searched high and he searched low, but no luck.

The fool said to the thieves, "Watch me steal his clothes, too."

"All right," they said. "Let's see you do it."

He killed the horse, cut off its head, and propped the head up in the water of the river nearby.

The peasant, still running about searching for his horse and wagon, saw the horse's head sticking out of the water and was overjoyed. "My nag must have drawn the wagon into the river." With that he took his clothes off and dashed into the water to lead the horse out. In the meantime the young thief stole the peasant's clothes and carried them to the other thieves.

When they saw what he had done, they said, "You're much too clever for us; you could trick us out of everything. So why don't you just go away? Here, take as much money as you like, but go away."

The young thief took a large sum of money, and went from one country to another, learning more and more about his trade, until he became a master thief. One day he came to a kingdom whose king had an only daughter—the most beautiful young woman in the world. The king had decreed that whoever could guess her name within four months could marry her, but anyone who guessed wrong would be sent to prison and fed only bread and water for four years. The young thief discovered that his two clever brothers had tried and failed to guess the princess's name and now lay in the king's dungeons.

"Ah," said the young thief, "I'll marry the king's daughter without having to guess her name." So he dressed in fine clothing and went to the palace, where he announced that he was a prince who wanted to marry the princess.

Now the king gave a great banquet, at which the thief was an honored guest. Everyone ate and drank the best of everything and the king granted the thief the usual four months to guess his daughter's name.

As the feast proceeded, the young thief stole the king's wine cup. When the servants were clearing the table, they noticed that it was missing and they reported it at once to the king. He decided that everyone at the banquet would have to be searched. The guests lined up, and the thief got behind a priest who wore a hood that hung down behind his back. The thief slipped the cup into the hood, and of course no one searches a priest, so the holy man went out of the palace with no trouble. The thief followed him and retrieved the cup from his hood.

After everyone at the banquet had been searched and the cup had not been found, the king's counselors decided that he should give another banquet a week later and strew gold coins on the floor. No doubt the thief would be among the guests, and when he tried to steal the coins he could be caught.

At the banquet the young thief saw the gold coins lying on the floor and noticed that no one bent to pick them up. Well, what do you think he did? He went out and took some axle grease from a wagon and put it on the soles of his shoes. Then he walked about over the coins and got them all because, of course, they stuck to his soles.

Well, since no one had seen anyone bending down, the king's counselors proposed giving another banquet a week later. At that time the princess, wearing her diamond earrings, would be put to bed in the garden. If he was there, the thief would certainly try to steal the earrings from her. But the princess would be given a piece of indelible chalk with which to mark the thief when he made the attempt.

And so it was done. The banquet was held, and after dinner the guests walked about in the garden and saw that the princess was sleeping there. The young thief waited until he was alone. Then he went up to the princess and gently removed first one earring, then the other. But as he did, she marked his coat with the chalk. Seeing what she had done, he grabbed the chalk out of her hand and went about marking the clothes of all the men at the banquet.

When the king and his counselors looked about to see whose coat had been marked, they discovered marks on everyone's, including the king's. And the earrings were missing.

His counselors then advised the king to hold another banquet. And for that occasion a cabinet decorated with fine gems would be on display, and a paper floor would be built leading to the cabinet. The thief would undoubtedly try to make his way to the cabinet, and he would fall through the paper floor into the cellar.

Well, during the banquet everything happened just as planned. The young thief stepped on the paper floor and fell into the cellar. What do you suppose he did then? He grabbed up a drum and some drumsticks and created such a tumult that everyone came running. And of course, one by one, the whole crowd fell through the paper floor into the cellar. So again nobody knew who the thief was.

The king, seeing what had happened, said, "I confess myself beaten. Whoever the thief is, he's cleverer than any of my counselors." The king described all the thefts to his guests. "And it's clear," said the king, "that the thief has not stolen anything for the sake of the theft but rather as a demonstration of his cleverness. I therefore decree that if he will reveal himself to us, he can marry my daughter without having to guess her name."

The young thief said, "How can one be sure you're not just saying that?" So the king issued a decree in which he promised that whoever had stolen the objects could marry his daughter. At that the young thief handed the king his wine cup, the gold coins, and the princess's earrings.

The king kissed him and said, "You are the man, and you will be my son-in-law."

Some time later, after the thief had been betrothed to the king's daughter, he and the king were talking. The king said, "You know, I really don't know who you are. Why don't you tell me about yourself?"

"Well," said the thief, "I'm the son of King So-and-So."

"Oh," said the king, "in that case, your two brothers are sitting in my prison." And the king promptly ordered that the two brothers be freed. Then he sent a messenger to the father of the prince inviting him to come to the wedding. The father came, though of course he thought it was one of his clever sons who was about to be married. Yet when he found out that it was his foolish son, he was very happy just the same.

After the wedding all the other imprisoned princes were freed too, and sent home.

The princess's father gave the thief a considerable portion of his kingdom. From then on, the young man was known as the Clever King, and his brothers were subject to his rule. And they all lived happily ever after.

34
The Orphan Boys

This happened a long time ago in a small town, a *shtetl,* where two orphan boys lived. They were named Berele and Shmerele and they had no home, no relatives, no parents. They were entirely on their own and grew up in the streets.

Well, there are do-gooders in every town. The do-gooders in this one couldn't stand to see two hungry children, abandoned by God and man and roaming about in their ragged clothes like blind lambs. And so the boys were put to work chopping wood, carrying water, and doing other such tasks, for which they were occasionally tossed food from the back door of a kitchen, like dogs. They slept in the *hegdesh,* the poorhouse, on bundles of shredded straw and covered themselves with ragged quilts.

The town sent them to *kheyder,* where the do-gooders decreed that they would sit apart from the other pupils. Even when the children played together, Berele and Shmerele were excluded from the games because they were orphans.

One day Berele and Shmerele decided that there was no future for them in the village, so off they went. As they traveled, people gave them a bit of bread here, a sip of milk there. A potato. A morsel of cheese. And somehow they managed to keep body and soul together.

"Best not to stay in one place," thought the boys. "Better to keep going."

One day Berele and Shmerele came to a forest and walked through it until they reached a fork in the trail. Standing there was an old man with radiant features, clearly possessed by the Divine Presence. "Good morning to you, children," he said. "What brings you into this forest?"

As if they were talking to their own father or grandfather, the boys told him of their suffering in the village and the griefs they had endured. The old man listened, his face glowing like the sun.

He stood musing after they had finished. Then, taking out his snuffbox, he put a couple of pinches into his nostrils, sneezed three times in a row, and then, taking a slim twig out of his breast pocket, broke it in two. Giving one piece to Berele, he said, "Take care of it. And carry it with you as you follow the road to the right. Keep going until the path is barred by a high fence that no one can climb. You'll find neither gate nor door that will let you in. Then take the twig out of your pocket, sit on it, and repeat three times:

Little stick, little stick, small as a tail,
Do what I bid you now without fail.

"Then the stick will rise into the air and carry you over the fence into a palace. You'll find a princess inside . . . and you'll find happiness there."

When he finished talking to Berele, he pulled a head of garlic out of another pocket and gave it to Shmerele. He said, "Carry this with you, my son, as you follow the left-hand path. Stay on it until you come to the capital city. When you arrive, everyone will be in mourning, for the king's only daughter is dangerously ill. Announce that you can heal her, but insist that they leave you alone with the patient. Then take out the garlic head and repeat three times:

Garlic, garlic, I know well,
Like an apple is your smell.
One and two and three and four,
Make her healthy as before.

"After that she will recover. And there, my child, you will find happiness. But remember," the old man said, addressing them both, "when you find happiness, you must not let it go to your head. Remember what your proper place is in the world. You must lead honorable and decent lives." Having said his say, the old man bade them both farewell and disappeared into the dense forest.

Berele and Shmerele looked around. They ate their last meal together, and embraced tearfully. Then Berele went off to the right and Shmerele to the left.

Berele traveled three days and three nights until he came to the high fence no one could climb. He pulled out the twig the old man had given him, sat on it, and said three times:

"Little stick, little stick, small as a tail,
Do what I bid you now without fail."

The twig rose into the air and Berele found himself standing inside a palace. He came to a room that gleamed and sparkled with gold, silver, and crystal, but there was no one in it. Berele went to a second room, which also gleamed and glistened with costly objects. A third room and a fourth were the same, shimmering with treasures but unoccupied. Finally he came to the last room and, with fast-beating heart, opened the door.

Like the others, this room was glittering and ornate, but there was also a woman dressed in the finest clothing standing in the doorway. She ran to him, embraced him, and kissed him as if she were his own sister. And she was so lovely. She clung to him and squeezed his hand and praised him for being brave. Berele thought he was in a delicious dream in which it seemed to him that his mother came from the other world to see her orphaned son. She hugged him and pressed him close to her heart. Then he snapped out of that fantasy and saw that there was a woman clinging joyfully to him. So he asked her why the palace was surrounded by such a high fence, and how it happened that she was there alone, and why she was so happy to see him.

She said, "You should know that I am the only daughter of a king. My father wanted to learn whether there really is such a thing as destiny. So he built this palace, and put the fence around it so that no man born of woman might enter. He stocked the palace with the best of everything. Food is handed in every day through a narrow opening. And my father has decreed that the man who can find his way in here will marry me. And that, my darling, is why I'm so happy to see you. You are my liberator, my destined groom."

The servant who brought her food that day saw that there were now two people inside and carried the news at once to the king, who came at once to the palace. He kissed his daughter and Berele, and the two were betrothed right on the spot. And when they were brought to the king's court, a truly regal wedding was performed. And Berele and his bride stayed in the royal palace.

Now let us return to Shmerele. He also traveled three days and three nights, until he came to the capital city. The entire town was in mourning, for the king's only daughter was dangerously ill. The finest doctors and professors of medicine had done all they could to save her, but without success. The princess lay unconscious and her death was expected at any moment.

Shmerele hurried to the king's palace and announced that he would cure the princess. The professors laughed, but Shmerele insisted that he could succeed where they had failed. So they quarreled fiercely until the sounds of the quarrel reached the king. "What harm can it do?" the king asked. "If she dies, it will have made no difference; and perhaps he might save her."

And so the king commanded that the young man be admitted to

the princess's bedside. Shmerele said, "Thank you, my lord king. I undertake to heal your daughter, but on the condition that everyone must leave the sickroom." The king was a little irritated by this but since he was a father, after all, and wanted his daughter healed, he yielded.

When Shmerele was alone in the sickroom with the princess, he took out his head of garlic and held it under her nose. Then three times he said:

> *"Garlic, garlic, I know well,*
> *Like an apple is your smell.*
> *One and two and three and four,*
> *Make her healthy as before."*

The princess opened her eyes, but she was still unable to move. So Shmerele held the garlic under her nose and repeated the spell once more. And he did this three times, until the princess had completely recovered.

On her cure the princess became so fond of Shmerele that she could not bear to let him out of her sight. And to show their gratitude, the king and queen betrothed him to her, and in a little while the marriage was celebrated in the royal court. And Shmerele and his bride lived on in the king's court.

From then on Berele and Shmerele lived happily and contentedly, honorably and decently, as the old man had urged.

Two Brothers Who Went to the Devil

Once upon a time there were two brothers, one rich and the other poor. The poor brother came to the rich one and asked for help, but the rich brother said, "You can go to the devil." So that's where the poor brother went.

As he traveled, he came to a river. There he found a man who carried people across but who couldn't get out of the water himself. "Where are you going?" the man in the water asked.

"To the devil," replied the poor brother.

"When you get there," said the man, "tell him how it is with me: I can carry everyone across the river, but I can't get out myself. Ask him what I must do to be able to climb out."

"Very well," said the poor man. Then he traveled on until he came to a large house full of young unmarried women. They asked him where he was going.

"To the devil," he replied.

"In that case," they said, "ask him why it is that there are no husbands for us."

"I will," said the poor man and went on his way.

Then he came to a young tree on which there were no leaves. "Where are you going?" asked the tree.

"To the devil," replied the poor man.

"Then do me a favor," said the tree. "Ask him why it is that I can't grow leaves."

"I will," said the poor man and went on his way.

He walked and walked until he came to a little house that was set upon chicken legs. An old woman sat on the doorstep spinning. "Hey, where are you going?" she said.

"I'm going to the devil," he replied.

"Ha," she cried, "you've come to the right place. He'll be back soon, and then he'll eat you up."

"Oh please, please hide me," begged the poor man.

"All right," said the woman. "I'll turn you into a needle and stick you into the window curtain." And that's what she did.

Around midnight came a noise, and the devil flew down the chimney.

He sniffed and sniffed and then he said,

*"I smell something, something good.
I know what it is, it's human blood!"*

With that, he searched everywhere in the house. But he didn't notice the needle in the window curtain.

The next morning the devil told the old woman about the adventures he had had the day before. "Not far from here," he said, "there's a leafless tree with a rich treasure buried under it. If the treasure were dug up, the tree would sprout leaves again.

"Another thing: I passed a house full of young women. If they swept the place and gave it a good cleaning, they would all find husbands.

"Oh yes, and I passed a man who carries people across a river but can't get out of the water himself. If he were to dip one of the people he carries into the river, he would be able to leave the water at last."

The poor man, just a needle stuck in the curtain, heard all this. In the morning, when the devil flew up the chimney again, the old woman returned him to his original shape. "Thank you for your help," he said, and away he went.

He went first to the tree, where he dug up the box of treasure buried at its roots. No sooner was the treasure in his hands than the tree sprouted leaves on all its branches.

With the chest of treasure under his arm, the poor man went to the house where the young unmarried women lived. "If you'll get me something to eat," he said, "I'll tell you what the devil advised you to do."

So they fed him, and when he was done eating, he said, "The devil's advice is for you to sweep the house clean. If you do that, you'll all find husbands." And it turned out to be true. They cleaned the house thoroughly and soon afterward they were all married.

The poor man, his treasure under his arm, went on until he came to the river. There he said to the man who carried people across: "The devil says that you should dip one of your passengers in the water. Then you'll be able to climb out."

The man in the river followed his advice. And when he dipped one of his passengers in the river, he was able to get out easily.

The poor man, carrying his treasure, went on home. There he built himself a new house and bought clothes for his wife and children. And from then on, he and his family were no longer poor.

But when his rich brother heard what had happened, he was very curious. He hurried over to his brother's new house and asked, "How did all this come about?"

"Simple," said the formerly poor man. "You told me to go to the devil and I went. When I got there, I followed his advice."

Hearing this, the rich brother was consumed with envy and decided to follow in his brother's footsteps. But in his case, when he came to the no longer leafless tree, the tree struck him with its branches. When he came to the house where the formerly unmarried women lived, they struck him with their kneading troughs. And when he got to the river, the man who formerly carried people across pushed him in. And from that day to this, the envious rich brother has had to carry people back and forth across the river.

36
The Snake Bridegroom

Once upon a time there was a very rich man who had no children. He went to a Hasidic rebbe and said, "Rebbe, pray to the Lord and ask him to bless me with children."

The rebbe said, "I will, but you must promise to hire twenty servants to care for the child that may be born to you."

"Certainly," said the rich man.

Not long afterward the man's wife conceived, and nine months later she bore a son. Promptly she sent to town for twenty servants. But when the boy was two years old she thought, "Why do I still need so many servants? I'll dismiss a few." And so she did. She let first one, then another go, until finally only one was left.

One day the rich woman stood at the stove warming milk when it occurred to her that she had sent the servant on an errand and no one was watching her boy. She hurried to his room just in time to see him falling out of bed. When he touched the ground, he turned into a snake and disappeared.

One year followed another, until eleven years had passed and the time came when the lost boy would have begun to use *tfiln*, phylacteries. Then one night he appeared outside his parents' window and cried, "Father, Mother. Get me *tfiln,* because it will soon be time for my *barmitsve.*"

"Certainly," said his father. "I'll get you the best *tfiln* in the world. Just come into the house and let me see you."

The boy said, "No, Father. That cannot be." And he went away.

In the morning the father went to the holy rebbe and told him all that had happened. The rebbe said, "When the boy comes again, set out a pair of *tfiln* on a chair."

Two nights later the boy came again and knocked on the wall. At once his father put out a chair on which he set a pair of *tfiln*. Just then a strong wind blew up and the *tfiln* disappeared; but when the father searched, no one was there.

On the boy's eighteenth birthday he came back again and said, "Father, I am grown now. It's time for me to marry. Get me a bride."

His father said, "Of course, my son. I'll get you a rich young bride. But won't you come into the house? I want to see you."

"That cannot be," replied the son, and he went away.

The next morning the rich man told the rebbe all that had happened. The rebbe said, "Today is Thursday. Harness your wagon and drive off in any direction you please. Travel until midnight and then stop wherever you happen to be, even if you are driving through water, even if you find yourself in the heart of a forest. Wherever it is, stop there."

The rich man did as he had been told, and at midnight when he stopped, it was in the middle of a forest. Two old people who lived in a hut not far away allowed him to spend the Sabbath with them. At his insistence they accepted the money he offered, and the old woman bought all sorts of food for the dinner table on Friday night. Yet the rich man saw that she put aside portions of everything and that she later carried them out of the house.

He watched her do the same thing on Saturday morning and again on Saturday night. Finally he said, "*Mumenyu,* auntie, why is it that you take away portions of every meal?"

"It's because I have twelve daughters," she said, "and we are so poor that not one of them has a dress. So I hide them in the cellar, and when God sends us anything to eat, I carry a part of it to them."

"In that case," he said, "let me have your oldest daughter to be my son's wife."

When they saw that he was not making fun of them but meant what he said, the old couple agreed. So the rich man took their oldest daughter away with him to be a bride for his son. As the girl was being led through the streets at her wedding, she heard people shouting, "She's going to marry a snake."

"That's strange," she thought. "They must mean that his name is Snake."

When the ceremony was over and she was brought home to her father-in-law's house, she was put into a fine room, and that night a

handsome young man came to it. "Now, my bride," he said, "what will you call me?"

"Why, I'll call you 'Snake.' Isn't Snake your name?"

For that, the handsome young man promptly strangled her.

When her body was found in the morning, the rich man went back to the hut for a second daughter and married her to his son. But she too called him Snake and was killed. And the same thing happened to each of the other daughters.

Finally it was the turn of the twelfth daughter. However, when the handsome young man came into her room and said, "Now, my bride, what will you call me?" she replied, "Why, what else shall I call you but 'my dear husband'?"

He smiled and said, "You, my dear, are my destined bride, and we shall live in happiness. One small thing I must ask you: never let firelight into our room." The girl agreed gladly.

Some time later the bride's parents paid her a visit. They found her living in fine, clean rooms. The mother said, "I am really curious to see what your husband looks like." And without her daughter's knowledge, she hid in the young couple's room when night fell.

All at once, there he was. When he took off his serpent shirt, the mother could see how handsome he was. She snatched the shirt up and burned it with a lighted match. Then still holding the match, she tried to see his face.

Furious, the young man turned to his wife. He broke his wedding ring in two, handed her half of it, and said, "Because of what she's done, I must leave you. When the two halves of the ring are united again, I'll return." Then he was gone.

Nine months later the young woman gave birth to a beautiful boy. When he was six she sent him to *kheyder,* where he turned out to be exceptionally bright. But the other children teased him, saying, "Your father is a snake, your father is a snake!"

The boy asked his mother, "Why do the children say that my father is a snake?"

"Never mind what they say," she told him. "Your father is a tall, handsome man."

The next day when he came home from school, he found his mother weeping over her half of the broken ring. He asked why she was crying. She said, "Your father promised to come back to us when the two parts of the ring are united."

Hearing that, the boy said, "Then I'm going to look for my father." He took his prayer book, put his mother's half of the ring inside it, and started off.

On his travels one evening, as he was reciting his prayers at an inn, he heard someone else saying prayers beneath the floorboards of the room.

The next morning he left his room, and while he was gone, his father came out from under the floorboards. Seeing the boy's prayer book, he looked into it and found the other half of his wedding ring. He closed the book and hid in a corner, and when the boy came back his father watched him wash his hands and heard him recite his prayers. Then the tall, handsome man stepped forward and said, "Tell me, my boy, where are you traveling?"

"I'm searching for my father," replied the boy. "See," he said, showing his half of the ring, "my father promised to return to my mother when the two halves of this wedding ring are united."

The boy's father said, "Watch." And with that he took out his half of the ring and matched it with the boy's, and the ring at once became whole.

"You must be my father," said the boy.

"I am," replied the man. "Now let's go home."

And so they went home together, and when they arrived there was great rejoicing. And the father and the mother and their son lived happily from that day to this.

37

The Princess and Vanke, the Shoemaker's Son

Once upon a time there was a king and a shoemaker. Now the king had a daughter and the shoemaker had a son and the children went to the same school. As it happened, the princess was a very poor pupil and Vanke, the shoemaker's son, was the best in the class. The two of them played together and studied together, the boy helping the princess with her studies, and in the course of time they fell in love.

One day the king, wanting to see how his daughter spent her days, rode to the school. There the girls were playing with the girls and the boys with the boys, but his daughter was playing with Vanke. That seemed shameful to him, so the king sent the princess to another school. She still wanted Vanke to help her, however, and he soon transferred to her school.

When the king next visited the princess at school, he found her playing with Vanke again. So he took her to a school in another city and left orders that no other children were to be admitted. But Vanke went to that city, applied to the school as a teacher, and was set in charge of her class.

The king again visited her school to see who her friends were. As before, he found her with Vanke. So he decided to take her out of school and marry her off.

The princess said to Vanke, "Though you and I love each other, my father is planning to marry me to someone else. Here, take this money to a sorceress and ask her to help us outwit my father."

Vanke rode away and found a sorceress, who gave him a ring. "Tell the princess to slip this halfway onto her finger," she said. "It will make her slightly ill. Then let her slip it all the way on and she will fall dead. When she has been buried, dig her up and take the ring off her finger. She will come to life again."

So Vanke returned home and gave the ring to the princess. On the day that was set for her wedding, she slipped the ring halfway onto her finger and became slightly ill. The doctors advised her to drink a little wine. Then she pushed the ring all the way down on her finger and fell dead. The doctors waited for five days, and when she still showed no signs of life, they buried her.

Afterward Vanke, fortified by a great deal of brandy, went to the cemetery and dug the princess up. As the sorceress had promised, she came back to life when he removed the ring from her finger. She lay ill in his house for several days, then recovered.

Now Vanke and the princess opened a shop to earn their bread. One day the king came in to buy some of the fine cloth that they sold. "You know," he said to Vanke, weeping, "your assistant looks just like my daughter. Oh, how I miss her!"

Vanke said, "Your highness must stop grieving. Why don't you hold a feast for the people of the town? It might lift your spirits."

The king took up this idea, and everyone came to the party except Vanke's shop assistant. The king looked everywhere for her and wept when he couldn't find her.

In the meantime Vanke set all the guests to telling stories. When it was his turn, he began, "Listen, my friends. Here's a problem for you to solve: A rich man had a vineyard, and one day its finest vine withered. Some visitors said to him, 'You have such a lovely vineyard, but that one withered vine mars its beauty.' So the rich man tore up the withered vine and threw it into the street.

"A poor man going by saw the vine and took it home. He planted it and tended it carefully. One day the rich man came along and, recognizing the now flourishing plant, said, 'Give me back my vine.'

"Now, people, what I want to know is this: to whom does the vine properly belong?"

"Why, to the poor man," everyone said. "To the poor man."

Then Vanke gave a signal and the princess came in. First she embraced Vanke, then the king, then her mother. "Now," said Vanke, "to whom does she belong? To me, who rescued her from death, or to somebody else?" Everyone said she belonged to him. So they were married and lived happily ever after.

38

The Foolish Youth and Elijah the Prophet

Once there was a couple who had an only son. He was a foolish youth—not at all gifted. Day after day he sat around on top of the oven doing nothing.

Well, nobody lives forever. The youth's father died. And the mother, it goes without saying, couldn't chop wood in the forest, so she begged her son, "Please, dear. Go into the forest. Cut wood. Earn something."

But it was as if she was talking to someone else. He kept sitting on the oven. But hunger accomplished what past pleadings couldn't. When, finally, there was nothing to eat, he took an ax and a saw and went off to the forest.

The youth cut wood and packed it up and carried it off to sell, the way everyone else did. As it turned out, his customers were very pleased with him, because no matter what the size of his bundle, he didn't charge more than one gildn for it. He wouldn't take more; that's how foolish he was.

One day when he went into the forest, there was no more wood to be found. He was leaning sadly against a tree when a poor old man went by. The man was Elijah the Prophet.

Elijah thought, "I really ought to give him something to bring him luck and make him happy." So he pronounced: "May whatever the boy says come to pass." Then the Prophet went on his way.

The foolish youth standing beside his tree said, "Ah me. If only this tree were to fall." He had no sooner spoken than the tree fell. The boy looked about. "As I live and breathe, the tree has fallen." Then he said, "If only I had a strong rope." He had hardly spoken than a strong rope fell over his shoulder. Fingering it, he said, "How nice it would be if I could carry the tree into town." At once the tree was properly tied and on his back, and he was on his way to the city to sell the wood.

As he walked past the royal palace, the king's daughter, a magnif-
icent young woman, was standing on the balcony. She saw a man
dragging a huge tree, roots, branches, and all. She burst into laughter
and cried out to her father, the king, "What sort of creature is that,
who can drag such an enormous tree?"

Irritated, the fool called up to her, "May you know as little about
why you are carrying a child as I know about why I can carry this
tree." And he went on to the market, where he sold the truly
enormous tree for—again—just one gildn. A fool.

But let's leave him now and talk about the princess. Not long after
the foolish youth went by with the tree, she discovered that she was
pregnant. She was beside herself. How could such a thing have
happened? Then she thought that perhaps she was imagining it. So
she went to the royal physician, who said, "It's not your imagination.
You're pregnant, my dear." She swore that she had no notion how
—or by whom—that could be. The physician replied, "A fact is a
fact. You're pregnant."

When the queen and the king learned about it—oh my, what a
stir. But a fact is a fact. At the end of nine months the princess had
a son.

Her parents studied the child's face, and it was clear that he did
not resemble the queen, or the king, or any of the king's ministers,
or his generals. Who was the father?

So the senate had a portrait painted of the child and hung in the
great hall. Then they gave a great ball, invited everyone in the city,
and searched the faces of all the guests. But the child resembled
nobody at all. Too bad.

Now what? Well, one of the senators had an idea. He said, "Perhaps there's someone who didn't come to the ball." And it turned
out that there was such a person: the foolish youth. So they looked
for him and found him on top of the oven.

"We're having another ball," they said. "Please come."

"I don't care for dances," he said.

So they brought him back by force to the palace, where the king
and queen looked closely into his face. He was just like the child.

They turned angrily to the princess. "Is this the fellow you've been with?"

She said, "Who? What? I have no idea who he is."

To make a long story short, the king would not believe her and he condemned her to be exiled. She and her child were put on board a ship together with the foolish youth, though he was shut off from them by a stout wall. The ship was supplied with food for a year, towed out to open sea, and set loose—with no helmsman, no sailors, no one.

The ship drifted for a year, and the fool just sat where he had been put. He had food, after all. But when there was nothing more to eat and he grew hungry, he looked about and saw that there was a thick wall enclosing him. "Oh," he said. "If only there was a hole in the wall." Even as he spoke, a hole appeared. He looked through it and saw the princess.

She asked, "How did you manage to make that hole?"

He said, "What makes you think I know how I did it?"

She said, "Well, if you make the hole larger, you can come over to me."

He said, "I don't mind. Let the hole be larger." And the hole enlarged and he climbed through it.

Now, the princess was nobody's fool. She knew that a youth who could make a hole with words instead of tools was no ordinary man. And she had been thinking about her pregnancy, about the youth with the tree who had passed by and about his words to her. She was beginning to understand. So she suggested, "Why don't you say, 'Let's land on the shore'?"

He said, "Well, why not? Let's land on the shore." And as soon as he had spoken, the ship pulled up to shore. After they had debarked, she suggested, "Why not say that you want a palace exactly like my father's?" So he did, and at once a palace exactly like her father's stood before them. Then she told him to say that he wanted costly furnishings, and soon they lacked for nothing.

And so the princess and the foolish youth lived as happily as birds for a while. One day she suggested, "Why don't you say that you want a bridge leading from here to my father's palace?" The moment he spoke the words, a bridge extended across the ocean right to the king's palace.

The king, when he learned of the bridge, commanded his servants to harness horses to his coach. "Let's see where this bridge leads," he said. So four horses were harnessed and all the ministers, generals, and servants got into the coach with the king and queen. And they rode off across the bridge. They rode and rode until they arrived at the other shore. There they got out of the coach and saw what looked exactly like the king's palace.

The king thought, "What's this? Have we turned ourselves around? Are we back where we started?"

Now, the princess and the youth had disguised themselves. So when the king saw them standing on the shore, he asked, "Who are you? And what are you doing here?"

They replied, "We're fisher folk." Then they added, "It's nice that you've come, since we're about to celebrate our marriage. Won't you be our guests?"

And so the marriage was celebrated. Do you think there was anything lacking? It was all exactly as if the richest of kings had arranged it. Golden dishes; golden spoons. And the wonderful foods that were served are impossible to describe.

A golden goblet set with gemstones was placed before the king, such a goblet that the king couldn't take his eyes from it.

Everyone ate and drank for a day and a night. Then, as the guests were leaving, the princess suggested to the fool, "Why not say that you want the goblet to fall into the king's pocket?" So the youth did, and the goblet did.

Well, the king and queen and their entourage drove off, and after a while the princess and her husband pursued and overtook them. "Don't take it ill," the princess said to the king, "but one of your people has gone off with the goblet."

Hearing this, the king grew angry and said, "Who would dare? I'll see that whoever has your goblet is put to death."

Well, they started to search everyone. The king, putting his hands into his own pockets, cried out, "Oh dear! Look, I have the goblet."

Everyone turned to stare. The king could not possibly have taken the goblet. And yet he had it!

The princess said to the king, "Do you see? Just as you have no idea how the goblet got into your pocket, so I have no idea how I got pregnant."

At first the king did not understand, but when the princess and her husband removed their disguises, the king flung himself into her arms and they embraced. Oh, what jubilation there was! They all got into the coach and rode home to the king's palace.

As for her husband, the fool, the king and queen had him educated and he turned into a proper man. And so from that time on they all lived happily ever after.

3 9
The King's Lost Daughter

Once upon a time there were two kings, one German and one Polish, and they always lived in peace.

It happened one day that the daughter of the Polish king disappeared. She was nowhere to be found, and the king had notices put up announcing that whoever could locate his daughter and bring her home could become her husband.

The German king's son went walking one day with his friend, a fisherman's son. When they saw the notices, the fisherman's son said to the German king's son, "Shall we look for the king's daughter?"

"Agreed," said the king's son, and off they rode.

They rode on and on until suddenly their horses stopped and refused to go any further. They beat them with whips and then with rods, but the horses would not budge. Then they heard a voice from on high saying, "Beat not your horses. They may not go any farther."

How were they to go on? This was a matter in which God was involved. Heaven itself. So they decided to send for a rabbi. When the rabbi came and learned what had happened, he bade them dig where the horses were standing. They dug and they dug until they uncovered a door. The fisherman's son and the rabbi opened the door and the youths descended through it into a cellar where they found a man wearing a *talis*, a prayer shawl, over his head and standing before a pair of black candles.

"What is it you wish, my children?" asked the man.

After hearing their story, the man said, "If you want to know where the king's lost daughter is, you'll have to swear by these black candles that you will never tell anyone I am here."

They swore by the black candles. Then he said, "Refill the hole and drive on until you come to a bridge. Under the bridge you'll find a golden rod. Swing the rod first to the right and then to the left. A road will appear before you, and you'll see a glass mountain in the distance. A horse will be standing on the summit of the glass moun-

tain. One of you must mount the steed and shut your eyes. The horse will run so fast that the rider will feel that his flesh is being torn from his body, but he must keep his eyes closed or else he'll fall down from the mountain."

The boys ascended from the cellar, refilled the hole, and rode off, along with the rabbi.

They came to the bridge and found the golden rod. The rabbi swung it back and forth, and a road opened before them leading to a glass mountain with a horse standing at the top. When they came close to the horse, the fisherman's son said to the prince, "You mount the horse."

But the prince replied, "I'm scared. You do it."

The fisherman's son climbed on the horse and shut his eyes, then felt himself flying with the speed of the wind. Finally the horse came to a stop beside a hut, and the youth dismounted. Through the window of the hut he saw the princess tied to a bed, while a red-hot oven glowed. And he saw a witch getting ready to throw the princess into the fiery oven. Without a moment's thought, he leaped into the room and so surprised the witch that he was able to kill her very quickly with his sword.

He flung the witch's body out of the hut, and it tumbled down the mountain and fell at the feet of the young prince, who was waiting there. The prince thought that it was the king's daughter, and that the fisherman's son had killed her. He grabbed the body, mounted his horse, and flew like the wind back to the Polish king.

Since the bloody corpse was unrecognizable, everyone believed the German prince. So the Polish king sent a troop of soldiers off to find the fisherman's son and take vengeance for the death of his daughter.

Meanwhile the fisherman's son untied the Polish princess and rode with her and the rabbi toward her father's castle. As they approached it, they saw a troop of soldiers coming to meet them. The rabbi said to the fisherman's son, "The German king's son must have accused you of killing the princess."

When the soldiers surrounded him, the fisherman's son revealed the princess to them and shouted, "This is the real princess!" And when the princess's face was washed, everyone could see that he told the truth.

The German king's son said, "She belongs to us both, because we both searched for her."

So it was decided that all three of them would lie in the same bed that night, and in the morning the princess would marry the youth whom she was found to be facing.

That evening there was a great banquet to celebrate the return of the king's lost daughter. Everyone ate and drank deeply—everyone but the fisherman's son, who took various good things and put them into his pockets.

When night fell, both youths and the princess went to sleep in one bed. The scent of chocolate and the other sweet things he had in his pockets wafted from the fisherman's son. But the German king's son gave off a fearful smell of drunkenness. Finally the princess couldn't stand it and turned her face toward the sweet-smelling fisherman's son. And when morning came, she was found pressed close against him, facing him.

And so they were married, and the German king's son was killed because he had tried to kill the fisherman's son.

40

The Magic Fish and the Wishing Ring

Once upon a time there was a childless king. Above everything he wanted to beget a child who would rule his kingdom when he was gone, but neither doctors nor magicians had been able to help him.

The king heard of a certain rare fish in such-and-such a river, and any woman who ate even a morsel of this fish would conceive a child. He sent at once for the royal fisherman and gave him four weeks to catch it. "If you bring me the fish, I will make you my viceroy," the king said. "If you fail, I will have you beheaded."

The royal fisherman went to the river eagerly, for he too was childless. And oh, what a catching of fish there was! At first he caught a big fish, then little ones. And each time he caught a fish, he examined it closely, but it was never the one he sought. At the end of two weeks he was catching no more fish, only worms and more worms.

Three and then four weeks were up and there was not even a worm left in the river. The fisherman was in despair when suddenly he heard a great splash. Turning, he saw a man standing in the water and holding a live fish. "Here is what you're looking for," said the man, who, of course, was Satan. "I'll let you have it on the condition that when he is thirteen years old, you'll give me the boy your wife will conceive after she has eaten some of this fish."

Without hesitation, the fisherman pledged to give the boy over Then, carrying the fish, he hurried to the king.

There was a great banquet, where the fish was served, and at which the king appointed the fisherman as his viceroy. And all the women who ate the fish, and whose husbands came to them that night, did conceive children.

Nine months later the queen gave birth to a daughter while the viceroy's wife gave birth to a son. The two children were raised together and startled everyone with their learning and talent. When they were not yet grown they became engaged, and it was generally agreed that after the king died, the two of them would rule the kingdom.

But the viceroy, the former fisherman, remembered what he had promised the man in the river and grew sadder with the years. One day when his son was twelve, the boy said, "Father, what is troubling you? Don't spare me, I can endure it."

So the viceroy revealed the truth about his pledge. "So be it, if it is my destiny," the boy said calmly. "But get me a boat, Father, and leave the rest to me."

When the day came that they were to separate, they went together to the riverbank and the son stepped into the boat his father had provided. Then the viceroy called out, "Satan, take what is yours and grant that I have fulfilled my pledge."

With a great splash Satan appeared. He acknowledged that the pledge had been met and turned to snatch the boat, but the son was such a skilled helmsman that he eluded Satan. They began a chase near and far, downriver and into the ocean, the devil almost but never quite catching the boy. At last Satan, exhausted, spat after the boat and sent it scudding across the sea to the edge of the world.

The vessel was cast up on the shore of a river, where the viceroy's son stepped out. For three days he wandered; on the fourth he came to a large city. He went into various houses, but they were all empty. He concluded, then, that there must be a council meeting in the king's court, and he walked down the main avenue till he came to the royal palace. Here too nobody was to be seen. He looked about and his eyes fell upon a tablet inscribed with these words:

Just as East
May not meet West,
Just so it is
Impossible that here
A human can appear.

And yet, should one
By some strange luck
Find his way here,
Then let him knock
Three times
With a hammer
On the anvil he'll find
In the large third chamber.

The viceroy's son followed the instructions. After the third blow on the anvil, a crowd of people seemed to start up out of the ground. They all filed by and bowed to him, crying, "Greetings to our liberator!"

When the queen came by, she explained that the people had, in the course of a war, been bewitched by their enemy and condemned to live underground. But now that he had broken the spell, he would be crowned king of this land.

And a few days later, that's what happened. He became king of the people he had freed, and in time he married their former queen and thus made her a queen again. He ruled happily for a long while, but then he began to think, "What have I got here? A king's throne? I could have had that at home. I would have married the princess and become a king, and I would have brought happiness to my parents in the bargain." And it struck him, too, that people at home must be mourning for him.

The queen noticed his unhappiness and said, "What's making you so gloomy?"

He told her, and she said, "If you really want to see your family and friends, I can arrange it. Here," she said, giving him a ring. "You have only to put this on and say, 'Take me to the land of my birth,' and it will take you there at once.

"But once there, you must tell no one about our country. If you do, dreadful things will happen to you."

"I promise," he said. And with that he put on the ring and gave the order, "Take me to the land of my birth."

Away he flew, and in an instant he was at home. Everyone was so glad to see him that a holiday was declared, during which the viceroy's son got so drunk that he forgot his promise to his queen. "In that other country," he bragged, "my wife is so beautiful that if you were to see her, your eyes would be dazzled. And . . . and . . . not only my wife . . . my cook, if she were here, would be the most beautiful woman in the land."

The king said, "Brag away. Talk is cheap. How do we know that you're telling the truth?"

"You want proof?" said the viceroy's son. "I'll give you proof." With that he put the ring on his finger and cried, "Bring me my wife and my cook."

And there, standing in the doorway of the banquet hall, stood his wife and his cook from that other country, and their beauty did indeed dazzle the people. No one, including her husband, noticed the displeasure behind his queen's smile.

A day or two later the viceroy's son was strolling in the country-side with his wife and cook. At a grassy knoll they sat down to rest, and the two women poured a glass of wine for him. The young man, expecting no evil, drank and fell instantly into a deep sleep.

Then the queen and the cook took away his clothes, the magic ring, and all signs of his identity. Leaving him sleeping on the grass, they disappeared forever.

When he woke and saw what had happened, he was too ashamed to go back into town. A kindly peasant gave him some old clothes, and for a year or two he wandered from town to town.

One day as he was traveling through a forest, he came upon three foolish brothers quarreling over an inheritance that consisted of a saddle that could seat seven people, a whip that could lash out of its own accord, and a piece of cloth that could make anyone invisible. "Why don't you let me help you?" the young man said. "Give me the saddle, the whip, and the cloth and I'll divide them in a way that will please you all."

"Very well," the three fools said, and gave him their inheritance. He seated himself in the saddle and, seizing the whip, cried, "Hey, brothers, can you still see me?"

"Yes," they replied.

"In that case," he shouted, "Saddle, carry me home. Whip, strike. Cloth, cover me." The whip struck at the brothers, the cloth made him invisible, and away he went until he was back in his home town. There he wrapped the saddle and the whip in the cloth and walked about.

Great crowds of people thronged the streets. The viceroy's son stopped a passerby and asked, "What's going on?"

"Where are you from? Why, the smallest child in town knows that the old king and queen are dead and we're having a wedding and crowning a new king today. Our queen was to have married the viceroy's son, but he disappeared."

When the viceroy's son heard this, he wrapped himself in the magic cloth and went at once to the coronation. The queen appeared leading her husband-to-be, who was about to be crowned when the invisible viceroy's son cried to his whip, "Whip, give him fifty lashes." Before everyone's eyes the whip set about beating the would-be king. Then the viceroy's son cried, "On, Whip. Give the queen fifty strokes!" And the whip turned on the queen, who wept and begged, "Whoever is beating me, please show yourself."

The viceroy's son threw off the magic cloak and the queen exclaimed, "It's him—he is the true king," and fell to the ground in a faint.

When she recovered, she and the viceroy's son were married, and he was crowned king with great joy on all sides.

41

The Hunchbacks and the
Dancing Demons

There were a couple of hunchbacked brothers who lived in the same village, but they did not get along. They were always mocking each other, quarreling, making each other's lives miserable. But you could cheer either one up by telling him that the other's hump was bigger.

One of the brothers was meaner and more spiteful than the other. At last the other, feeling that his bad-tempered brother was shortening his days, decided to leave the village. He gathered together such rags as he had—an old shirt, a pair of trousers, some scraps of cloth for his feet—and put them in a sack. With the sack over his humped shoulder and a stick in his hand, he started off one morning at dawn.

He traveled from village to village, from town to town, from city to city. He wandered through woods and over fields, till one day he was forced by bad weather to spend the night in an open field. He was lonely there all by himself, but what else could he do?

Then, in the distance, he saw the protruding tip of a roof. He walked toward it and found that it was an abandoned hut, so he went inside. It had a broken-down bed with a bit of littered straw for a mattress, and putting his sack down, he flung himself on it and went to sleep.

Toward midnight he was awakened by a loud noise. Opening his eyes, he saw a crowd of carousing demons making a great racket. As they beat a drum and danced about, they stuck out their tongues, squealed, whistled, and howled.

All at once they came upon the hunchback. They hauled him out of bed and made him join their circle. He danced about with a will, making the same strange cries, and this pleased them very much.

Everyone danced until it was almost one o'clock in the morning. Then the chief of the demons said, "You're a great fellow; we'd like you to visit us again. And to make sure you come back, we want you to leave us a pledge."

The hunchback offered them his shirt and trousers, but they said, "No, we don't want them." He offered his sack, but still they said, "No."

"What can I give you?" he asked. "I haven't got anything else except my hump."

"That's it!" cried the chief of the demons. "Your hump. Now, that's undamaged goods. There's a pledge we can accept." Then all the demons formed a circle around the hunchback, though when he looked around a moment later, nobody was there. And not only were the demons gone, but when the hunchback touched his shoulder he found that his hump was gone too.

The former hunchback, his head held high and his shoulders thrown back, strode through the streets of his village. He was met by his mean-tempered brother, who looked him over and said, "Where have you left your hump?"

The other described all that had happened—the hut and the demons and the dancing. "And that," he concluded, "is how I got rid of the hump."

"Where's the hut?" the mean hunchback asked eagerly.

His brother provided instructions on which paths and trails to take, and the hunchback started off. He walked on and on until at last he came to the hut. There he found the bed littered with straw, just as his brother had described it. He too went to sleep and, just at twelve o'clock, the demons arrived and began their dance. There were the same strange cries, the drumming and whistling, the tapping of feet, just as he had been told.

This time too the demons took the hunchback into their circle, and he danced along with them, matching their cries. They were delighted with him. A few minutes before one o'clock, when their carousing was ended, the chief of the demons said, "You're an honorable fellow. You kept your word and came back to us, so now we want to return your pledge."

With that he gave the other demons a signal, and they formed a circle around the mean hunchback. And when they found that he already had a hump on his back, they stuck the pledged hump on his chest, so now he had two.

42
The Princess of the Third Pumpkin

Once upon a time there were a king and queen who had an only son. When he was eighteen years old, they sent for him and said, "Dear son, it's time for you to be married." And the son replied, "If you find a bride for me, I'll gladly marry." The king ordered the most beautiful maidens of the country to be brought before the prince, but the young man was not pleased with any of them. So the king proclaimed that anyone who could procure a bride for his son would be richly rewarded.

An old woman came to the palace and said, "Lord king, I have a maiden for you who is unique in all the world."

"Let's see her," said the king.

The old woman said, "Let the prince get up at dawn. Let him put on his coat and take his knife and a bottle of water, and let him go into the king's garden. There he will see three pumpkins growing on a single vine. Let him take his knife and cut one off. The most beautiful princess in the world will emerge from it. Let him give her water to drink and she will at once be willing to be his bride."

The king thanked her and commanded that she be given a place in the little hut in the courtyard that was near the royal kitchen. Then the king called his son and told him what he had to do to get a bride. The prince followed the king's instructions: He got up at dawn and put on his coat. He took along his knife and a bottle of water and went into the royal garden. There he saw three pumpkins growing on a single vine. He took his knife and cut one off. A naked princess as lovely as a sunrise stepped out of the pumpkin and cried, "A drink, a drink, a drink!" But the princess escaped before the prince could give her water from his bottle. So he cut a second pumpkin from the vine, and again a beautiful naked princess stepped out. She cried, "Oh, a drink, a drink, a drink!" But before the prince could give her water, she escaped. So the prince cut the third pumpkin from the vine, and from it stepped a naked princess, uniquely beautiful in all the world, who cried, "Oh, a drink, a drink, a drink!" And the prince quickly put his bottle to her lips and she drank her fill and stayed.

The prince took his coat off and wrapped the princess in it, then set her on the branch of a tree and started off to tell the king that he had found a bride. Meanwhile the princess sat on the branch of the tree.

Now, the branch overhung a well, and a gypsy woman came to it for water. She looked into the water and cried out, "Oh, how lovely I am!"

The princess on the branch cried, "A curse on you! You? Lovely? It's I who am lovely."

The gypsy looked up and saw the princess sitting in the tree. So she dragged her out of it, took the coat, and threw her into the well, after which she donned the prince's coat and perched herself in the tree.

And now the joyful king and queen came running and looked up at the bride. "Oh my, a gypsy," they thought. But they pitied the prince and said nothing to him. They sent for clothes and had the gypsy dressed and taken to the palace. And the gypsy with her spells made the prince believe that she was the beautiful princess, and preparations began for the wedding.

One day the king's cook went to the well to get a pail of water. As he pulled it up, he saw a golden fish swimming in the pail. He took it to the kitchen and cooked it, but he threw the scales outside. Now, the old woman who lived in the hut near the royal kitchen looked out and happened to see the scales. She gathered them up and sewed them together to make a little shoe. She hung it up on the wall of her hut before she went to bed that night.

When she woke in the morning, she was astonished to see that the hut had been tidied, her breakfast had been cooked, and her bread was already baked. She sat down to spin flax. She spun and spun until she fell asleep. When she woke, she discovered that all her flax had been spun.

She was curious to know who was helping her, so she decided to stay up all night and find out. She got into bed, closed her eyes, and pretended to be asleep. Late at night she opened her eyes and saw a princess lovely as the world come out of the golden shoe. The princess heated the oven, baked the bread, and tidied the hut.

The old woman got silently out of her bed and stole over to the wall. She snatched the golden shoe and flung it into the fire. The princess, seeing this, set up a clamor. But it was too late. The little golden shoe had burned up, and the princess had to stay with the old woman.

One day the princess said, "I'm very bored. Give me some work to do." So the old woman went to the king and said, "I'm very bored. Give me some work to do." So the king gave her some thread and told her to crochet a tablecloth out of it. The old woman took the thread back to her hut and gave it to the princess, who sat down and crocheted a tablecloth in the design of a garden. And in the middle of the garden she crocheted a portrait of her own face.

The old woman took the tablecloth to the king, who liked it so much that he had it placed on the table at a banquet for the prince and his wife. As the company sat eating and drinking and having a pleasant time, the prince looked at the tablecloth and saw the picture of the garden and the princess's portrait. "Who crocheted that tablecloth?" he asked. The king said, "The old woman who lives in the hut near the kitchen." The prince commanded that she be brought at once. The old woman came and the prince said, "Was it you who crocheted this tablecloth?" "No," she replied. "Not I, but the princess of the golden shoe."

The prince ordered her to bring the princess, so the old woman went home and came back leading her. The prince instantly recognized his betrothed, uniquely beautiful in all the world. He fell on her neck and wept as he embraced and kissed her. The gypsy bride, the false princess, was driven out of the palace, and the prince and princess were married and continue to live happily unto this day.

43
The Orphan Boy Who Won the Bride

Once upon a time there was a man who lived in a nobleman's domain. The man and his wife had been childless for many years so he went to a rabbi in a nearby town and said, "Rabbi, my wife and I want a son. Won't you pray for us and ask the Lord to bless us?" The rabbi said, "Yes, I will." So he prayed to the Lord and his prayers were answered: The man's wife became pregnant and bore a son. Of course, the overjoyed parents invited the rabbi to the circumcision feast.

When the boy was five years old, his parents died and there was no one to care for him. So the nobleman took the child into his own home and raised him himself.

The boy, eager to make himself useful, learned how to build things. Using a saw and a plane and a hatchet, he made sleds and wagons. Several years went by in this way and by the time he was twelve years old he had quite forgotten how to speak Yiddish. One night the boy's father appeared to the rabbi in a dream and said, "Rabbi, my son no longer knows what he is. Take him away from the nobleman and instruct him in Judaism." The very next day the rabbi went to the nobleman and pleaded for the boy to be given to him, but the nobleman refused.

Well, one way or another, the rabbi got the boy away from the nobleman and undertook to raise and instruct him. He taught him the rites of Judaism: when to wash his hands, how to make the blessing over bread, and so on.

When the boy was seventeen, a letter came inviting the rabbi to a wedding in a distant land. The youth said, "Rabbi, take me with you. I want to go, too."

But the rabbi said, "How can I take you? You don't have the right clothes. You can't go traveling, ragged as you are."

"Never mind that," replied the youth, "they'll find out who I am soon enough."

The rabbi said, "You can't come. I haven't got enough money for both of us." Then off he went on a ship, leaving the youth behind.

Or so he thought. But just before the ship weighed anchor, the boy, ragged as he was, slipped aboard and the ship sailed away. They were in mid-ocean before they knew it, and a great storm came up and blew the ship far out of its course until it came to rest, becalmed in the Congealed Sea.

Days went by and they stayed in the Congealed Sea, where there was nothing but derelict ships to be seen, and nothing to eat. Then one day a great storm blew up and broke the ship free and drove it across the ocean until it came to an island where they dropped anchor.

The hungry passengers decided to explore the island hoping to find berries and fruit to eat. The youth came upon an apple tree, which he climbed. He ate some apples and threw some down for the others who ate the fruit and then fell asleep beneath the tree. Meanwhile the youth, too, dozed up in the branches where, a little while later, he was awakened by the stirring of a breeze.

Startled, he looked around, then he called excitedly, "Rabbi, rabbi, you should see the stones that are up here."

The rabbi called back, "What do you see on the stones?"

"I hardly know," the youth called down, "it looks like very beautiful writing."

"Copy down what you see on a piece of paper and throw it down to me," said the rabbi.

The youth did what he was bidden. He copied down what he saw on a piece of paper and threw it down to the rabbi, but just then the rabbi and the other passengers went aboard the ship and sailed off, leaving the youth behind in the tree.

Well, he made himself as comfortable as he could and settled down to wait. That night a rabbi appeared beside him in the tree and taught him all of the Torah—and all the commentaries as well—so that he became a great scholar.

At daybreak, he spotted a ship passing by. He stood up in the tree and waved his hands and shouted, "Help, help, help!" Fortunately, the people on the ship saw him and sent a boat that took him off the island and brought him back to the ship which, as it happened, was also going to the town where the wedding was to take place.

When he arrived there, the youth took up lodgings in a poor man's hut. He passed himself off as a merchant looking for goods to buy, and the poor man who owned the hut said to him, "I've been invited to a wedding. Why don't you come with me?"

"How can I go to a wedding?" said the youth. "Look how ragged I am."

"Never mind," said his landlord, "I'll find you some clothes."

The landlord kept his word. He found the youth some clothes and they went to the wedding together.

At the reception before the wedding, even the rabbi who had raised the youth was unable to recognize him in his new clothes. The youth stood near a circle of rabbis and learned folk who were discussing and arguing various deep points of Torah commentary. At one point the prospective bridegroom gave a learned address to the assembled guests. The youth stood by silently, an enigmatic smile on his face.

The discussion, the disputation, the arguments went on and the youth, all the while, stood by with an enigmatic smile on his face. Finally, one of the rabbis was affronted and said angrily, "You, young man. You, with the grin on your face. If you have something to say, say it."

The youth then put such subtle, such profound questions to the company that no one was able to answer them. Everyone was so delighted with his performance that the mother of the bride-to-be said to the father, "Now that's the sort of husband our daughter should have."

"You're right," her husband replied. With that they canceled the betrothal on the spot and engaged their daughter to the learned stranger.

When the time came for the wedding, the youth insisted that it be celebrated in the poor man's hut where he was staying.

"How can that be?" he was asked. "It's such a tiny place."

"Never mind," he said. "Everyone will fit."

The preparations were made. The hut was decorated as well as it could be. When the musicians arrived, the youth said, "Don't play yet. We won't have music until twelve o'clock."

Meanwhile more and more people came, and lo and behold, no matter how many entered the hut, there was always room for more. The entire population of the town came in, and the hut simply grew larger and larger.

Then all at once the sky turned dark and a gale blew up. The wedding guests ran outside and saw an enormous cloud descending from the heavens. When it reached the ground, the youth's father and mother stepped down from the cloud, and they were followed by King David and all his musicians.

"Now play!" cried the youth to his musicians.

And they did, and the food was served, and the dancing began, and I too was there and had a good little glass of brandy.

From my beard it dripped,
But none I sipped.

As for the island—it was *ganeydn,* the Garden of Eden.

44

Forty Hares and a Princess

Once upon a time there was a king who had an only daughter. A great many officers and generals wanted to marry her, but the king said to himself, "If I give her to one of them, all the others will be angry." So he thought of a plan: he would put a gold ring on her finger and set her up in a high place, and whoever could snatch the ring would become her husband. So that's what he did. And men came from all over the world to try and snatch the ring from her finger, but none succeeded.

One day a shepherd boy in ragged clothes showed up. He approached the princess sitting on her high perch, and with a great bound he snatched the ring from her finger. The king and the courtiers, seeing how shabbily he was dressed, were unwilling to let him marry her. But what was to be done?

"Well," they said, "to tell the truth, there's another test you must pass. You see these hutches? Inside are forty hares. We want you to drive them into the woods each day and bring them home at night. But be warned: not a single hare must be missing. If you fail the test, you're a dead man."

"Hmm," said the boy to himself, "forty hares aren't easy to control. And even if I drive them into the woods, how can I drive them back? Yet if a single hare is missing, I'll pay with my life.

"Still, if I want to marry the princess I'll have to try." So he turned the hares loose and managed, one way or another, to get them all into the woods, but there they ran off in all directions. "Ah," he thought sadly, "I'm a fool . . . and a dead man. I'll never be able to round them up."

As he walked gloomily through the woods, he chanced to look down and saw a whistle lying on the ground. He picked it up and blew on it. Immediately all forty hares came running to him. "Hmm," he thought, "a fool with a little luck is only half a fool. Let's see. I wonder if they'll follow me to an open field."

So he started off piping on his whistle, and the hares all followed him to the field. "Well, they seem obedient," he said. "Let's see if I can turn them into soldiers. Hey, there," he called to one of the hares, "you can be a sergeant. And you," he said, pointing to another, "you can be a platoon leader." He pointed to a third and said, "And you can be a squad leader."

Then he shouted, "Fall in." And when they had lined up, he taught the hares how to march in formation.

Back at the king's court, a huge crowd gathered to wait for the execution. But lo and behold, there was the shepherd boy, marching at the head of his hares, like a military troop. He marched them to their hutches and cried, "Fall out!" and all forty went into the hutches and settled down for the night.

The king and his courtiers counted all the hares and found that not one was missing. But they didn't want this ragamuffin to marry the princess, so what were they to do? By hook or by crook, they decided they had to make him lose a hare.

The next day when the shepherd had marched the hares out of the palace, the king himself, wearing a disguise, followed him to the woods. There he said to the boy (who recognized him at once), "Who owns these marching hares?"

"They are the king's," replied the shepherd.

"Sell me one."

"I won't sell any. I don't need the money."

"Well, what do you want?"

"If you'll kiss the place beneath the sergeant's tail," said the shepherd, "I'll give you a hare."

So the king agreed. And when he had kissed the place beneath the sergeant rabbit's tail, the shepherd gave him a hare.

The king started off with his animal, feeling pleased because now they could kill this upstart.

Meanwhile, that very same thought had occurred to the shepherd. "Well," he said to himself, "let's see what my whistle can do." He blew on it and lo and behold, the king's hare leaped out of his arms and ran back to the shepherd.

When the king returned to the palace empty-handed, he was too embarrassed to confess that he had lost the hare. So he said, "That shepherd refused to sell me one."

Hearing this, the queen said, "I'll go tomorrow; he'll sell me a hare."

The next morning the shepherd gathered his army of hares and marched off to the woods, where he passed the time by drilling them. He beat on a drum and the hares marched to its beat.

Meanwhile the queen in her coach rode into the forest, approached the shepherd, and said, "Sell me a hare." He replied, "I won't sell any of my hares. But if you'll kiss the place beneath the tail of my platoon commander, I'll give you one."

Well, she was the queen, after all, but she was determined to cheat him out of one of his hares. And though the place beneath the hare's tail was soiled, she kissed it.

The shepherd said, "That hare is a platoon commander. You'll have to do better than that. Give him a really good kiss." And so she kissed the place again. Then he said, "Which of my hares do you want?"

"Whichever hare you say," she replied.

"Choose one for yourself."

She tried to pick one up, but it wouldn't allow itself to be caught. The shepherd said to the hare, "Come here." And the hare came obediently. The shepherd said, "Lie down." The hare lay down and the queen caught him. "Hold him tight so he won't run away," said the shepherd.

The queen got into her coach and commanded the coachman, "Drive as fast as you can, before the shepherd changes his mind."

The coachman said, "If you had some powdered English salt to put on the hare's tail, it wouldn't run away."

"Well, I don't," she said, "so let's get moving."

As they sped away, the shepherd sounded a note on his whistle and the hare tore itself from the queen's grasp and ran back to him. The queen sat stunned, and when she got home, she too lied. "The shepherd won't sell any of his hares. Nor will he give them away."

That night the king and queen and their courtiers talked and talked and decided to send the princess to him the next morning. Since the shepherd wanted to marry her, they reasoned, he would surely give her a hare. And if he came home missing a hare, he was a dead man.

In the morning the shepherd got up and went to the forest to drill his army of hares.

The princess, his bride-to-be, started off carrying preserves and other delicacies, as well as a bottle of brandy to make the shepherd tipsy. In addition, the queen had given the princess some powdered English salt to sprinkle on a hare's tail.

The princess arrived in the forest and said to the shepherd, "See, I've brought you some preserves and a little bit of brandy. Eat, drink; let's be jolly together."

The shepherd had a little glass of brandy and ate some of the preserves. A while later the princess said, "I have to go now. But it would be so nice if you gave me a hare. I'd love to have one to play with at home."

"The platoon commander will be unhappy if I give you a hare," said the shepherd, "but if you kiss him three times on the place beneath his tail, he will most likely agree."

The princess thought, "Well, the platoon commander won't tell anyone. And if I get home with the hare, the shepherd will be a dead man, so I might as well kiss the place under the tail three times." And so she did. And the shepherd gave her a hare.

She got into her coach and they started off quickly. She was just reaching for the English salt when the shepherd sounded his whistle. The hare leaped out of her arms and ran back to its master. "Oh, dear," she said to herself, "I kissed the place beneath the hare's tail three times and still I have no hare. What excuse can I give?"

Back at the palace she said that the shepherd had refused to give her a hare. Everyone sympathized, but the king and queen each guessed what had happened.

So, the royal family and their courtiers were in a turmoil. "What's to be done with this shepherd?" they asked. "How can we get rid of him?" And they devised another plan.

The next day they sent for him and said, "There's one more test before you can marry the princess. If you fail to perform it, you will be killed and that will be the end of you. Now listen. Tomorrow there will be a great banquet, and at its height we'll tell you what you must do. Go now, and be at the banquet tomorrow."

The banquet took place the next day and there was a huge crowd there. At the height of the festivities, the king called the shepherd to the podium and announced: "Ladies and gentlemen. As his last task to fulfill before he can marry the princess, the shepherd here will fill this sack with words. If he fails, it's off with his head."

The shepherd looked into the sack, then he looked at the audience and wondered, "How can a sack be filled with words?" Then turning to the audience, he said, "So you want a sack full of words. Well, let me put these words into it." And he began to tell the story of his experiences with the royal family.

"I thought," he said, "that the king was honorable and his word was good. So I snatched the ring from the princess's hand, but did I get the princess? Oh, no. I was given forty hares to tend, and threatened with death if I lost one. And so I tended them. I did what I was supposed to do. But did the king keep his word? No. He came to me in the forest and said he wanted to buy a hare . . ."

Here the shepherd interrupted himself and turned to the king. "Will your royal highness look into the sack," he said, "and tell me if it's full yet?"

The king started nervously forward and the shepherd resumed his story: "I say the king wanted to buy one of the hares. But I told him that I didn't sell hares. If he wanted a hare, he would . . ."

"Enough," shouted the king, "enough. The sack is full. There are enough words in it." So the king gave permission for the wedding, but the shepherd overthrew the king instead, and ruled long and well in his place.

And that's enough words for now.

45
The Merchant's Son and the Demons

Once upon a time there was a rich old man who had an only son. When the old man felt that he was dying, he sent for his son. "Dear child, I am leaving you well provided for," he said, "but before I die, promise me that after I'm gone you will never travel anywhere by sea."

"I promise," the son said, and with that the old man died.

Well, time passed and the son lived on his father's wealth, until one day a letter came to him from a merchant far across the sea. "Dear Sir," the letter said, "Here in my country there is a fortune waiting for you, money that was owed to your father. It would be a pity for so much money to go to waste. Why don't you come and get it?"

Without a moment's thought the merchant's son left his wife and child, hurriedly boarded a ship for that land beyond the sea. He had not traveled far when a storm blew up. The winds howled, the waves tossed, and all at once there was a terrible shudder and the ship began to sink.

It was then that the merchant's son remembered the promise he had made to his father and began to repent from the bottom of his heart. Then suddenly he was assailed by a terrible dizziness and fainted dead away. As he lay there in a trance, his father appeared before him and said, "Well, my son, is this how you keep your promises?"

"Father, father," begged the son, "forgive me. Oh, forgive me. Take pity on me—if not for my sake, then for my wife and my only son."

The winds howled, the waves tossed, and the youth prayed. At last his father said more kindly, "Very well, listen to me. When you come to, you will find yourself clinging to a log. Just hold on, and it will keep you afloat until it drifts ashore. There you will find an eagle waiting for you. You must let the eagle take you where it will." Having said that, his father disappeared.

And lo and behold, that's what happened. When the young man came to, the ship was nowhere to be seen and he found himself in the water clinging to a drifting log. It was sunset. Soon it would be dark. Just then the rich man's son heard the cries of beasts nearby and realized that he was near shore. So he turned the log loose and swam toward the land.

He dragged himself ashore, and suddenly there was a whoosh and a whirl and a spiral motion before his eyes. Before he knew what was happening, he was high in the sky, caught in an eagle's beak and being carried higher and higher. When he looked down, he saw tiny trees in one place, in another, small streams. If he should chance to fall from such a height, there would not be an unbroken bone left in his body. "Oh Lord," he cried, raising his eyes to heaven, "please don't let me fall."

With that he felt the beat of the great eagle's wings gradually slowing, and felt how they were descending lower and lower until the eagle landed. On the ground the creature opened its beak and flew away.

"Where in the world am I?" said the rich man's son as he looked around. At that moment he heard the voices of children in a *kheyder,* reciting their lessons. He followed the sounds until he came to a little house. He went in and saw a *melamed* sitting around a table with his pupils. He approached the teacher, put his hand out, and greeted him politely. To his dismay he was told by the teacher that he was in the land of the demons.

The rich man's son wept bitterly. Pitying him, the teacher said, "Stay here with me. I'll hide you from them."

And so he did. But one day the rich man's son had an impulse to go out for a walk. He had hardly taken two steps when a couple of demons seized him and took him to the court of Ashmodai, King of the Demons.

"And who may you be?" said Ashmodai sternly.

"A poor man who has been driven by misfortune into your country."

"A mortal, eh? A mortal!" roared Ashmodai, his eyes glowing so fiercely that the merchant's son was certain he was about to be swallowed whole. "Your kind and my kind are not the best of friends. The question is, shall I kill you now or later?"

The rich man's son stood trembling while Ashmodai continued to mutter to himself. Finally the King of the Demons said, "Hmmm. Hmmm. Well . . . you seem a likely sort. In your case I think I'll make an exception." He added: "I'm going to need someone to take charge here when I go off to fight my new war."

And so, as the weeks passed and Ashmodai prepared to go off to war, the rich man's son settled down in the demon's kingdom. With each passing day Ashmodai grew fonder and fonder of the mortal and trusted him more and more.

One day Ashmodai sent for the rich man's son. "Well, sir, I'm off to war. Here, take these," he said, handing over a great bunch of iron keys. "You can go anywhere you like except into the last room over there—the one that is opened by this key," he said, clinking the smallest key in the bunch. "That room is forbidden," he said grimly.

The demon turned on his heel and marched his army off to war.

Left alone, the rich man's son wandered from room to room admiring the wealth and luxury he found everywhere. Finally he came to the room into which he had been forbidden to go. He paused, terribly tempted to open the door with the little key, whose clink he seemed to be hearing once again.

But it was not the sound of the key he heard. Oh, no. It was a sound much more beautiful. A sound so enchanting that he pressed himself against the door to hear it better. It was a woman singing. For a while he listened; then, overcome by the melody, he unlocked the door and went in.

The woman turned, and he saw that she was as dazzlingly beautiful as her song. And she, the moment that she saw him, flung her arms around him and kissed him.

Then, all at once, there was a dreadful racket. Suddenly Ashmodai stood in front of them, red and wrathful, his eyes flashing, his sword drawn, ready to kill. "You," he raged, "you! Were you not warned to stay out? Were you not told this room was forbidden?"

The young woman who, of course, was Ashmodai's daughter, seized her father's arm. "No, Father," she cried. "Don't kill him, for he will be my husband."

At these words Ashmodai calmed down and sheathed his sword. The very next day the demon's daughter and the merchant's son were married, and within a year she gave birth to a son, whom they called Shloyme.

One day as the couple were playing with their child, the rich man's son heaved a deep sigh.

"Why are you sighing?" asked Ashmodai's daughter.

"I'm sighing for the wife and son I left in the country I came from," he answered.

"Poor man," said Ashmodai's daughter. "Would you like to pay them a visit?"

"Oh yes," he replied.

"Well," she said, "why don't you go? But you must promise not to stay longer than three months."

"All right," he said. "But how will I get there?"

"No problem," said Ashmodai's daughter. And with that she sent for an old demoness to take her husband back to his home. The old demoness seized the merchant's son and flew with him through the air so swiftly that he was back in his own country within hours. And there she left him.

His wife and child were delighted to see him, and he was so overjoyed to be there that he completely forgot his promise to return after three months. When the time was up, demons appeared in his dreams. They bore letters from Ashmodai's daughter, letters which he ignored. "You disregard your promise at your peril," the letters warned, but he continued to stay where he was.

Finally his son Shloyme appeared to him in a dream, saying, "Father: Mother and a pack of devils are at the town gate. If you don't come home, she will destroy the town." Frightened awake, the rich man's son hurried off to the rabbi and told him the whole story. The rabbi convened a rabbinical court to deliberate over the matter. After several hours the court decreed that it was forbidden for a mortal and a demoness to marry. "And so," said the rabbi, "Ashmodai's daughter must give you a divorce."

When Ashmodai's daughter heard this news, she appeared before the rabbinical court and said, "Very well. What must be, must be. I will give him the divorce. But I want one thing before we part: I want to give him one last kiss."

The rabbinical court granted her request, and the rich man's son, poor fellow, suspecting nothing, stepped up to her and offered his face to be kissed. But Ashmodai's daughter put her hands to his throat, and when he lay dead at her feet, she cried, "If I can't have him, she can't have him!" And with that she disappeared.

46
The Ram, the Basket, and the Stick

There was a poor man who had many children and couldn't give them anything to eat. One day he was walking along looking for food when he came to a magic forest. He rested there and then went on his way. Before long he met four forest people. When they saw him, one of them said, "Let's kill him," but the others said, "No, he deserves to be helped in any way we can."

They gave him a ram and told him, "If you say to the ram, 'Serve me,' it will give you whatever you want."

The man took the ram home and said to his children, "Take your places at the table." The children sat down and the man told the ram, "Serve us a meal." And at once they all had whatever they liked and as much as they wanted.

Now, the poor man had a rich brother. When the rich man learned that his poor brother had such a wonderful ram, he came to him and said, "Here, I'll give you a pair of oxen and wheat. Plow your land with the oxen, then sow the wheat, and you'll have food for your children and money left over to heat your house." The poor man gave his brother the ram for the oxen. But when he got home, he realized that there was nothing for his children to eat, so he killed the oxen and fed the meat to them. When the meat was gone, he and the children were left with nothing.

He started off once more to look for food. Again he came to the magic forest where he had rested, and this time he met five forest people. Seeing him, one said, "Let's kill him," but the other four said, "No, let's help him in any way we can."

And so they gave the poor man a basket and told him, "Whenever you need food, say 'Basket, fill up,' and the basket will provide what you need."

The poor man took the basket home, and when he got there he said, "Basket, fill up." And the basket filled up with all sorts of good things, so once again there was plenty to eat.

When his rich brother heard about the wonderful basket, he crept into the poor man's house and stole it from him. Again the poor brother and his children were left with nothing to eat.

And so the poor brother went to the magic forest where he had rested twice before. This time he met three forest people, one of whom said, "Let's kill him." But the other two said, "No, let's help him all we can."

Then they gave the poor brother a stick and told him, "If anyone harms you, say 'Stick, strike!' and the stick will obey your command."

He thanked them and went home, taking the stick. Not long afterward he invited the whole town to a big celebration. His rich brother was there, showing off the ram and the basket. Seeing this, the poor man went up to the balcony of the banquet hall, took out the stick the three men had given him, and called, "Stick, strike my brother!" And the stick flew down and beat the rich brother until he cried out, "Take the ram; take the basket. They belong to you."

Then the poor man said, "Stick, stop beating." And the stick stopped.

So the poor man took back his ram and basket and became the richest man in town.

47
The Golden Feather

Once upon a time there was a well-to-do householder who had twelve sons, eleven of whom were clever while one was a fool. The same man owned a mare that had twelve colts, eleven of which were handsome while one was ugly.

The father lined up the twelve horses before his sons, and the eleven clever sons chose the eleven handsome horses. The ugly horse was left for the fool, and at this the fool began to cry.

But the ugly horse said to him, "If you'll stop crying and do everything I ask, I'll tell you how to turn me into a handsome horse."

"All right," said the fool, "I'll do everything you ask."

"First wash me and comb me," the horse said. "Then I'll be handsomer than any of the other horses."

So the fool washed and combed him, and the horse turned very handsome. "Now," said the horse, "harness me up and we'll take a drive."

The fool harnessed him up and they drove off. As they went along they saw something glistening in the roadway. The fool said, "Stop. I want to know what that is." The horse stopped and the fool saw that the bright thing was a golden feather from some sort of golden bird.

The fool wanted to pick the feather up, but the horse said, "Don't do it. I didn't tell you to pick it up. If you do, you're only asking for trouble."

The fool said, "I'm not listening to you. I want the golden feather."

"But," said the horse, "you promised you'd obey me, and I tell you that if you take it, you'll have more troubles than you ever dreamed."

But the fool wouldn't listen. He picked the feather up, and they went on their way into a dense forest, where they became lost. And the darker it grew, the brighter the feather glowed. The fool was delighted.

"Go on," said the horse, "be happy. Your troubles will come soon enough." But the fool ignored him.

They went deeper into the woods, until all at once they saw a hut. The fool said, "Stop here, horse. Let's go to the hut and spend the night there."

"No," said the horse, "don't do that."

But the fool ignored him and went into the hut, where he found three young peasant women sitting. "Can we spend the night?" he asked.

"We can't say," they replied. "Our mother is a witch whose name is Bobe Ha. She'll be home soon and you can ask her yourself."

The fool showed them the golden feather, which lighted up the entire hut. The peasant women shivered with pleasure and said, "It's a truly beautiful feather, but we can't give you permission to spend the night. You'll have to wait until Bobe Ha comes back."

Just then Bobe Ha showed up with a great noise—rat-a-tat-tat, rat-a-tat-tat—for one of her feet was made of iron.

The young women said, "They want to spend the night." Then they showed Bobe Ha the golden feather, and she said to the fool and his horse, "Yes, you may spend the night. But you'll have to sleep on the floor with your heads at the threshold."

The fool said, "That's all right, we'll sleep on the floor with our heads at the threshold." Then Bobe Ha ran off once again to the woods.

The household settled down to go to sleep. The three young peasant women lay in their usual places, while the fool and his horse lay down on the floor with their heads at the threshold.

A little while later the horse said, "Ah, we're in trouble. I warned you not to pick up the golden feather. I said it would get us into trouble. Bobe Ha would never have let us pass the night if we hadn't had the feather."

"Well, what can we do now?" asked the fool.

"I'll tell you what to do," said the horse. "Carry her three daughters over to our side of the hut. Put them down in our places, with their heads at the threshold, and we'll lie in their places."

The fool did as he was told. He put the three sleeping daughters on the floor with their heads at the threshold, and he and his horse lay down in their places.

Suddenly, in the middle of the night, Bobe Ha came hurrying back from the forest. She dashed up to the threshold and gave such a terrible stamp with her iron foot that the shattered heads of her daughters flew off in all directions. Then she ran back into the forest.

The horse said to the fool, "Quickly, harness me up. Take the golden feather and let's get away. Drive me as hard as you can."

The fool harnessed the horse as quickly as he could. Then he grabbed up the feather and off they went.

The next morning, miserable indeed was Bobe Ha when she came back to her hut from the forest and saw what she had done with her iron foot. "Woe is me," she wailed. "I hacked my own daughters' heads off. And those two have escaped with the golden feather. Oh, woe. Oh, woe." And she started off in pursuit of them. She chased them and they ran for dear life, and as they ran they heard the rat-a-tat-tat of her iron foot.

"She's chasing us, she's chasing us!" cried the fool.

"Yes, I hear her," said the horse. "Didn't I tell you that troubles would follow if you picked up the feather? But you wouldn't listen. Well, don't panic, I've got an idea. Fill a pitcher with water and throw it over your head, and it will turn into a river that she won't be able to cross."

The fool did what he was told. He filled a pitcher with water and threw it over his head, and it turned into a broad river. When Bobe Ha came to the river, she couldn't cross it. So she ran back home, snatched up a pot and ladle, and used them to quickly empty the river. Then she raced on in pursuit of the fool and his horse.

She ran after them and ran, and they fled with all their might, and as they ran they heard again the rat-a-tat-tat of her iron foot. "She's chasing us, she's chasing us!" cried the fool to the horse.

"Yes, I hear her. Didn't I tell you that troubles would follow if you picked up the feather? But you wouldn't listen. Well, don't panic, I've got an idea. Pluck a handful of twigs and throw them over your head, and they'll turn into a forest so dense she won't be able to push through."

So that's what he did. He plucked a handful of twigs and threw them over his head, and they turned into a dense forest that she couldn't push through. Back she went to her home, where she grabbed a hatchet and used it to chop a path through the forest. Then she raced on in pursuit of them.

She chased them and they fled with all their might, and as they ran they heard again the rat-a-tat-tat of her iron foot. "Help," the fool begged the horse. "Help! What shall we do? We're doomed."

The horse said, "Hush. Don't panic, I have an idea. Take a heap of sand and throw it over your head, and it will turn into a high mountain that she won't be able to climb."

So that's what the fool did. He took a heap of sand and threw it over his head, and it turned into a high mountain. When Bobe Ha came to it, she couldn't climb over. Back she ran to her house, grabbed a spade, and used it to shovel the mountain away. Then she raced on after them.

Again they heard the rat-a-tat-tat of her iron foot. The fool cried to the horse, "Do you hear? Oh, woe is me. Oh, woe!"

"Hush. Don't panic," said the horse, "I have an idea. Chop some wood into kindling, start a fire, and let the wood burn down to coals. Then take the coals and pour them into a hole outside the forest and put a thin wire across the hole. When Bobe Ha comes out of the forest and sees the coals, she'll try to walk over the wire to get to the other side, but the wire will bend and she'll fall onto the coals and burn to death."

So that's what the fool did. He chopped some wood into kindling and built a fire that he allowed to burn down to hot coals. Then he poured the coals into a hole near the forest and set a wire across the hole. When Bobe Ha came out of the forest and saw the hot coals in the hole, she tried to cross over the wire. But it bent, and she fell on the burning coals and burned to death.

Well, now that they were rid of Bobe Ha, the fool and the horse turned around and went back home. When they got there, and when the fool's brothers saw how handsome his horse was and how brightly the golden feather shone, they liked him even less than before. But the horse, seeing the look of envy in their eyes, said to the fool, "You'll have to leave home. Harness me up and let's run off as fast as we can, because your life is in danger here."

So the fool harnessed the horse, and they ran away until they came to a large village surrounded by fields. The fool plowed and sowed the fields and became very rich. He sowed rye and ground it to flour, and the horse carried loaves of bread to the city, where the fool distributed them to the poor, and everyone was very happy.

And he had the dear horse to thank for all that. Oh, was that a horse. What a horse that was! A horse in a million!

.   .   .

PART FOUR

Justice,
Faith,

and
Everyday
Morals:
Pious
Tales

Storytelling was not only a pleasure for the father, but a must. . . . Teach through entertaining. Train children through story telling. "Thou must narrate" was a commandment of God.

—From a turn-of-the-century Jewish folklore
journal

We turn now to a body of religious tales with ethical messages. Like wonder tales, they are told as fiction and often begin, "Once upon a time."

Some of these tales, called *mayses mit a muser-haskl,* "stories with a moral," serve as guides to proper conduct, making explicit statements about acceptable and unacceptable behavior. While most wonder tales describe the adventures of young men and women and end with their marriage, most *mayses mit a muser-haskl* focus on married people with families and deal with aspects of moral life: generosity, piety, humility, hospitality, and kindness on the one hand, and stinginess, cruelty, meanspiritedness, immorality, arrogance, and pride on the other. In these tales, just as in the magical tales, the characters are generally all good or all bad, virtuous or wicked, humble or haughty, generous or selfish. The tales teach the Golden Rule and demonstrate that the virtuous will be rewarded and the wicked punished.

Beyond general ethics, they teach the specific commandments on which Jewish piety is built. The 613 *mitsves,* commandments, that appear in the Bible, as well as the laws formulated through later rabbinic interpretation, make up the structure of belief in the Jewish community. A number of the tales illustrate such commandments: "honor the Sabbath" (Exodus 20:8, 23:12); "provide for the poor" (Deuteronomy 15:8); "keep your vows" (Deuteronomy 23:23); and "honor the aged" (Leviticus 19:32).

The benevolent visitation of the prophet Elijah, who wanders the earth in various guises, brings help to the pious and the needy. When the helper is not Elijah, he is often a *lamedvovnik,* one of the thirty-six holy men in each generation for whose sake God allows the world to continue to exist. The *lamedvovnik,* a hidden saint, is usually a simple man like a water carrier or a poor teacher.

The tellers of pious tales generally make sure to drive home their ethical point. Some end their tales with an aside to the listener: "Now, it was *hakodesh borekh hu,* the Holy One, blessed be He, who did this for the pious man because he had not violated the Sabbath." Or, "Let those who have wealth refrain from taking things for granted, since the Almighty may retrieve it at any moment and give it to someone else, even as He gave the treasure to this poor family." It seems clear from endings like these that some of the tales were originally part of a sermon.

Of course, these sometimes ponderous "codas" were not appreciated by everyone. Sholem Aleichem wrote in his memoirs: "The children would have listened to all of [grandfather's tales] with delight if he had not had the unpleasant habit of squeezing a moral, a *muser haskl,* out of each tale: 'one had to be a pious Jew and have faith in God . . .' The moral would be followed by a lecture and then he would start upbraiding us . . . for wanting only to fish night and day . . . and get into mischief."[1] The coda can also take the form of a popular proverb, such as *ver es grobt a grub far yenem, falt in im aleyn arayn,* "he who digs a pit for another, falls into it himself"—or it may be a quote of a Biblical or Talmudic passage. The moral can even appear at the beginning of the story, making it an "explanatory" tale that illustrates the truth of the statement.

In terms of atmosphere the pious tales are among the most "Jewish" of the stories in this collection. Time is marked by the observance of the Sabbath and the yearly cycle of holidays—Succos and

Passover, Purim and Yom Kippur. Religious rituals and customs are carefully observed: the men don *talis* and *tfiln* (prayer shawl and phylacteries) at prayers; the women bathe monthly in the *mikve* in accordance with the laws of sexual purity. The settings in most cases are the small villages and towns of Eastern Europe, peopled by the traditional small-town types: the *melamed* (*kheyder*-teacher), the *parnes* (community leader), the *arendarke* (innkeeper's wife), the water-carrier, the merchant, the *yeshuvnik* (Jewish villager), the *porets* (the Polish squire), and the rebbe (the Hasidic spiritual leader).

Of course, no religious community would be complete without its *apikorsim,* its skeptics and heretics, and from them come some sharply satiric and antipious tales, like "Holding On to One-Quarter of My World," and "Water Wouldn't Hurt," in which the wonder-working rebbe describes a ritual for saving a man's burning house, but adds urgently that water won't hurt, either.

If the pious tales served to regulate religious life from within, they also offer powerful testimony to the threat from without. A second group of tales in this section reflects the persecution to which Jews were subjected. The most insidious charge was the blood libel, by which Jews were accused of killing Christian children to get their blood for ritual purposes. From the twelfth century on, these charges were periodically leveled against Jews. Up to modern times they directly inspired anti-Semitic riots that devastated many communities. The most famous of the modern blood-libel trials was the Mendel Beilis case, which affected Jews throughout Eastern Europe from 1911 to 1917. Despite the fact that the twelve peasants on the jury declared Beilis not guilty, up to the eve of the 1917 revolution the Russian government was still trying to prove its case against Beilis and the Jewish people.

In the tales of persecution that appear in this section, the villains include viceroys, courtiers, kings, and local priests. The helpers of the Jewish community include a *lamedvovnik,* a rabbi, and a good emperor—and always the anti-Semites receive their just desserts. One such story is "A Shocking Tale of a Viceroy," told as a pseudo-historical account set "in Amsterdam, a long, long time ago." Actually, although Jews in neighboring countries suffered from blood libels, there were apparently never any in Amsterdam. But there is a Yiddish proverb: *af a mayse fregt men nisht keyn kashes,* "Don't ask questions about a story." The "Shocking Tale of a Viceroy," unhistoric though it is, no doubt served to comfort people in their real dealings with a hostile environment in Eastern Europe. And indeed there were lessons reiterated in the persecution tales: don't despair, justice will prevail, innocence will be proved, and the libelers will be punished. Through these tales and through the didactic "stories with a moral," the community and its traditions were strengthened.

48

The Tale of a Stingy Woman

Once there was a village woman, an innkeeper's wife, who was very rich. It never occurred to her that she would die one day, and so she never contributed anything to the community—no charity, no alms, nothing. The villagers, therefore, watched her like a hawk and waited for a chance to get even.

Well, no one is immortal. Her husband—God keep us from the same—her husband died. Naturally he had to be buried. But she, stingy woman that she was, devised a scheme to save the cost of burying him.

Luck was with her, because a butcher who used to come to her inn to buy cattle and fowl was there on the night her husband died. She took the butcher into another room, gave him food and strong drink, and got him good and drunk. Really very drunk.

Then she put him to bed. A drunken man—does he have any idea of what's happening to him? She dressed her husband's corpse in the butcher's clothes and dressed the butcher in white graveclothes. He, poor sodden fellow, slept through it all.

When she was finished, she sent word to his wife that he had died at the inn. The members of the burial society arrived. Well, what was to be done? They could hardly demand money from the butcher's impoverished wife. So they carried the corpse out and buried it. And that's how the stingy woman got her husband buried without spending a penny.

Some two or three days later, the butcher woke up and saw that he was dressed in white. Wondering what sort of trouble he had gotten into, he ran off to his wife. (Isn't it the truth? When trouble comes, that's what men do.)

"Sheyne," he called, "open the door. It's me."

"Oh, woe, oh sorrow. What do you want of me? Go back to your resting place."

"Dear wife, what are you talking about? What's happened to you?"

She shrieked, "Go back! Go back to your resting place."

Seeing that she would not let him in, he ran off to the rabbi. "Rabbi, open up," he said.

"My son," said the rabbi, "you have received all the proper rites due a pious Jew. Go back to your resting place."

The butcher, finding how bad things were and seeing that no one would let him get near, went to the cemetery. Where else could he go?

Meanwhile, though he was in the graveyard, the butcher grew terribly hungry. He looked around (it was early in the morning) and saw local women passing by with baked goods in baskets. He leaped out at them. When they saw what they thought was a dead man, they dropped their baskets and ran off, leaving him with plenty to eat. Then a villager who was carrying eggs came along. As soon as he saw the butcher, he dropped his basket of eggs and ran off. So the butcher sat at his ease, dining happily on bakery goods and eggs. Just then someone carrying a little barrel of brandy drove up. Seeing what he thought was a corpse, he dropped the barrel and ran off. So now the butcher had loaves of bread, eggs, and brandy.

But sooner or later, things turn bad. He couldn't sit there forever. So he went once more to the rabbi's house: "Rabbi, what's going on here? I'm a living person. What does everyone have against me?"

The rabbi asked, "Where have you been? Where do you come from?"

The butcher explained that he had gone to the inn. That the woman had gotten him drunk. That he had slept for three days. That when he woke up, he found himself dressed in white. "When I came home to my wife, she cried, 'Go back to your resting place.' Then I came to you, and the same thing happened."

Finally everyone understood the innkeeper's trick. There was an uproar in the town, and this time they decided to make her pay. The town trustees directed that her husband's grave be dug up at her expense and that the corpse be carried back to her home. And so for once, she had to pay many times over for her stinginess.

49
The Wheat Poured In at the Door

Once upon a time a very charitable man had a daughter who was about to be married. So he went to the market to buy food for the wedding feast. Everyone knew him. People said, pointing, "There goes the charitable man, there goes the generous man." Then someone said to him, "There's an orphan in town who has nothing for her wedding." So he bought a trousseau with the money he had intended to use for his own daughter, and he led the orphan to the wedding canopy. Having bought the orphan's trousseau, he had no more than a gildn left. Since he was a dealer in wheat, he bought a gildn's worth of wheat. He put it into a cupboard in his pantry and went off to the synagogue. When he came back, his wife said, "Look, there's wheat pouring in at the door," and indeed, his pantry was so full of wheat that it had overflowed into the house. And that's how he became a rich man.

50

In Heaven and Hell

Borekh bar Zorekh and Berl bar Shmerl were business partners in St. Petersburg. They were as close as brothers, but they had to part because the business made it necessary for one of them to move to Moscow. So, taking heaven and earth as their witnesses, they swore an oath that whoever died first would return to tell his friend what it was like in the "other" world.

It happened one day that Berl was in the street when he saw a man on horseback coming toward him, and the rider was Borekh. "Stop!" shouted Berl, "Stop! Stop!" but the horseman went by and disappeared. Though Berl jumped into a cab and pursued him, Borekh was not to be found.

"Something's not right," thought Berl. And so he sent a telegram to Moscow asking for news. The reply informed him that Borekh had died, and that his funeral had taken place at precisely the moment when Berl saw the rider. And so Berl was confident that he would soon hear from the other world. But a year went by, then a second, a third. And still nothing.

One day when Berl was on a boulevard in St. Petersburg, his dead friend Borekh came up, took him by the elbow, and started to lead him away. "God preserve me," said Berl. "Tell me how it is with you, brother, and then let me go home." But Borekh made no reply. He continued to lead Berl by the arm through fields and woods until at last they came to a desert. "There," said Borekh, pointing, "you will find a cave. Walk ten yards down and then ten yards up and you'll come to the Garden of Eden. That's where you must ask for me." Then he disappeared.

Berl did as he had been told and entered the Garden of Eden, which turned out to be a tumbledown hut. Inside were a number of men reciting their prayers. It was raining, and water dripped into the room through the thatch. The place was dark, filthy, slippery. "Dear God in heaven," thought Berl, "this is the Garden of Eden?"

Then he asked, "Where can I find Borekh bar Zorekh?"

"In the next room," came the reply.

So Berl went into the next room where, seated on rickety benches before wobbly bookstands, he found a number of men studying Torah. In still another room he came upon a group of Hasidim sitting beside a broken brandy bottle, singing wordless tunes or going into ecstasies. "Is Borekh bar Zorekh here?" Berl asked. "Oh, he's in hell," came the reply.

"In hell?" said Berl to himself. "And this is what you call heaven?" Aloud, he said, "And where is this hell of yours?"

"Go that way," someone said. "You'll find another cave. Crawl ten yards down and then ten yards up and you'll come to it."

Well, Berl crawled—what else could he do?—down and then up and finally emerged from the cave and looked around. Amazing! A building forty cubits high, forty cubits wide. A palace, just like the riding hall in Mohilev, with a soldier in front of it wearing a fine uniform and carrying a shiny rifle.

Berl asked the soldier, "This is hell?"

"Yes."

Berl went in. He came to a huge, magnificently decorated hall. An orchestra was playing, and young men and women were dancing.

"Has anyone seen Borekh bar Zorekh?" asked Berl.

"He's in the next room," came the reply.

Berl went into the next room and found a group of people seated around a table playing cards and drinking cognac. But Borekh was not among them. "In the next room," he was told, so Berl went into a third room and there found him, Borekh bar Zorekh, his partner, sprawled like a king in an armchair, a glass of tea in one hand, a cigar in the other.

"Hey," cried Berl, "is this what you call hell? And you call that other place the Garden of Eden? Why the devil didn't you let me know how well things are going for you? And why did you have to walk me through all those dreary wastes?"

Borekh said, "How well things are going for me? Is that what you say? Ah, brother, look closely at my lips and gums. Do you see how seared they are?

"Do you remember how on Sabbath afternoons, we used to light the samovar so we could drink hot tea on the Sabbath? And how we smoked cigars on the Sabbath? Well, at the instant I died, I was set down beside a steaming samovar and a cigar was shoved into my mouth. And my doom is that I must alternately take sips of scalding tea and choking puffs from the cigar. Sip and puff. Sip and puff. Without stopping, without end."

"But what about the dancers in the great hall? And those others drinking cognac and playing cards?"

"Ah, it's the same for them. 'Play and drink. Drink and play. Dance, brother, dance.' Should any of them tire of dancing, there's a tormenting angel with a whip who lashes away, crying, 'Dance, brother! One, two. Hup. No rest for you!'"

The moral of the story is clear, isn't it? You smoke and light the samovar on the Sabbath at your peril.

5 1
The Miracle of the Tree

There is a tale of a pious man who had a beautiful garden filled with trees behind his house. One day a hole suddenly appeared in the garden. The man prepared to go and fill it, but as he was about to begin he remembered that it was the Sabbath. "What to do?" he pondered. "If I fill the hole now, I'll violate the Sabbath."

He thought it over and finally decided to keep the Sabbath. Then a miracle occurred: a tree grew out of the hole, a tall tree whose branches spread over the garden. And it bore three kinds of fruit, which nourished the pious man's family.

Now, it was *hakodesh borekh hu,* the Holy One, blessed be He, who did this for the pious man because he had not violated the Sabbath.

The Poor Man's Ruble

On a Sabbath many, many years ago, a poor man went to the synagogue to pray. He saw a pile of gold lying in the synagogue courtyard, but not wishing to violate the Sabbath, he left it alone. When he returned for the early-evening service, he saw the gold again, and again left it where it lay. However, on Saturday night, when he left the synagogue and could at last touch money, all he found was a single ruble. He took it home and gave it to his wife.

In the same town there was a rich man who had to make a long sea voyage to acquire merchandise. The poor man's wife gave the ruble to the rich man and asked him to buy something for her. On his journey the rich man bought many goods, but he forgot about the woman's ruble until his ship was about to sail. He hurried ashore thinking, "I'll buy the first thing that comes my way."

He met a beggar carrying a sack. The rich man asked him, "What have you got in the sack?"

The beggar replied, "Three young cats."

"How much do you want for them?"

"One ruble."

So the rich man bought the cats and sailed away. A storm came up at sea and the ship was blown into the harbor of a city full of very wicked people. When a stranger came to their shores, their practice was to lock him in a building swarming with mice, who then tore him to bits. They threw the rich man into that building, but he turned his cats loose and they killed many of the mice and chased the others away.

In the morning the people found the rich man very much alive and with three cats for company. The people said, "How much do you want for those cats?" He replied, "Three sacks full of gold. Also, I want to be sent home." They gave him three sacks of gold for the cats and sent him home.

Safely home, he asked the poor man's wife where she had gotten her ruble. She said, "My husband gave it to me." He asked the husband, who replied, "I saw a pile of gold in the courtyard of the synagogue, but because it was the Sabbath I didn't take any. In the evening, all I found was a single ruble."

The rich man brought a sack of gold and poured it out before the poor man. "Was the pile of gold you saw as big as this?" he asked. "Bigger," said the poor man. The rich man poured out a second sack of gold, and the poor man said, "Still bigger." Then he poured out a third sack, and the poor man said, "That's the size of the pile I saw." So the rich man gave him all three sacks of gold and the poor man became very rich.

5 3

Blood and Water

Once there was a king who went to the river to bathe. When he came to its bank, he saw that half of the stream was water but the other half was blood. And there was a man in the middle trying to cross over from the blood to the water.

So the king called together priests, rabbis, and other holy folk and asked them what it meant. Strangely, none of them could see anything in the river but water.

Then the king sent for the greatest rabbi in the city, and this rabbi saw exactly what the king saw. "Half of the river is the blood that has been spilled," the rabbi said. "And the other half is the tears that Jews have wept. The man in the middle is your father, who is trying to go from hell into paradise. But to do this he must wade out of the Jewish blood he has shed, and the river will not let him."

A Letter to God

Once upon a time there was a king whose treasurer was one of the most honest men in the world. He managed the national budget, collected taxes, and accounted scrupulously for every penny. The king valued him highly, and this irritated one of the courtiers. "My lord king," the courtier said, "you have to expect a little larceny when your treasurer is a Jew."

"What are you talking about?" said the king. "He's an honest man."

The courtier said, "Put him to the test; dismiss him. I'll bet you that his standard of living doesn't change. Then you'll know that he's been stealing from you."

The king allowed himself to be persuaded. One day he said to his treasurer, "Yankl, I can't keep you in my service any longer."

The treasurer wondered what he had done wrong. "My lord, have I not served you faithfully?" he asked. "Is there even so much as a penny missing?" But the king wouldn't hear a word; he simply told him to pack up and go.

"Where will I go?" Yankl said. "I'll starve to death. Have pity on me and my family."

The king's heart was touched. But still he thought, "I have to test him." A peasant's wagon was sent for, and Yankl's furniture and everything else he owned was piled into it. Then the king gave his former treasurer five rubles and sent him away.

Yankl came to a village, where he moved his family into a hut. And now his life turned dismal. It was just before Passover, and Passover, as everyone knows, is a serious matter. There's no end to the things one needs. Yet Yankl was penniless, with no job to be had anywhere.

His wife said, "It's almost Passover, and we have nothing for the holiday meals. Why don't you write a letter to God in heaven? Tell Him it was like this and this—in short, the whole story; and ask

Him to send us some wine and *matse* and meat and dishes—and everything else a Jewish home needs on Passover."

Yankl looked at his wife in surprise. "Listen," he said, "you can write a letter to anyone at all—even to the king. But you can't write a letter to the *reboyne shel oylem,* the Lord of the Universe."

But she wouldn't let the matter rest, and finally he thought, "What can I lose, after all?" And he sat down and wrote that he had been an official in the court of King So-and-So; and that he had served him faithfully and had been dismissed just the same; and that he and his family were hungry; and that here it was, nearly Passover; and would God please send wine and mead and meat and fish . . . Here Yankl listed everything that was needed.

Then he tied the letter to the leg of a bird and the bird flew over cities and towns and from country to country. Flying thus one day, the exhausted bird saw a palace and lighted to rest on one of the window ledges.

Now this was the palace of a very great emperor, the greatest of the kings of the world. And the emperor happened to see the letter tied to the bird's leg. He commanded that the bird be caught and the letter brought to him, and then he read the tale of the man who had faithfully served his king but had been dismissed; and now he was poor and it was almost Passover time and therefore he begged God to send him wine and mead and meat and fish and utensils and everything else that was needed.

So the great emperor commanded his servants to gather all the things listed in it and pack them into two big chests.

The emperor wrote a letter saying, "I am sending the things you asked for," and placed this and his ring in one of the chests. Then a guard delivered the two huge chests, setting them quietly in front of Yankl's door in the middle of the night, and went away.

In the morning when Yankl got up, he tried to open his door but could not and finally climbed out through a window. Seeing two such large chests, he was afraid that something dreadful was in them, that someone might be about to make a blood-libel accusation against him.

He went to call the village magistrate, who ordered the chests opened, found the letter, and read it. "God sends wine and mead and meat and fish and utensils to such-and-such a person."

What joy there was in Yankl's home! He was determined to make a Passover feast fit for a king.

The envious courtier came just then to find how Yankl was celebrating Passover. He looked in the window and was dazzled by what he saw: the best of everything. So he ran off to the king to report. "The Jew is presiding over his Passover feast as if he were a king— and it's all at your expense." The king got into his carriage and drove off to see for himself. And when he caught sight of Yankl at the head of his bountiful table, the king was outraged. "Now, there's a Jew for you. A shameless rogue! He complained to me that he was penniless, and look at him, stuffed with money."

The king ordered Yankl arrested. His house was searched and everything was taken away from him. The king personally took the ring from Yankl's hand and put him and his wife and children into prison. They were given only bread and water, and Yankl was beaten to make him confess where he had hidden "all the other things he had stolen." And when the poor man, weeping and wailing, said that he had never stolen so much as a penny from the king, and that it was God who had sent everything, he was beaten all the harder. "Don't invent tales," he was told.

It happened then that the great emperor was traveling through his domains to see whether he was being well served and justice was being done. His custom was to visit all the prisons and listen as the inmates told him why they were there.

When the emperor came to Yankl's country, Yankl's wife said, "Listen, dear husband: write a letter explaining why you were arrested. Tell the whole story." So he wrote it all down, and when the emperor entered the prison, he stood to one side and handed him the letter. The great emperor read it and commanded that the king be brought to him. "Why did you arrest this man?" the emperor asked. "He was stealing me blind," the king said.

Just then the emperor saw his own ring on the king's finger. "Whose is that?" he asked.

"It's mine," the king said. "The Jew stole it from me."

Now the great emperor told the king the whole story. And the king bowed his head and said, "I am guilty, sire."

But the emperor was not satisfied. "Who knows," he said angrily, "how many innocent people you've arrested." He ordered all the jails emptied, and he imprisoned the king and the envious courtier and had them fed on bread and water. And he made a king of Yankl, who leads a happy life to this day.

The Seven Good Years

A story is told about a man who lost his fortune and became so poor that he had to earn his living as a hired laborer plowing other people's fields. As he worked behind the plow one day, *Elyohu hanovi,* the Prophet Elijah, appeared to him and said, "You are destined to have seven good years. When would you like them? Now, while you are still young, or later, when you are old?"

The poor man said, "You must be a sorcerer, but there's no way I can pay you for this prophecy."

Three days later Elijah came again and repeated the question. And the poor man gave the same reply, because he still thought that Elijah was a sorcerer who expected to be rewarded. On the fourth day Elijah came once more and said, *"Hakodesh borekh hu,* the Holy One, blessed be He, has ordained that you shall have seven good years. Tell me: When do you want them? Now, or when you are old?"

The poor man said, "I pray you, let me go home first and ask my wife." So he went home and told his wife everything, and she said, "Let's take them now."

The man went back to the field, where once again Elijah the Prophet came to him and asked, "When do you want your seven good years?"

The poor man replied that he wanted them now.

Elijah said, "Go home. When you get there you will be blessed with wealth."

Now, the poor man's children were playing on a dung heap, and there they found a treasure: enough money to feed them all for seven years. They called their mother, who rejoiced and said to her husband, "See, the Holy One, blessed be He, has been gracious and sent us seven good years. Let us now, as pious people do, practice charity throughout our seven years, and it may be that God will show compassion toward us later."

And so they did. They gave alms to many people.

The man's wife told her youngest son, "Dear boy, keep a record of the sums we have given away." And the boy wrote everything down.

When the seven years were almost up, Elijah the Prophet appeared to the man and said, "The time has come for me to take back what I have given you. I want you to return the money."

The man said, "I will give it back only with my wife's permission, because I did not accept it without her permission." Then he went to his wife and said, "The old man is here again, and he wants me to return what he gave."

The wife said, "Ask the old man whether he wants to take the money in order to give it to someone else. And ask him if he has found anyone who is as charitable as we have been. If he has, I'll restore the money so he can give it to those who will make better use of it."

The Holy One, blessed be He, noted their words and knew of the good works they had performed. And He rewarded them with even more money, so that He might confirm the saying, "Let there be acts of charity."

Let those who have wealth refrain from taking things for granted, since the Almighty may retrieve it at any moment and give it to someone else, even as He gave the treasure to this poor family. May God's Holy Name be blessed forever. Amen.

5 6

Set a Trap for Another

Once upon a time there was a merchant whose dishonest clerk stole some of his goods. The merchant, seeing the theft, decided to get even.

When the clerk's wife gave birth to a son, the merchant sent a peasant to the clerk's house to steal the child and bring it to him.

The merchant put the baby in a chest and carried it a great distance away. Then he threw it under a bridge not far from a hut.

The man who lived in the hut was a fisherman. As he passed by the bridge, his eyes fell on the chest. He took it home, opened it and found the child. The fisherman and his wife decided to raise the child.

A considerable time went by and the child grew into a handsome youth. It happened once that the merchant spent the night in the fisherman's hut. Here he saw the youth who greatly pleased him, and he decided to give him his daughter for a wife; and it was arranged that when the merchant returned from abroad, the young man would come to his home.

Later that night, the fisherman told the merchant how he had found the boy and decided to raise him. The merchant, remembering his clerk's son, regretted promising his daughter in marriage to this young man. But he said nothing to the fisherman. Instead he wrote a letter to his wife instructing her to hire a peasant to kill the young man. He sealed the letter with wax and gave it to the youth to deliver.

When the young man came to the town, he decided to spend the night in the synagogue. As he was falling asleep, the letter fell out of his pocket and the rabbi picked it up. The rabbi opened the letter, read it and then tore it up. The rabbi wrote a second letter instructing the wife to welcome the young man warmly.

In the morning, the young man went off to see the merchant's wife and gave her the letter. A few days later, the vengeful merchant returned from his foreign travels and was surprised to see that the young man was still alive.

This time, he paid a peasant a large sum to dig a pit beside the door into which the young man should fall so that he might be killed. But the young man left the house through a second door and did not fall into the pit.

The merchant, seeing that the youth was no longer in the house, went to inspect the pit, but he slipped and fell into it himself. The peasant, unaware that it was the merchant in the pit, slew him.

He who digs a pit for another—falls into it himself.

Ver es grobt a grub far yenem, falt in im aleyn arayn.

57

A Succos Tale

A father had two sons. One was both pious and good. He always shared whatever he had, and he was so generous that he sold his own houses and lands so that he could give money to the poor. His brother, on the other hand, was a stingy ne'er-do-well.

Once at Hoshana Rabba time, the seventh day of the Succos holiday, when everyone's fate for the coming year is irrevocably sealed, the generous man's wife handed him their last ten rubles and said, "Go to the market and buy what the children need for the festival."

As the man walked along, he met the trustees of the charity fund. "How fortunate to see you," they said. "It happens that we're collecting money for a poor bride. Perhaps you can help."

"Of course," he said. "Of course." And he gave them the ten rubles.

"Oh Lord," he thought, when he realized what he had done, "how can I possibly go home and face my wife empty-handed?"

Instead he walked sadly to the *besmedresh,* where he saw children playing with *esroygim.* He gathered the citrons together and put them in a sack, which he slung over his shoulder. Then he carried it down to the river and boarded a ship that was going to the capital city.

Now the king of that country was very sick, and none of his doctors could find a remedy that would help him. One night he dreamed that he would be cured if he ate the citrons over which Jews prayed and uttered blessings during the Succos holiday.

The next day the king issued a decree: "Let citrons be found!"

Soon afterward it happened that some of the king's servants went to the riverbank to search the passing boats that came from far away. They hoped to find a merchant who had citrons to sell, and indeed, on one of the boats they came upon the *tsadek,* the pious man, sitting on his sack.

"Hey," they said, "what sort of merchandise do you have in the sack?"

"I'm not a merchant," he replied. "I'm just a poor man, and I have nothing to sell."

"Let's see what you've got," they said. With that they searched his sack and found the citrons. "Hey," they said, "what do you call these?"

"Those . . . oh, those are citrons over which Jews recite prayers and blessings during the Succos holidays."

"Well now, as it happens, that's just what we're looking for," said the servants. With that they took the poor man and his merchandise to the king. And the king ate the citrons and was cured.

To reward the pious man, the king commanded that his sack be filled with gold. Then he said, "Is there anything else you want? You have only to ask."

"It would be nice," said the pious man, "if I were allowed to buy my properties back. And . . . and . . . oh yes. If it's not too much trouble, would you decree that the people come out to greet me when I get back to my home town? Not, God forbid, because I want honor for myself, but because I want them all to know how you were healed by God's miracle and how I was helped through you."

"Let your wish be my decree," said the king. And that's what happened. When the pious man arrived at his home town, the populace welcomed him with great honor.

The *tsadek*'s mean-spirited brother was among those in the crowd. As he and his children approached the riverbank, a sudden wave caught them up and dragged them into the water—where they drowned.

And the generous *tsadek* inherited all their property and lived as a wealthy man all the days of his life.

5 8
Only Eleven Little Fish

Once there was a man and wife who were very poor. They had nine children. That made, including the two parents, eleven all together.

How did they make a living? The man used to go to the river to catch fish, but he never caught more than eleven at one time. His family lived on these eleven fish—one for each of the children, and one each for the husband and wife.

The husband said, *"Reboyne shel oylem,* O Lord of the Universe, how can anyone fill his belly with a single fish? If one of us should happen to die, I would be able to eat two fish. As it is, all I ever get is one." He repeated this prayer so often that God finally yielded, and one of the children died.

The husband was pleased that two of the eleven fish would now be his. But when he went to the river the next day, he caught only ten fish. God did not send him anymore.

So the husband said, "You see, when there were eleven of us, I caught eleven fish; and now that we are ten, I catch only ten fish. What have I accomplished?"

This was God's way of showing that it is wrong to pray for the death of children. It does not matter how many children there are in a family; He provides for them all.

5 9

A Passover Tale

Once upon a time there were two brothers, one rich and the other poor. And they had an old mother who lived with the poor son. Well, it was just before Passover and the poor man had none of the things necessary for the Passover service. So he said to his mother, "I'll tell you what: I'll carry you to the rabbi's house where we'll stand under one of his windows and listen to him conduct the service." So the old mother set herself on his shoulders, and they went to the rabbi's house and heard the whole service under a window.

Meanwhile the poor man's wife, who had been sleeping, woke up and didn't know where she was. There were signs of wealth everywhere. She was lying on a luxurious bed, and her children were dressed in fine clothes. The table was richly set and piled with every sort of fine food. And there was a crowd of cooks preparing marvelous dishes.

Just then her husband, the poor brother, came home with his mother on his shoulders. He too didn't recognize his house, since there was a mansion where it had stood. So he went around by another street, but the mansion was still there. He said to his mother, "We might as well go inside. They won't beat us if we do."

He carried her in, and his wife, dressed in velvet and silks, hurried to greet him. The children looked like the children of noblemen, but they came up and kissed their father and grandmother. Then all took their places at the table and conducted the Passover service as God had commanded.

The next morning the rich brother remembered his mother and brother. He called a servant and, giving him a few pieces of *matse* and a small flask of wine, said, "Take this to my brother, the poor man." So the servant went to the poor brother's house and came upon the mansion. He entered and found the poor brother and his wife and children dressed in fine clothes. The servant was amazed, but he said nothing. He took out the few pieces of *matse* and the flask of wine and gave them to the poor brother who said, "I'm not poor anymore, so I don't need these. Now I'm richer than he is."

The servant went back to his master, returned the bits of *matse* and the flask of wine, and said, "Your brother has become a wealthy man." The rich brother refused to believe it and said, "No doubt you stumbled into some wealthy man's house."

The servant said, "Go see for yourself."

The rich brother went to the mansion and saw that the story was indeed true. He asked his brother, "How did you become so rich?"

"God helped me," was the answer. The rich brother, seeing that he would learn nothing this way, thought, "I'll find out more from a woman."

He went home and told his wife, "Go to my brother's house and get his wife to tell you what made them so rich." And when she went to the mansion, the poor brother's wife said her husband had carried his mother on his shoulders to the rabbi's house so they could hear the Passover service. "God Himself then blessed us with riches," she said.

On the second day of Passover, the rich brother paid a visit to his mother. "Set yourself on my shoulders," he told her. "I'll take you to the rabbi's house, and we can stand under a window and hear the service."

His mother said, "My son, why should we do that? Your brother was a poor man and had to stand under the rabbi's window to hear the service, but you are rich." The rich brother pressed her so hard, however, that at last she climbed onto his shoulders. And off they went to the rabbi's house to stand under one of his windows and listen.

In the middle of the service, they heard sounds of bells, people running, and shouts of "Fire! Fire!" The rich brother asked, "Where's the fire?" And he was told that it was such-and-such a rich man's house—his own. He flung his mother off his shoulders so violently that she died on the spot. Then away he ran to the fire, but he couldn't save a thing. It all burned, and he became a poor man.

And for the rest of his days the poor brother lived a rich and happy life with his wife and children.

6 0
A Shocking Tale of a Viceroy

This story took place in Amsterdam a long, long time ago. That city belonged to an emperor who lived far away. It was ruled by a viceroy, in the same way that a district governor rules in Russia.

Nowadays taxes are paid by each person directly to the state. But long ago, things were different. A tax collector "farmed" the taxes and paid the king a certain amount. Later the collector got a commission from the state.

Now, this viceroy, one of the wickedest of the wicked and a big spender as well, was always in need of money.

Where to get it?

Where else but from the Jews of Amsterdam? So they endured a great deal from him.

There was a rabbi in that city, one of the great rabbis of the kingdom. He was as cherished and treasured as a precious stone. He lived to a ripe old age, then became ill and took to his bed. People, knowing that his end was near, mourned greatly. For who could possibly take his place? "Rabbi," they asked him, "who will lead the congregation when—may you live to a hundred and twenty—you pass on?"

The rabbi said, "I've taken care of everything." Then he died and was buried.

When they read his will, this is what they found: "Let messengers be sent to such-and-such a town, where a rabbi by the name of Kashmen lives. Let him be made rabbi of the Jews of Amsterdam."

So two messengers were chosen to find Reb Kashmen and bring him back to Amsterdam. They rode and rode, visiting towns and villages until, by the help of God, they arrived at their destination and put up at an inn.

When they had eaten and rested, they approached the innkeeper. "Tell us, sir, where does the rabbi, Reb Kashmen, live?"

The innkeeper said, "I've lived here for I don't know how many years, and there's never been a rabbi with that name."

So the messengers asked the same question of other people, who all said the same thing.

Concluding that their rabbi must have been mistaken, they returned home. Back in Amsterdam a special assembly was called, and the people decided that their rabbi would not have made a mistake about something in his will. So two new messengers were dispatched to that town to examine the matter thoroughly. There they went from house to house and searched the village from one end to the other, but no one had ever heard the name of Reb Kashmen. They were on the point of returning home when one messenger said, "Maybe we ought to go to that settlement over there—those few houses in the open fields."

They went there and came to a small hut. An old woman and a girl sat there plucking feathers. The messengers said, "Good evening."

"Good evening and a good year," came the reply. "What do you want?"

One of the messengers asked whether Rabbi Kashmen lived there. The old woman nodded and the messengers were delighted.

"He'll be here soon, most likely," she said. They decided to wait. As they waited, the door opened and an old man came in. The woman went to the oven, from which she took out a dish of food. The old man washed his hands, recited a blessing and sat down to eat. He paid no attention to the messengers—as if they were not there.

When he had finished, they approached him. "Our rabbi of blessed memory," they said, "enjoined us in his will to bring to Amsterdam a certain Reb Kashmen so that he may take our rabbi's place."

Reb Kashmen said not a word, nor did he look at them. It was as if they were invisible, as if no one were speaking at all. He rose, walked into his room, and went to sleep.

The messengers, seeing that they would accomplish nothing, said good night and went away. They returned the next morning, but no matter what they said, he kept silent. Even when they nagged at him, he remained mute as a wall. Then they begged for his pity and said they would not leave without him.

He replied, "Why are you burdening me? I don't understand any of this. You want me to come? Very well, I'll come. Just stop tormenting me."

That was what they were waiting to hear. They put the old man and his wife and daughter into their wagon and drove off.

When they arrived in Amsterdam, how happy everyone was! Reb Kashmen was welcomed with a parade. He was given a fine house with large rooms. Joy reigned, but the rabbi was silent even though people were dying to hear him say a few holy words. Finally, after much coaxing, he said, "Dear friends, I don't know anything." This offended everyone. "What kind of a rabbi is this?" cried the synagogue officers. "He must be crazy."

So the people began to put distance between themselves and Reb Kashmen. And finally they moved him out of the fine house and installed him with his wife and daughter in a small room at the city's edge. And the community chose another rabbi.

Now, the viceroy was a great carouser and gambler, a man who danced all night at balls, who poured out money like sand. And now, on top of everything, he had acquired a mistress, so he needed even more money.

Where to get it?

He went to the tax collector, Reb Azriel, and said, "Because of this and that, and such-and-such, I need a few rubles."

Reb Azriel handed him some money, and the viceroy went away. Not an hour later he came back again, and then again, and again. Finally, Reb Azriel said, "I can't give you any more."

The viceroy banged furiously at the collector's door, calling, "I'll rise against you the way Haman* rose against you." And he stormed off to the chief priest. Together they plotted to take a dreadful vengeance on Reb Azriel and all the Jews. Just before Passover, they killed a Gentile boy and put his body, along with several bottles of blood, into Reb Azriel's house. Then they shouted, "The Jews have killed a boy!" So they ordered a search of Jewish houses, and when the murdered child was found, the old tax collector was taken in chains to prison. Meanwhile the wicked viceroy wrote to the emperor: "The Jews have risen against the state; they are slaughtering our children."

The emperor replied, "Do what you like," which was all the viceroy wanted to hear. So he issued a decree that on Yom Kippur, the Jewish Day of Atonement, the inhabitants of all the towns and villages must gather to see Reb Azriel hanged. The decree also said that anyone could do what he liked with the Jews.

As the day of the hanging approached, the cries and lamentations pouring from the Jewish homes would have restored hearing to the deaf. Feverish prayers to our Father in heaven rose from the synagogues. Finally it occurred to someone to consult Reb Kashmen. A delegation was sent to his room, where they found him wearing his *talis* and *kitl,* his prayer shawl and robe, and intoning his prayers with so much grief that the group was afraid to move. Seeing them, he said, "Go quickly and command everyone to eat the meal that precedes our fast, as if tomorrow were Yom Kippur."

The Jews did as he commanded, and that evening everyone gathered in the synagogue. And when Reb Kashmen, standing at the

---

* Haman is the anti-Semitic viceroy at the court of King Ahasuerus in the Book of Esther, which is read every Purim.

podium, recited the *kolnidre* prayer, it is said that the walls quivered and the heavens shook. And each time he spoke, thunder roared, after which came the sounds of the congregation's weeping and lamentations.

When the *musef* prayers were finished, Reb Kashmen addressed the people. "My brothers, an evil decree hangs over us, but God's compassion is great. I am going to the emperor. Wait for my return." With that, he vanished.

Far away, the emperor had just eaten and was strolling in his garden. Growing weary, he sat down on a bench and fell asleep. He dreamed that he was drowning in a river of blood, and each time he struggled to the bank, the viceroy thrust him back. At last he was saved from drowning by a little old man, a Jew, who ran up and drove the viceroy off.

Now, the journey from Amsterdam to the emperor's palace ordinarily required some days, but Reb Kashmen accomplished it in an instant. The emperor was just waking. Seeing that Reb Kashmen looked like the Jew who had rescued him in the dream, the emperor said, "Holy man, I feel evil around me. Can you explain it?"

Reb Kashmen answered, "Great Emperor, it is clear that someone wishes you ill, and you know who it is: your viceroy. He and your generals have plotted your death. Command that his house be searched; papers that are in a drawer there will prove his guilt.

"And, Great Emperor, you should also know that the viceroy is tormenting the Jews of your kingdom. He has exacted tribute from us and has not given you a groshn. He squanders it all even as he skins us Jews alive.

"Now he has killed a Gentile boy and thrown the corpse into Reb Azriel's house, creating a blood libel. Great Emperor, stand by us. Issue a proclamation to delay the execution while you determine whether I am telling the truth."

The emperor called in his general. "Take a regiment of soldiers," he said, "and go to Amsterdam. Delay the decree. Search the viceroy's house. If you find proof of wickedness, carry out whatever sentence he deserves."

Reb Kashmen returned miraculously to the synagogue. It was time for *nile,* the concluding Yom Kippur prayers. When the late-evening service was done, he said, "Brothers, go and break your fast. Let those of you who have food give it to those who have none. Things will be well. Reb Azriel will be saved."

In the morning after daybreak, crowds of Gentiles began to gather on all the roads from all corners of the land. Whole villages arrived bringing ladder-wagons to carry away Jewish property. They were armed with scythes and rakes and axes. But no Jews appeared anywhere. They had shut themselves up in cellars and attics.

The gallows had been erected in the market square, and there the Gentiles massed. At the time decreed, Reb Azriel was led in. The chains on his feet made it hard for him to walk, so he was driven along with blows from gun butts. He went quietly. So much goodness glowed in his face that the Gentiles fell silent and did not touch him.

As the guards were setting Reb Azriel under the gallows to throw the noose over his neck, the viceroy—that Haman—said, "Do you want to live? Then become a convert."

Reb Azriel raised his eyes to heaven and cried, "*Shma Yisroel,* Hear, O Israel." Then he was silent. As the executioners were about to begin, shots were heard and the crowd saw riders approaching. The general arrived and handed the emperor's orders to the viceroy. The noose was removed from Reb Azriel's neck. The general quietly signaled his men to watch the viceroy, and his riders surrounded the viceroy's palace. When the soldiers began to search, they found papers describing a plot to kill the emperor and usurp his kingdom. So the viceroy was hanged on the gallows that had been prepared for Reb Azriel.

The Gentiles scattered like mice, while the Jews left their hiding places and crowded into the streets, kissing and embracing each other for joy.

It was clear that the instrument of their happiness was Reb Kashmen, yet he was nowhere to be seen. They went to his room, but it was empty. Riders were sent out on all the roads, and they found him at last in a forest. Throwing themselves at his feet, they said, "Holy Rabbi, don't leave us."

Reb Kashmen said, "There is no further need for me here. I must go wherever Jews are troubled, wherever a Haman has risen."

Then he and his wife and daughter disappeared.

When the emperor returned to Amsterdam, he was sorry to hear that Reb Kashmen was gone. "I didn't even get to thank him," he said.

From that time on, the emperor bestowed many favors on the Jews. He excused them from taxes, and there was prosperity and abundance on all sides. And they all thanked the Creator and lived happily.

This shocking tale has been told so that later generations may know and remember what once came to pass.

61

The Leper Boy and Elijah the Prophet

Once upon a time a poor leper boy used to sit on a box in the middle of a great square, and people who went by gave him what bits of food they could. One day a carriage drove up and out stepped a man —it was Elijah the Prophet—who said to the boy, "I'm an uncle of yours and I'm going to make you respectable."

"Good, Uncle," said the boy.

Then Elijah took the boy with him in the carriage and they rode off to a forest. There he pulled the boy's hat off and threw it up into a tree, and the boy's skin turned clean and healthy. Then the Prophet washed the boy, dressed him in fine new clothes, and had him apprenticed to a baker.

Some time later Elijah visited the boy and asked, "How is it, being a baker?"

"Not so good," said the boy. "I often burn my hands."

"Well, what would you like to be?" asked Elijah.

"Uncle dear," said the boy, "maybe I'd like to be a tailor."

So Elijah apprenticed him to a tailor.

Some time later the prophet visited the boy and asked, "How is it, being a tailor?"

"Not so good, Uncle dear. I keep sticking myself with the needles."

"Well, what would you like to be?" asked Elijah.

"Uncle dear, maybe I'd like to be a shoemaker."

So Elijah apprenticed him to a shoemaker.

Some time later he visited the boy and asked, "And how is it, being a shoemaker?"

"Uncle dear, being a shoemaker isn't working out too well either. I keep banging my knees and smearing my hands."

"Well, what would you like to be?" asked Elijah.

"I'd like to be a barber-surgeon."

So Elijah had him trained as a barber-surgeon.

Some time later he visited the boy and asked, "How is it, being a barber-surgeon?"

"Uncle dear, not good. I'm at everyone's beck and call. I'm constantly running around setting leeches on patients."

"Well, what would you like to be?" asked Elijah.

"I think I'd like to be a doctor," replied the boy. And so Elijah had him trained as a doctor.

Some time later he visited the boy and asked, "And how is it, being a doctor?"

"Uncle dear, that's not so good either. For a doctor there's neither night nor day. I'm constantly running to the homes of my patients."

"Well," said Elijah, "what would you like to be?"

"Uncle dear," said the boy, "I think I'd like to be a merchant."

So Elijah had him trained as a merchant. But being a merchant didn't please the boy either, and he asked for a career in the army. Elijah had the boy trained successively as a company commander, a battalion commander, a brigade commander, a corps commander, and an army commander. Always the boy was unhappy, either because he was too low on the chain of command or because his responsibilities were too heavy.

Finally Elijah said, "Well then, what would you like to be, my son?"

"I'd like to be the czar," said the boy.

"Very well," said Elijah. "Be the czar and rule the country well."

Some time later Elijah visited the boy and asked, "Well, what's it like, being the czar?"

"Not too good," replied the boy. "I've got to worry about the whole country."

"Well, my son, what would you like to be?"

"Uncle," replied the boy, "Maybe I'd like to be God Himself."

"Well," said Elijah, "let's go up to Heaven, and we'll hear what God has to say about it."

"Perhaps now you'll understand," said God to Elijah the Prophet, "that sometimes I actually know what I'm doing. And now you, Elijah, come over here with me. As for you . . . you leper . . . creep back to your box where you belong."

6 2
The Trustees

Once there was a man and his wife, Khaim and Shifre, who had two
children. One Saturday morning while Khaim was off in the synagogue, the children were taken suddenly ill and died.

When Khaim came home, he sat down to eat and said to Shifre,
"Where can the children be?"

"They're playing with other children in the neighbor's courtyard,"
Shifre replied.

After Khaim finished his *tsholnt,* his Sabbath bean and barley stew,
he went back to the synagogue and stayed for the late-evening
prayers. When he returned, he sat down to eat but the food somehow did not agree with him. So he asked Shifre again, "Have the
children been home since this morning?"

"Yes, they were only just here. They ate and then went back out
to play."

While Khaim ate, Shifre asked his opinion about a matter of
religious law. "If someone leaves something in the care of someone
else and then later comes to reclaim it, is the person to whom the
thing has been entrusted required to give it back?"

Khaim said, "What a question! Of course he must give it back. At
once, without another word."

"In that case," Shifre said, "come with me into the other room. I
want to show you something."

When Khaim followed her and saw that the children were dead,
he began to tear his hair.

"Hush," Shifre said. "You said it yourself. If one entrusts something to another person and then comes and asks for it again, it must
be given back. God entrusted the children to us and now He has
taken them back again."

6 3

A Tragic Tale

Once upon a time there was a brother and sister who were very rich. Because they did not want their fortune divided, they decided they would never marry but would live with each other.

The sister became pregnant, and people in the town began to talk. Fingers were pointed at the couple as at the most sinful pair in the world. And when the day came that the sister gave birth, anger blazed up against them so that they had to move away. They sold their possessions and divided the money, and each of them went to a different town. In her new home the woman let it be known that she was a young widow. And to hide the fact of her sin, she decided to get rid of the infant. She wrapped it up and put it into a basket along with two thousand rubles. Then she wrote a letter explaining that the child was Jewish and that the money would belong to whoever raised him.

After the woman had left the basket at the door of the synagogue, the first person to come along was the *melamed,* the schoolteacher. He unwrapped the baby boy, found the money and the letter, and decided to raise the child himself. With the help of a wet nurse, the infant thrived and grew.

The child was hardly three years old when he asked to be sent to *kheyder,* where he soon showed signs of genius. This made the other children unhappy, so they called him "bastard." One day when he was demonstrating formidable scholarly powers and the rabbi was praising him, another pupil called out, "If we'd been found in the synagogue, we'd be as smart as he is."

Now, this distressed the boy terribly, and, with tears in his eyes, he insisted that the teacher tell him the truth. The *melamed,* seeing that it would be worse if he did not, showed him the letter and told him everything. So the boy packed his things and took the two thousand rubles, which the teacher had saved for him. Then he went away to study in a distant city, where nobody knew his secret.

When he was nineteen, his mother too came to that city. She was very rich and wanted a husband, but because she was already some forty years old, she could not expect to marry a wealthy young man. So she went to the head of the yeshiva, who proposed the nineteen-year-old genius to her as a groom. And soon they were married.

But sometime after their wedding, when she was returning from the *mikve,* the ritual bath, certain signs appeared in her that showed she was impure. The young man pleaded with her to tell him if she had any sin on her conscience, and finally she told him everything.

Early the next morning the young man went away, taking with him what was left of the two thousand rubles. He wandered through villages and towns until he came to a village inn, and there he stayed.

By day he was not seen at all; he appeared only at night. The innkeeper thought his behavior suspicious and began to spy on him. He found that the young man usually walked far into the forest, put on a *talis* and *tfiln,* and beat his chest and wept as he prayed. At last the innkeeper told him that it was a sin to punish oneself so severely, but the young man explained that he was doing penance.

A while later, the young penitent noticed a vacant cellar near the inn. He begged the innkeeper to lock him in there and throw the key away. The innkeeper wouldn't hear of it, but when the young man offered him a hundred rubles, he allowed himself to be persuaded. He gave the penitent two loaves of bread and a pitcher of water, locked the cellar, and threw the key away. Then he forgot about him.

It happened that a *tsadek* died in a certain town and the townspeople did not know who was worthy to take his place. But before the saintly man expired, he told them to send the most distinguished of the congregation out to search for a man locked in a cellar, because that man was worthy to be their rabbi.

The townspeople traveled here and there until they found the penitent in his cellar. They asked him to be their rabbi, but at first he refused. When they explained who it was that had sent them, he told them to come back in a month. At that time he agreed to become the rabbi of their town, and people began traveling to him from all over to get his blessing or his advice.

Among them came the woman who was both his mother and his wife. He had a divine presentiment that she would arrive, and he gave orders that no richly dressed woman was to be admitted into his presence. She saw, however, that there seemed to be some objection to her wealthy clothes, so she dressed herself anew like a poor woman. When she was at his door, he cried out, *"Reboyne shel oylem,* O Lord of the Universe, why dost Thou punish me?" And she fell dead on the spot.

He sat for the prescribed days of mourning on her behalf, and when he was asked why, he replied that it was because she had died in his house.

6 4
Upon Me

There once was a Polish noblewoman who had a large estate. There was a hut in one of her woods in which an old woman lived. She was a lonely old woman who had no relatives and who lived on what bits of cooked and baked food the rich woman gave her. But the old woman never said humbly, "Thank you, my Lady." And this bothered the noblewoman—how could a person be so ungrateful as never to say thank you.

She thought about it and said to herself, "I'll teach her the difference between 'mine' and 'yours'." So she baked her a large handsome braided loaf of white bread, a *koyletsh,* into which she put poison. When the old woman came, the lady gave her the loaf. The old woman was so pleased by the size and the quality of the loaf that this time she said twice, "May the Lord repay you, my Lady." And went away. When she was gone the Lady burst out laughing. "We'll see whether he'll repay me or you."

The old woman meanwhile, when she got home, was so pleased with the loaf that she decided to hide it. A little while later the Lady's son was hunting in the forest and was caught in the rain. Remembering that there was an old woman who lived in a hut nearby, he ran to it.

The old woman was so delighted to see him that she took the hidden loaf out so that she could treat him with it. When he had eaten of the loaf he felt very sick. The old woman was frightened and ran to the Lady's house. "Lady, what have you done? What misfortune have you brought down upon me?"

The Lady understood at once what had happened and said, "Upon me. Upon me."

The Ballad of the Faithful Wife

Once upon a time a man
Left his wife. It was his plan
To travel far, to travel near,
And he was gone for many a year.
Khane, his lovely wife, was left
Alone, abandoned, all bereft.

One day the man returned, disguised
So well he was unrecognized:
"Lady, tell me, tell me, pray,
Have you fine clothes and do you stray?
And tell me lady, do you sin?
Do you lust for other men?"
"I've no fine clothes. I do not sin.
I do not lust for other men."

He had a brilliant ring, so bright
Thirty ounces was its weight.
It was worth its weight in gold
And it was bright and very old.

"This ring so bright is yours to wear
If you'll forget your husband dear."

"The ring is brilliant and it's bright
And thirty ounces is its weight,
It's worth, no doubt, its weight in gold
And it's lovely, and it's old,
But it's not for me to wear—
Instead I'll mourn my husband dear."

He had an apron, long and white
And smooth when washed, a lovely sight,
And long it was, down to the ground,
The finest apron ever found,
And worth a hundred rubles clear.

"This apron, lady, is yours to wear
If you'll forget your husband dear."

"The apron's surely long and white
And smooth when washed, a lovely sight,
And long it is, down to the ground,
The finest apron ever found,
And worth a hundred rubles clear.
But it's not for me to wear—
Instead I'll mourn my husband dear."

"Ah well for me and for my life
That I'm your husband, you're my wife.
I thank the moon, I thank the sun,
I thank the Lord for what He's done.
I thank thee, Lady, with this kiss
And thank my God for wedded bliss."

66

The Iron Chest

One day a *parnes,* a community leader, was traveling home from a large city, and it happened that he had to go by night. Driving along, he fell asleep and his horses took a wrong turn. He woke and saw that he was lost, but it was too dark to find the right road. So he drove straight on until he came upon two men who were digging a hole. At first he feared they might be robbers, but it turned out that they were respectable peasants. When he had greeted them, he asked, "What are you digging for?"

"We're digging up a chest filled with gold coins."

"And whose chest is it?"

"It belongs to your son-in-law," was the reply.

"Can you change some copper coins into gold for me?" asked the man.

"Certainly. Why not?"

He gave them forty copper coins and they gave him three gold ones in exchange.

By then it was almost dawn, and the *parnes,* taking care to remember the place where the peasants were digging, drove away. After great difficulty he found the right road again and made his way home. He told no one of his adventures, however.

Several years went by. The *parnes* had a daughter for whom various matches had been proposed, but she had rejected them all. This made her father unhappy, because some of the young men were very rich. As time passed, the *parnes* became ever more impatient to know who his son-in-law would be.

He thought and thought about it and finally settled on a plan. He dropped one of his gold coins on a path that led to the synagogue, vowing that whoever picked it up would be his son-in-law.

The next morning when he went to check, the coin was gone. He dropped a second coin and it too disappeared; then he dropped a third, with the same results. So the *parnes* announced in the synagogue that he had lost three gold coins that had been left to him by his grandfather and that he wanted whoever had found them to come forward.

Now, a water carrier lived in that town, a man with a blind father whom he led to the synagogue three times a day. And it was this water carrier who had found the gold coins. He acknowledged in the synagogue that he had found them, then hurried home and brought them back to the *parnes*.

The *parnes* returned to his own home greatly dejected. To think that he would have a water carrier for a son-in-law! A man so unschooled that he hardly knew how to hold a pen. Still, to honor his vow he went to the water carrier's parents and asked them to let their son live with him. "I'll teach him how to write properly, and furthermore, I'll put him to work in my business."

But the water carrier's parents refused, because the blind father needed his son to guide him to the synagogue. The *parnes,* however, promised to hire someone to do that.

So the water carrier went to live with the *parnes* and studied diligently, and it was not long before he learned a great deal. Nor was it long before he and the daughter were in love, and they decided to marry, even though they feared that it would make the *parnes* unhappy.

After the wedding the son-in-law and his bride continued to live in the *parnes*'s home. One evening the *parnes* took a spade and asked his son-in-law to go with him to the place where he had seen the men digging long ago. He pointed out the exact location, but though the son-in-law dug and dug, he found nothing. Finally they went home.

Nevertheless, the *parnes* was determined to have a wealthy son-in-law. So he made him go back to the spot where he had dug before and dig even deeper. Again without success. This time the *parnes* was so angry that he drove the young couple out of his house.

The man and his bride rented a cellar, where they set up a little ironmonger's shop to earn their living. Once when the husband was away, a peasant came into the shop and asked for three whetstones to sharpen his scythes. He explained that he couldn't pay money, but that he had an iron chest at home which he would give in return. "Good," said the wife. Soon afterward the peasant came back bringing an old iron chest all covered with cobwebs. He tossed it into the shop and then went away in a great hurry.

When the husband, the former water carrier, came home that evening, his wife told him the whole story. So he went to work on the dusty chest and, after some struggle, wrenched it open. You can imagine their astonishment when they saw it was crammed with gold coins exactly like the ones he had picked up on the path to the synagogue. The husband and wife ran out of the shop in search of the peasant, but he was nowhere to be found.

So the two of them went into town to see the rabbi. They gave him a great deal of money and told him to build a large synagogue of the finest materials. But until it was finished, they said, he must keep their identity as donors a secret.

And that's what the rabbi did. The synagogue was built and some three years later it was ready. The entire congregation gathered to get their seat assignments, but two seats, one in the men's section and one in the women's, were left unassigned.

The *parnes* too came to the synagogue and greeted people warmly. His daughter and son-in-law stood off by themselves, for the *parnes* had not spoken to them since he drove them from his house. The rabbi delivered an address from the *bime*. Then the young couple were led to the unassigned seats, and the rabbi announced that they were the ones who had donated the money for the synagogue.

The *parnes* fell at his son-in-law's feet and begged his forgiveness. The congregation asked the couple to tell them the whole story of the whetstones and the chest and the fortune. Then the *parnes* told everyone how the peasants had foretold that he would have a rich son-in-law. The father and his daughter's husband were reconciled and became good friends. And the young couple lived out the rest of their lives in honor and prosperity.

6 7

Water Wouldn't Hurt

An exhausted Hasid came running to his rebbe. "Rebbe, help. Take pity. My house is burning."

The rebbe calmed the Hasid. Then, fetching his stick from a corner of the room, he said, "Here, take my stick. Run back to your house. Draw circles around it with my stick, each circle some seven handbreadths from the other. At the seventh circle, step back seven handbreadths, then lay my stick down at the east end of the fire. God will help you."

The Hasid grabbed the stick and started off. "Listen," the rebbe called after him, "it wouldn't hurt also to pour water. Yes, in God's name, pour water. As much water as you can."

6 8

The Unlearned Villager

There was a well-known rabbi, I've forgotten his name—I got this story from my father, of blessed memory. This rabbi was once on a journey. It was a Friday, and when he passed the home of a Jewish villager, a *yeshuvnik,* he decided not to travel any further. So he sent his servant in to ask whether he, the rabbi, could spend the Sabbath there.

"In my house?" stammered the villager. "I don't know. There's another *yeshuvnik* not far from here. The rabbi could certainly spend the Sabbath with him."

This reply seemed strange to the rabbi. Jewish villagers in the old days were generally very hospitable. In particular it was odd that a Jew wouldn't feel honored at having such an important Sabbath guest. So the rabbi sent his servant into the anteroom to eavesdrop on the conversation inside the house.

The servant heard the wife cry to her husband, "Fool! Stupid oaf! Where's the harm in having a saintly guest for the Sabbath?"

And the husband: "Wicked woman, do you want to shame me? You know I don't know how to make the blessing over the wine."

The servant reported the conversation to the rabbi. The rabbi said, "Tell the man that I don't want to spend the Sabbath with the other villager because once, long ago, when I was his guest and made the blessing over the wine, he blessed it again. And I don't want to stay with a man who isn't satisfied with the way I bless the wine."

"Ah," said the villager happily, "in that case let the rabbi spend the Sabbath here with us."

6 9
Holding On to One-Quarter of My World

In the course of a great flood, a boatman helped a *tsadek* across a river. The holy man, seeing what an uncouth fellow the boatman was, pitied him and felt inclined to lecture him a little. "My son," he said. "Is this really your trade?"

"Oh, I also work on the timber rafts," said the boatman.

"But do you at least *koyveya itim letoyre?*" asked the holy man.

"What does that mean, Rebbe?"

"I'm merely asking whether you take time for studying the Torah —even so much as a chapter in the Mishnah."

"Rebbe, I can't pay expenses with the Mishnah. I have to feed my children."

"Ah, ah, ah," groaned the holy man. "A Jew without study is deprived of a quarter of his world. And I'm sorry to say that's what you've done. But tell me, do you at least recite the Psalms?"

"Rebbe, if I recited the Psalms, who'd carry the logs?"

"Ah, ah, ah," groaned the rebbe. "If only you recited the Psalms. Because a Jew who doesn't recite the Psalms has wasted another quarter of his world."

A while later the rebbe said, "Tell me, my son, do you recite your prayers?"

"A flood washed away the hut where I kept my prayer shawl and prayer book. And now I work with a troop of raftsmen, so I don't get to pray."

"Ah, ah, ah. So you've wasted still another quarter of your world."

Just then the boat struck a rock and capsized. "Rebbe," cried the boatman, "can you swim?"

"No," groaned the sinking rebbe.

"In that case, you've wasted all four quarters of your world. But never mind. Grab on to me and I'll pull your whole world to safety."

70

The Poor Rabbi and His Three Daughters

There was a poor rabbi who had three daughters. They owned but a single dress among them, so that two daughters always had to stay in bed on top of the oven while one showed herself in town.

Their house was cold and damp. There was only a crust of bread lying in a cupboard drawer. Scratching about on the floor was a scrawny rooster, not one of your better-class roosters at all. Meanwhile the rabbi sat in a corner, singing a rapturous melody as he studied.

One day a stranger who wore a *shtrayml* and had the look of a holy man came in and greeted the rabbi. He sat down and asked whether there might be something to eat.

The rabbi found the crust of bread and gave it to him. Then he called one of the daughters lying on the oven and told her to have the rooster killed so that they could prepare food for the holy man.

The girl put on the dress, tucked the rooster under her arm, and started off to the butcher's.

But the rooster broke loose and started to fly away. The girl ran after it, trying to catch it. She ran and the rooster kept leaping and fluttering away. They came to a fence where she was sure she had him, but the creature flew right over it.

So she tried to climb the fence, but her dress caught and the skirt ripped from top to bottom.

At this she wept and wrung her hands. How could she show herself in town with such a tear in her dress? Then she tried to find the rooster, but there was no sign of him anywhere.

Her heart ached and tears gushed from her eyes. How, in her condition, would she even get home?

When she had cried herself out, she stood leaning against the fence, utterly spiritless.

Meanwhile night fell, but she continued to stand alone in the dark. All at once she caught a glimpse of something bright under the trees. And the thing grew brighter and lovelier, gleaming until it dazzled her.

She began to think of stories she had heard about hidden treasure discovered by deserving people. But she remembered too that it was frequently demons who deceived the gullible with false treasure.

Her heart pounding, she called in a trembling voice, "If that's a real treasure, then let it come closer. If it's the work of a demon, let it sink into the ground."

The thing began to shine brighter and brighter, then to move closer and closer, glowing and glittering and shimmering until it was quite near.

So she picked up the ends of her torn skirt and, in spite of her fear, gathered up whole fistfuls of gold.

Back in the rabbi's house, everyone sat wondering where she was. They were ready to send someone in search of her, but the other daughters couldn't get down from the oven because they had no clothes.

It was very late when she finally staggered home, exhausted and with her torn skirt loaded with gold. As soon as she entered, they began to scold her. But the holy man, the guest, quieted them and told them that God had seen their poverty and suffering and had sent them a treasure to bless them.

·   ·   ·

PART FIVE

Nitwits,

Wits,

and

Pranksters:

Humorous

Tales

Nakhman the tailor liked to whip out a humorous anecdote or a tune in the vestibule of the *besmedresh,* the House of Study. Sometimes I'd stray away from my grandfather, who stayed put in his corner at the back of the *besmedresh,* near the old wall clock whose pendulum went back and forth, back and forth. I'd sneak out into the vestibule and join the group of shoemakers and tailors who surrounded Nakhman, and I'd listen to his jokes and proverbs and tales.

—Memoir from Pumpyan, Lithuania, the 1920s

$\mathcal{S}$hort tales, quips, and capers, merry and satiric, are a beloved genre of Yiddish folklore. The language is rich with synonyms like *vitsik-maysele, shpasik-maysele, khokh-mele, shtuke,* and *shpitsele* for such stories. These are the tales about jesters and pranksters, shlemiels and shlimazls, clever adventurers and rascals, riddle solvers, masters of repartee and Talmudic hairsplitters. As Yehoshua Ravnitski, one of the collectors of the *vitsike-mayselekh,* pointed out, whenever people, young or old, got together for a family or holiday celebration, or just happened to meet, swapping funny anecdotes was a favorite pastime. One person began by telling a *vitsik-maysele* related to whatever was being discussed. Another capped this jest with one about the same or a similar subject, only to be followed by a third person with another "suitcase of quips"—and so it would proceed, on and on.[1] And then there was the *batkhn,* the master of ceremonies at weddings, a real specialist in humorous stories. Before the ceremony he helped create a solemn mood with tear-jerking improvisations, but after the service he donned the cloak of the comic entertainer and told merry stories into the night.[2]

Every ethnic group seems to enjoy stories about simpletons, and some tell whole cycles of tales about entire towns of numbskulls. Thus there is the ancient Greek Abdera, the English Gotham, the Danish Molbo, and the German Schildburg. In Yiddish folklore Khelm, a real place in Poland, figures as the most famous of such towns.[3] My father, born in the Ukraine in Letitshev, was fond of telling stories about *Khelemer naronim* (fools of Khelm) or, as they were affectionately, if ironically, dubbed, *Khelemer khakhomim* (wise men of Khelm).

These "wise men of Khelm" lived in a world of their own. Children loved to hear and adults loved to tell about their absurd and inappropriate behavior. Stories like "The Hill Pushed Away" were favorites. Khelmites were sure to misread every Bible verse and misinterpret every injunction—always at great cost. They also had a penchant for ignoring reality, and a positive talent for overlooking the laws of nature, as in "The Rolling Stone" and "How Khelmites Lighted Up the Night."

In addition to the cycle of humorous tales about the not-so-bright denizens of Khelm, Yiddish folklore also has cycles of humorous anecdotes pegged to specific, real-life *vitslers,* or pranksters. If the Khelmite fools are the subjects of jests, the *vitslers* are the creators of jests, although at times the *vitsler* pretends to be a fool himself, in a jest of his own creation. While the Khelmite misunderstands reality, the *vitsler* manipulates it.[4]

Each of our three *vitslers* comes from a different region: Hershele Ostropolyer from Volin in the Ukraine, Motke Khabad from Vilna in Lithuania, and Froyim Greydinger, *the galitsyaner vitsler,* from the region of Poland known as Galicia.[5] Hershele Ostropolyer (1757–1811) has been described as a kind of jester at the Hasidic court of Rebbe Borukh Mezhbizher. Although some claim that Froyim Greydinger lived in the nineteenth century, others place him a century earlier, claiming that he supplied Hershele with jokes, anecdotes, and proverbs. Motke Khabad (1820–ca. 1880) is best known for his relationship with the Vilna Gaon, Elijah ben Solomon (1720–1797), a towering figure of rabbinic Judaism and an opponent of Hasidism. According to one tradition, Motke was said to have helped raise the spirits of the Gaon. The other has it that the Vilna Gaon, angry with Motke on one occasion, "cursed" him to live by his *khokhmes,* his wit and pranks.

Hershele, Motke, and Froyim are basically poor folk whose pranks are a way of coping with poverty. They are given to mild teasing, as in "The Congregation Loves Jam," or to droll and mischievous displays of absurd "logic," as in "Reb Hershele and the Goose Leg." But frequently, as in "Motke Khabad Needs a Place to Live," a blacker humor, a darker tone of unhappy social satire underlies the tales. Like the parables told by itinerant preachers, the stories have an implicit, if not explicit, moral and often attack the bigotry and hypocrisy of the powerful within the Jewish community. It is not uncommon to find that the same tale is told now of one, now of another of these three figures.

Other tales here offer a cross section of Yiddish folk humor. Some tell about numbskulls like Khushim ("Simpleton"), who would feel right at home in Khelm. Others are about Anyman/Anywoman: there are, for example, the shlemiel/shlimazl simpletons, like the foolish innkeeper so easily parted from his money by "The Visitor from the World Beyond"; sly scoundrels like the tailor who wanted to become a cantor; gifted riddle solvers like Moshke or "The Clever Girl"; women who demand the religious prerogatives of males and are ridiculed for doing so. There are anecdotes about misused logic, like "Then Where's the Cat?" and misplaced conclusions, like "What Makes Tea Sweet?" which poke fun at casuistry and parody the subtle argumentation (*pilpl*) employed in studying the Talmud. In addition, there are the lovely cante fables, in which a melody becomes part of the story.[6] The teller repeats a song again and again within the frame of the narrative. This way the audience can learn the tune and sing along.

The Clever Girl: A Riddle Tale

Once upon a time there was a *porets*, a nobleman who had three leaseholders on his domain. One leased his woods and another his mill, while the poorest of the three held the lease on the inn.

One day the nobleman sent for the three leaseholders and said, "I'm going to ask you three questions: What is the fastest thing in the world? What is the fattest thing in the world? And what is the dearest thing in the world? Whoever gives me the right answers within three days will be granted his leasehold for ten years without fee. But whoever gives the wrong answers will be driven from my estate."

The first two leaseholders—the one who had the forest and the one who had the mill—didn't take long to think the questions through. Both concluded that the fastest thing in the world was the nobleman's horse; the fattest thing in the world was his pig; and the dearest thing in the world would undoubtedly be the woman he marries. And they were satisfied with their answers. But the poor innkeeper returned home in great perplexity because he had no idea what to say.

Now, the innkeeper had a beautiful and talented daughter who asked, "What makes you look so worried, Father?" He told her about the nobleman's questions and said, "How can I help looking worried? I have no idea what the answers are." "There's nothing to worry about," she said. "They're simple enough: Thought is the fastest thing in the world; the earth is the fattest; and sleep is the dearest thing of all."

At the end of the third day, all three leaseholders appeared before the nobleman. He immediately dismissed the first two from his estate because their answers were wrong. Turning to the innkeeper, he said, "I like your answers very much, but I know they didn't come out of your own head. Tell me the truth: who told you what to say?"

The innkeeper confessed that his daughter had given him the answers.

The nobleman said, "If you have a daughter that clever, I want to see her. Let her come to me three days from now. But I want her to come neither walking nor riding, neither dressed nor naked. And I want her to bring a gift that is not a gift."

The innkeeper returned home more downcast than before. His daughter said, "Now what's wrong, Father? What makes you look so worried?" So he told her what conditions the nobleman had imposed. "Never mind," said she. "There's nothing to worry about. Now, here's what I want you to do. I want you to buy a fisherman's net, a goat, a pair of doves, and a couple of pounds of meat."

And he bought all the things she asked for.

Then she stripped and wrapped herself in the net, so that she was neither dressed nor naked; she mounted the goat and of course her feet dragged, so that as she went along, she was neither riding nor walking. She carried the doves in one hand and the meat in the other, and in that fashion she made her way into the nobleman's courtyard.

When the nobleman, who was watching from his window, saw her enter, he unleashed his dogs. But she threw them the meat and walked calmly past them into the house, where she said to the nobleman, "I've brought you a gift that is not a gift." And she released the doves, who immediately flew out of the open window.

"I want to marry you because you're so clever," said the nobleman.

"But we can be married only on one condition: that you won't meddle in the decisions I make when lawsuits are brought before me." She promised not to meddle, and so they were married.

Some while later as she was standing beside an open window, she saw a weeping peasant pass by. "Why are you crying?" she asked. He said, "Listen. One of my neighbors and I own a stable in partnership. I own a mare, and my neighbor owns a wagon. Now, the mare gave birth to her foal under the wagon, and my neighbor claimed that the foal was his. So we asked the nobleman to decide between us, and the nobleman said the foal belongs to my neighbor. That's why I'm weeping."

She said, "Let me tell you what to do. Get yourself a fishing rod and line and stand in the sandy place just below the nobleman's window. Pretend that you're catching fish in the sand. When the nobleman asks, 'How can you possibly catch fish in the sand?' you must say, 'If a wagon can give birth to a foal, then I can catch fish in the sand.'"

The peasant did as she said, and when the nobleman heard his reply, he understood at once that his wife was involved. Turning to her, he said, "Since you haven't kept your part of our agreement, I want you to take the finest and dearest thing that you can find in the house and go back to your father."

"All right," she said. "But before I go, I want us to have one last meal together." Well, he agreed to that. There was plenty of wine at the table, and she saw to it that he got good and drunk. When he passed out, she ordered the servants to put him into a carriage. Then she stepped into it herself, and they were driven off together to her father's house.

The nobleman woke up sober and saw where he was. "How did I get here?" he asked.

She said, "You told me to take the finest and dearest thing I could find in your house. I could find nothing finer or dearer to me than you."

"In that case," said he, fondly, "let's make up and go back home."

And from that time on, they grew old together in wealth and honor.

Then Where's the Cat?

The cat in Khaim the *melamed*'s house was a rotten pest. One day Khaim's wife bought a kilo of butter and left it on the table, and the cat ate it up. The wife made a terrible racket and threatened to kill the cat.

The *melamed* said in the cat's defense, "But you didn't actually see what happened, so how do you know it was the cat that ate it?"

Then he had an idea. "I'll weigh the cat," he said, "and we'll see if it ate the butter." So they weighed the cat and it weighed precisely one kilo.

"Then it's true," said Khaim's wife. "The damn thing ate the butter."

"Hmm," said Khaim. "It's true, the butter's there all right. But then where's the cat?"

7 3
The Best for My Wife

A *melamed* went to the butcher shop to buy some meat for his wife, who was in childbed. He asked the butcher to cut him a nice piece. "The best you have," he said. The butcher showed him some meat, saying, "See how nice and fat it is."

"If fat is so desirable," thought the *melamed,* "I'll buy some fat instead."

The butcher handed him some fat, saying, "It's like pure olive oil."

The *melamed* handed the fat back and went off to buy olive oil. The grocer, as he handed it to him, said "This olive oil is as pure and clear as water."

"In that case," said his customer, "let me have some water."

7 4
The Coat of Patches

Once there was a man so poor that he couldn't support his wife and six children. They were hungry and cold. The man thought, "What good is a life like this? I'll have to do something about it." He decided to go out into the wide world to beg for alms. So he said farewell to his family and started off.

He wandered through woods and forests, from villages to towns, and collected a great sum of money in coins, which he then changed into banknotes. But how could he carry them safely? Well, he hid them inside his coat, beneath patches that he sewed over each bundle of bills.

Eventually he had so much money that his entire coat was covered with patches. Of course it didn't all happen at once. Years went by before the body of the coat was covered with patches. Then he had to sew patches on the sleeves, on the collar, and inside, on the lining.

So the years passed. He didn't write letters and his wife and children, long convinced that he was dead, stopped mourning for him. They grew poorer every year. The mother took in laundry and scrubbed floors, while the children did what they could to earn something for the family. And thus thirty years went by.

The husband had a real stock of capital by now. And he thought, "How much longer must I wander? I'll go back to my wife." So he bought an expensive coat with a fur collar and dressed himself up like a rich man. He made a parcel of the patched coat and took it with him. When he arrived at his *shtetl,* nobody recognized him. He went into his house and asked his grown children, "Where is your father?" They said, "Our father went wandering in the wide world. Probably he's dead."

He said, "No, he's not. Children, I am your father," and embraced them. Immediately the house was filled with a joyful commotion. "Khaim Yankl is back! He's a millionaire!" The whole town was in an uproar.

When his wife, who was not at home, heard the news, she refused to believe it. Still, she started back to the house. Meanwhile her husband put the patched coat into a kitchen corner and went off to the synagogue to recite his prayers. The wife came in and saw the prayer shawl he had forgotten, and recognized it at once. So she started in to prepare the midday meal. As she was working in the kitchen she came upon the patched coat. Picking it up, she said, "Ugh. What an ugly thing," and threw it aside.

Just then a poor man came in and asked for alms. She had nothing to give him, yet she was unwilling to send him off empty-handed. Then she remembered the patched coat and said, "Perhaps you could use this coat. It's not much, I know." But the poor man snatched it up and put it on, saying that it would do very well to keep him warm, and went on his way.

When her husband came back from the synagogue—ah, what joy

and happiness! They embraced; they talked. When they had finished eating, the husband took out a knife and a sharpening stone and began to sharpen the blade.

This terrified the family. How could they be sure he was not a robber in disguise? They had heard of stranger things. And so they crouched in various corners of the room while one of them stood near the door so that he could go for help if necessary.

When the man had sharpened his knife, he went to the kitchen and looked in the corner where he had put the coat. Not there. He asked his wife if she had seen it. "Yes, and I gave it to a poor man," she said. When he heard that, he fainted dead away.

They brought him to, and he said, "My whole fortune—all the money I collected over thirty years—is in that coat." His wife fainted dead away.

Her husband put on his new coat and went to a store where he bought a fiddle, which he carried to the town square, where he played it as he sang, "I'm a fool, I'm a fool." A crowd gathered and somebody said, "Khaim Yankl, what's the matter with you? Playing the fiddle in the middle of the day!" But he kept on playing and repeating, "I'm a fool, I'm a fool." People came running from all sides crying, "Khaim Yankl has gone mad." The whole town gathered to watch.

The poor man who had taken the coat saw that a crowd had gathered and also came to watch. Recognizing his coat, Khaim Yankl cried even more loudly, "I'm a fool, I'm a fool, I'm a fool." Turning to the poor man, he said, "Let's exchange coats." Everyone laughed. Just think what a crazy man will do! A fine coat with a fur collar for a patched rag!

The poor man was delighted by Khaim Yankl's offer, and the two of them traded coats on the spot. Fearful that Khaim Yankl might change his mind, the poor man ran off as fast as he could. Khaim Yankl meanwhile walked along, wearing his tattered coat, playing the fiddle, and singing, "You're a fool, you're a fool, you're a fool."

When Khaim Yankl got home, he unstitched the patches on the coat and took the money out. And from that time on he lived like a rich man.

The Bishop and Moshke: Another Riddle Tale

A bishop was once very angry at a Jew named Moshke. So he went to the king and complained about him. He insisted that Moshke be given a good thrashing.

"All right," said the king. "But first I want to put three questions to you. If you give me the right answers, you can do what you like with Moshke. And you can have three days to think about the answers. The first question is: Where is the middle of the earth? The second is: How many stars are there in the sky? And the third: What will I be thinking when you come back to see me?"

The bishop agreed to this test and went home. He thought and thought, but he couldn't light on the answers. Then it occurred to him that he would ask Moshke. "It's true," he thought, "I'm planning to do him harm, but he doesn't know it. I have a feeling that he can guess the answers, and that I can get him to tell me what they are."

So the bishop called Moshke to his house and told him what the questions were. Moshke said, "Give me a little time to think." He thought and thought and thought. Then he said, "Take off your clothes and hang them in the next room. Then run naked around the room seven times. After that I'll be ready to tell you the answers."

The bishop did as he was told. And Moshke went into the room where the bishop's clothes were and put them on. Then he left to see the king. The king stared and stared at him.

"What are you thinking?" Moshke said. "I know what you're thinking. You think that I'm the bishop, but I'm not. I'm Moshke the Jew."

The king was amazed that he had answered one of his questions right. He said, "Very well, I'll ask you the other questions now. If you answer them correctly, you'll discover what you have earned."

Moshke said, "Very well, ask me."

The king said, "Where is the middle of the world?"

Moshke thought for a while, then tapped his foot and said, "It's right here."

"How do you know?" asked the king.

"If you don't believe me, be good enough to measure it for yourself." When the king heard that, he decided it was the better part of wisdom to believe him.

"And now," said the king, "here is the last question. How many stars are there in the sky?"

Moshke thought for a while. He reckoned and reckoned. Then he said, "There are ninety-eight thousand, seven hundred and sixty stars."

The astonished king asked, "How is it that you know the number so precisely?"

Moshke replied, "Count them for yourself and see whether I'm right."

"Your cleverness has just saved your hide," said the king. "And because you were able to answer all of my questions, I'm going to make you my chief counselor. And now we'll take a droshky to the bishop's house. We can let him know that I've given you the right to do to him what he was going to do to you."

The king and Moshke drove to the bishop's house, where they found that worthy running naked round and round a table. At the sight of him the king burst out laughing.

The end of the matter was that the bishop was given a good thrashing and Moshke lived on in the king's favor.

Good Manners and Foolish Khushim

Until he was sixteen, Khushim the Fool lolled about on top of the oven and never went anywhere. His mother said, "Khushim, why don't you get out of the house? It'll do you good to rub shoulders with other people."

"All right, Mother," he said. So he left the house and went out into the street, and there he saw a crowd. He pressed his way into the middle of it and started to rub against the people, for which they beat him soundly. When he came home weeping, his mother said, "My son, when you mingle with people you have to greet them. If it's morning, you say 'Good morning.' If it's afternoon, you say 'God be with you.' If it's evening, you say 'Good evening.' When you take your leave in the afternoon, you say 'Good day,' and if it's night you say 'Good night'."

"Good, Mother," said Khushim. "I'll do as you say."

He went out into the street, and there he saw a funeral procession. He ran up to the mourners and cried, "Good morning. God be with you. Good evening. Good day. Good night," for which they beat him soundly.

When he came home weeping, his mother said, "My son, if you come upon a funeral procession, you're supposed to weep. And if the deceased is a young man, you say, 'Woe, woe. Such a young tree to be felled in its prime.' And if he's old, you say, 'May he rest in paradise'."

"Good, Mother," said Khushim. "I'll do as you say."

He went out into the street, where he saw a wedding procession going by. The musicians were playing, the relatives of the bride and groom were dancing. Khushim, seeing them, cried out, "Woe, woe. Such a young tree to be felled in its prime. May he rest in paradise," for which they beat him soundly.

When he came home weeping, his mother said, "My son, if you

see a wedding procession, you cry 'Congratulations!' and you sing and dance."

Khushim said, "Good, Mother. I'll do as you say."

He went out into the street and came to a house on fire. People were standing around it weeping and wailing. Khushim called out "Congratulations!" and began to sing and dance, for which they beat him soundly.

When he came home weeping, his mother said. "My son, if you see a house on fire you're supposed to grab a bucket of water and put out the flames."

Khushim said, "Good, Mother. I'll do as you say."

He went out into the street, and there he saw a house with smoke coming out of its chimney. So he grabbed a bucket of water, climbed up on the roof, and poured the water down the chimney, for which they beat him soundly.

When he came home weeping, his mother said, "My son, you may as well loll about on top of the oven. There's no point in your rubbing shoulders with the rest of the world."

7 7
Khushim and His Bride

When Khushim started off to see his prospective bride, his mother said, "My son, cast an eye on the girl to make sure there's nothing wrong with her."

At the bride's home when Khushim was seated at the table, he took an eye out of his pocket and cast it at her, for which they beat him soundly.

When Khushim's mother came home, she found the house in an uproar, filled with neighbors complaining that Khushim had cut the eyes out of a kid, a calf, and a sheep, for which they beat him soundly.

His mother said, "My son, when you talk in the home of a possible bride, try to make your conversation well-rounded."

When Khushim returned to the prospective bride's house, he shouted, "A plate, a bowl, a barrel, a basin, a frying pan," for which they beat him soundly.

When Khushim came home weeping, his mother said, "My son, here is my calf. Take it to the young woman and she will be reconciled with you." Khushim took the calf up in his arms and started off. As he went along, the calf began to bellow and kick so violently that it broke out of his arms and escaped, leaving him with his face all bruised.

Khushim returned home weeping. His mother said, "My son, you don't carry a calf in your arms. You tie a rope to it and make it follow you." Then she gave him a piece of meat and told him to give it to the prospective bride as a gift.

Khushim took the meat, tied a rope to it, and dragged it along through the streets. Dogs quickly gathered around it, and before long they had eaten it all up. Khushim returned home weeping bitterly.

His mother said, "My son, you're supposed to put meat into a basket. You put the basket on your shoulder and carry it that way." Then she told him to invite the young woman to a meal.

Khushim went to the home of the prospective bride. There he grabbed a basket, shoved the young woman into it, put the basket on his shoulder, and carried it home, for which they beat him soundly.

Then his mother said, "You may as well loll about on top of the oven. There's no point in your going to a prospective bride's house any more."

7 8
The Tale of a Leaf from the Tree of Knowledge

Once upon a time a peasant lost his way and found himself in a desert. Suddenly there was a windstorm that caught up dust and sand and a mixture of all sorts of things and whirled them round and round. When the storm was over, the peasant came upon a path that led him to a village.

As he walked along, he was amazed to feel himself becoming wiser and cleverer, so that he could now understand things around him better than he ever had before.

After a while when he grew tired, he sat down to rest and took his sandals off. But as he did so, he felt himself becoming as dull and ignorant and boorish as before. Yet the minute he put the sandals back on, he turned sensible and wise again. So it was clear to him that the sandals had brought all this about.

Now, the explanation was that the windstorm had blown a leaf from the Tree of Knowledge out of the Garden of Eden, and the leaf had stuck to the bottom of one of his sandals.

The peasant came to a town in which the king's daughter was very sick. All the doctors had despaired of her life, and the king was bracing himself for her death. Then he was told that there was a certain crude peasant who promised to cure his daughter if they would let him in.

The peasant, using a variety of remedies that he understood because of his new wisdom, began to cure the princess. Slowly she became conscious again, and after a few days she was entirely well.

The king, as was to be expected, rewarded the peasant magnificently. He also kept him in the palace for several days so that the royal physicians could determine whether he had cured the princess with authentic remedies or through something unnatural—magic, for instance. The doctors testified that the peasant's remedies were well and wisely chosen.

Then the king asked the peasant how it was that he, an ignorant man, had been able to surpass the wisdom of the greatest court physician.

"It's my sandals," said the peasant simply.

The king demanded, "What kind of joke is that?"

"I'm not joking," said the peasant. "All my wisdom comes from my sandals. If anyone were to put them on, he would be as smart as I am."

The king promised half his kingdom and much more if the peasant would let him have the sandals.

Now, it stands to reason that a king cannot wear dirty sandals, so he gave them to his servants to be cleaned. And in order to get them clean, they threw away the leaf from the Tree of Knowledge.

So when the king put on the sandals, he was neither wiser nor more sensible than he had ever been.

Reb Hershele and the Goose Leg

One Friday when Reb Hershele Ostropolyer was eight years old, he crept into the family food locker, stole a leg from a roast goose, and ate it. Soon afterward his mother went to the locker and saw that one of the goose's legs was missing. She knew at once that this was her son's work, so she gave him a scolding for taking the leg without permission.

"Maybe the goose only had one leg," said Reb Hershele.

His mother replied, "Where have you ever seen a one-legged bird?"

That evening Reb Hershele went to the synagogue with his father. As they were walking, Reb Hershele saw a stork standing on one leg. "See, Father," he cried, pointing to the stork. "Mother says there are no one-legged birds."

"That bird," replied his father, "habitually stands on one leg; his other leg is hidden beneath him. Watch me drive him off—you'll see." The father picked up a stone and threw it at the stork. The bird quickly lowered its other leg and flew away. "So you see that your mother is right."

"Ah," said Reb Hershele, "Maybe if you drove the roast goose off, you'd see its other leg."

8 0

Hershele Ostropolyer and the Sabbath Caftan

It happened that a hungry Hershele Ostropolyer came to a town one day. There he learned that the town's richest man was marrying off his only daughter. "Hmm," thought Hershele, "it wouldn't hurt to look in on the wedding." But the rich man's servants refused to let such a ragged man into the house. So Hershele Ostropolyer hurried to a friend's house and begged him, with tears in his eyes, to lend him his Sabbath caftan. The friend took his new caftan out of the chest and let Hershele put it on. And when Hershele went back to the wedding, he was welcomed and seated in a place of honor. But no matter what good things he was given to eat or drink, he emptied them out on the caftan. Finally someone said, "What are you doing, Hershele?"

"I'm only doing what's proper," Hershele Ostropolyer replied. "After all, it's the caftan, not I, that's being honored here."

8 1

Why Khelmites Are Fools

Once upon a time a new Torah reader, a *balkoyre,* came to Khelm just as the annual cycle of readings from the Torah was to begin. The *balkoyre* was not much of a scholar, and instead of reading "*Breyshes, boro elohim es hashomayim*"—"In the beginning, God created the heavens"—he read "*Breyshes, boro elohim es . . . hashoytim*"—"In the beginning, God created fools." And since that time, for better or worse, Khelmites have been fools.

The Angel Spills the Jar of Fools

Since no angel ever has to perform two assignments at once, one angel carried a jar filled with intelligent souls, while another angel carried a jar filled with foolish souls so that every town could have its town fool.

One day the angel with the jar of foolish souls happened to be passing Khelm. Since the region thereabouts has many hills and valleys, the angel lost his footing, slipped, and spilled the whole jar near Khelm. And since that time, all Khelmites have been fools.

8 3

A Shoyfer in Khelm

One day a stranger arrived in Khelm, a very muddy town, and lost one of his boots in the mud. He looked everywhere but couldn't find it. Later a Khelmite found it, but since no one in Khelm wore boots, people didn't know what it was. So they took the boot to the rabbi, and a meeting was called. Everyone looked at the boot, and the rabbi declared that it was a *shoyfer*, a ram's horn, because a *shoyfer* is long at the bottom and round at the top. So the Khelmites placed the boot inside the *ornkoydesh*, the Holy Ark, in the synagogue.

It happened that the same stranger came back to Khelm and went to the synagogue to pray. When he saw his boot in the Holy Ark, he cried, "That's my boot! Let me have it."

But the Khelmites wouldn't believe him. They shouted that it wasn't a boot, it was a *shoyfer*. Well, they took the quarrel to the rabbi, who ruled that the boot was a *shoyfer,* but that the stranger should be paid eighteen zlotys just the same for his distress. And that's what was done. The stranger was paid eighteen zlotys and Khelm "blows the *shoyfer*" with a boot.

8 4
The Hill Pushed Away

There was trouble in Khelm. There was no water. People who wanted it had to go to a well several versts away. In summer you could die of thirst.

The people of Khelm decided that no one could go on living like that. A solution had to be found. There had to be a closer well. So they decided to push away the hill that stood between them and the well. The entire village took sticks and spades and pushed. They pushed and pushed, but they couldn't tell whether they had budged the hill. So they decided to take their jackets off and pile them up in a wagon. Then the pile could serve as their marker. So that's what they did; they took their jackets off. And they pushed and pushed, but while they pushed, they couldn't see what was happening behind them.

What was happening was this: a rider came by and, finding a wagon piled with clothes, he harnessed his horse to the wagon and drove away with it, clothes and all. The Khelmites meanwhile kept on pushing. At last one of them turned around and saw that the wagonload of clothes was a long way off. They all stopped work and gazed at their marker, which was moving farther and farther into the distance. They concluded that the hill had decided to move of its own accord. Thus there was no point in pushing anymore, because the hill was moving toward the well by itself.

They went to get their clothes, but no matter how much they walked, they couldn't overtake the wagon. To this day the Khelmites have no jackets, and they still hope to overtake their marker.

8 5

How Khelmites Lighted Up the Night

The Khelmites were troubled by the night. When it was dark they often fell and broke their arms and legs. One day they heard a man from Vilna saying that even the nights in Vilna were bright. So they held a meeting at which they formed a fine plan. First they had to wait for a moonlit night. Finally it came—and what a night! A night of nights! The moon shone so brightly that it simply begged to be blessed, so they blessed it in proper form. Then, seeing the moon's reflection in a barrel of water, they took a board and quickly nailed it over the barrel.

Later, when it was the new moon again and the night was pitch-black, they opened the barrel, meaning to take their moon out of storage. But lo and behold, when they looked into the water, there was no moon to be seen. "Alas, alas," they cried, "someone has stolen our moon!"

8 6

The Melamed's Trunk

In the synagogue in Khelm this is inscribed on the *balemer*, the platform from which the Torah is read:

A *melamed* is forbidden three things:

> 1. *He may not live on a hill.*
> 2. *He may not have a suitcase on wheels.*
> 3. *He may not eat strudle.*

You see, it had been the custom in Khelm for boys to be examined orally Friday evening on their lessons. One Friday morning a *melamed* came to tutor the son in a Khelmite's house. He noticed a strudle in the kitchen and asked the servant, "What's that?"

"A strudle," she replied.

The *melamed* went home and, giving his wife a two-zloty coin, told her to bake a strudle. Instead she used the money to buy her son a pair of shoes. When the *melamed* asked, "Where is the strudle?" she told him what she had done, and he flew into a rage.

Now, as it happened, there was an open trunk on wheels standing nearby. The two of them quarreled so fiercely that they fell into the trunk. The lid closed, the trunk began to roll and, since their house was on a hill, it rolled with all possible speed until it reached the market square. When people saw the rolling trunk, they set up a hullabaloo. They shuttered their shops and ran to the synagogue, where they caused the *shoyfer* to be blown. Finally, in God's good time, the trunk stopped rolling. The rabbi and all the town's Jews moved hesitantly toward it. When the trunk was opened, the *melamed* and his wife leaped out.

And that's why the rabbi and the community leaders established the three rules and caused them to be inscribed on the *balemer* of the synagogue.

8 7
The Rolling Stone

There is a huge stone on a high hill in Khelm. It happened once that the Khelmites wanted to move the stone down from the hill. What did they do? They gathered up the entire population and started to drag the stone. When they had dragged it halfway down, a stranger went by. Seeing what they were doing, he laughed at them. "Why are you dragging the stone?" he asked. "Just give it a shove; it'll roll downhill by itself." The Khelmites, heeding good advice, dragged the stone back to the top of the hill. Then they pushed it, and it did indeed roll to the bottom by itself.

8 8
A Cat in Khelm

People in Khelm didn't know about cats, and they lived with mice crawling in and out of every nook and cranny. At mealtimes each householder had a rod at his table to drive the mice away. Then one day a stranger came to Khelm and described a creature he had seen, an animal called a "cat" which, if it was introduced into a house, drove the mice into their holes. The town of Khelm asked him to find such a creature, and then bought the cat from him for the enormous sum of eighteen zlotys. But the Khelmites didn't know that a cat could run away. Well, the cat was put on watch in a house, and the townspeople were delighted to see that it scared off the mice. But one day someone left a window open, and the cat took it into its head to leap out onto a roof.

So the Khelmites called a meeting to figure out how to catch the cat. They decided to set the house on fire to make the cat jump to the ground. So they burned the house down, but the cat sprang to the roof of the next house. So they burned the second house down. But the cat sprang to the roof of a third house. So they burned the third house down. And so on, until they destroyed half their town.

89

Khelmites Who Refused to Tread on Snow

Once upon a time a stranger came to Khelm and was taken ill. He needed to be led to the hospital, but it happened to be winter and the Khelmites, who dearly loved the whiteness of snow, didn't want him to spoil it with his footprints. So they called a meeting to discuss the problem. At last they arrived at a solution: they put the sick man on a board, and four of them simply carried him to the hospital.

90

The Sundial

It happened once that the people of Khelm made a sundial. But a rainstorm came along and drenched it. So the Khelmites built a roof over their sundial to keep it from getting wet.

91

A Khelm Compromise

It happened once that the Khelmites had to build a new ritual bath, a *mikve*. When the frame was finished, they turned their attention to making the floor. It was at this point that a quarrel erupted and they broke up into two groups. One group said that it was necessary to plane the floor boards so that people shouldn't get splinters in their feet. The other group held that the floor boards must not be planed, otherwise they would be too slippery and people would fall. Finally they decided to consult the rabbi and do whatever he told them to. Well, the rabbi of Khelm listened attentively to what each side said. Then he ruled as follows:

"Of course, the floorboards ought to be properly planed, but to keep people from slipping, they must be laid planed-side down."

92

A Bridge in Khelm

A river flowed right through the middle of Khelm. It occurred to several merchants that a bridge over it would be good for business on both sides of the river. But some of the younger people objected. They said: "Of course it would be nice to build a bridge, but let's not do it because it would be good for business; we should build it solely for aesthetic reasons. We'll be glad to contribute to the building expenses for beauty's sake, but we won't give a penny for the sake of trade." Still others, even younger people, said, "A bridge!

That's a good idea, but not for the sake of trade or beauty but to have someplace to stroll back and forth. We'll be glad to contribute money to build a bridge for strolling." And so the three groups began to quarrel, and they are quarreling still. And to the present day Khelm does not have a bridge.

9 3
Sowing Salt

Once there was a shortage of salt in Khelm. What to do? The townspeople thought and thought without resting night or day. Then the rebbe, a mighty thinker, had a thought. "Let us go out to the fields, and let us sow salt." The whole town went out to the fields carrying the last specks of salt they had left. They went to work sowing salt, and after they were done, the rebbe said that he would stay in the fields to guard the crop.

At night the rebbe lay down to sleep. As he slept, a wolf came by and bit his head off. In the morning the whole town turned out to see how the salt was doing. They found the headless rebbe in the field and wondered where his head could be. They sent messengers to the rebbe's wife with the question: "Do you recall—did the rebbe have a head, or not?" She said she couldn't remember.

So they went to the cantor of Khelm, who said he couldn't remember either. People gathered in clusters discussing whether the rebbe had had a head or not. Some cried, "He did," others, "No, he didn't."

They were about to come to blows when a man arrived from another town. "What are you arguing about?" he asked, and they told him about the salt and the rebbe and the rebbe's head. When he had heard the whole story, he said, "If your rebbe was prepared to sow salt, it's proof that he didn't have a head. You can bury him without further ado."

Two Cows for a Melody

Once upon a time there was a husband and wife who had two cows, one black and the other red. One day the husband was driving his cows through town when he saw a man who was playing this melody on his fiddle:

He went up to the man and said, "Teach me how to play that melody."

The fiddler said, "What will you give me if I do?"

"Anything you want," said the man, "Just as long as you teach me how to play it."

And so the fiddler played:

Then the man gave the fiddler his red cow, and the fiddler taught him how to play the tune.

The man went on his way until he came to another fiddler, who was playing this melody:

The man went up to the fiddler and said, "Teach me that melody."

The fiddler said, "And what will you give me if I do?"

"I'll give you my black cow," said the man.

So the fiddler taught him how to play it.

When the man came home, his wife asked, "Shepsl, where is the red cow?"

The man replied:

Then she asked him, "Shepsl, where is the black cow?" to which the man replied:

Froyim Greydinger, the Magic Stick, and the Pot of Soup

Froyim Greydinger—surely you know him, the Galician wit—journeyed once from village to village trying to earn what he could. In the course of his travels he came to an inn. There he asked the innkeeper's wife to give him something to eat, but she replied that she herself had nothing to eat.

"Bitter news," Froyim thought as he mulled over what to do about his empty stomach. Looking about, he saw—I should tell you that it was a Thursday—he saw some meat and a freshly killed hen on a cutting board in the kitchen. Smiling, he said to himself, "Aha, so that's how things are." Now that he knew who he was dealing with, he was ready to take her on.

Picking up a stick, he toyed with it for a moment and then said, "Do you see this stick, ma'am? With this stick and a pot of water, I could cook you a fine soup."

The woman was instantly curious. "What kind of stick is that?"

"Oh," said Froyim with assumed naïveté, "if I stir a pot of water over a fire with this stick, I can cook up any sort of dish at all."

The moment the woman heard that, she could think of nothing but the stick and how he would make a soup with it. She filled a pot with water, and Froyim set it on top of the stove and started to stir it. He stirred and talked, talked and stirred. "It's an amazing stick," he said. "Many's the time it has saved me from having to go to bed on an empty stomach."

When the water in the pot had come to a boil, he said, "Tell me, ma'am, would you happen to have a bone, some chicken giblets, and some salt?"

"Of course," she said. "What a question." And she handed him a fine marrow bone, some giblets, and salt. Froyim put them all into the pot and continued to stir. He talked and stirred. A moment later he said, "Perhaps you have a carrot, some cabbage, and some groats?"

"Some!" said the woman. "No need to be stingy with them. The Lord be thanked, I have a gardenful of vegetables." With that she handed him some groats and vegetables, and Froyim put them all into the pot and stirred and talked. Talked and stirred. When he was done, Froyim poured himself a bowl of soup. Tasting it, he smacked his lips with pleasure. Seeing that, the innkeeper's wife could hardly keep from drooling. "Can I taste it?" she asked.

"By all means," said Froyim.

He poured a bowlful for her and another one for himself, and even so there was more left over. She tasted it and said, "I have to admit that I haven't had such a fine soup in a long time. What a wonderful stick! Perhaps you'd like to sell it?"

"Heaven forbid. Never. The stick was part of my inheritance. And yet, hmmm. You're such a fine woman. You have such a generous heart. Hmm. Suppose . . . let's just suppose I could sell it, how much would you give?"

"Let me see," said the innkeeper's wife. "Would a ruble do?"

"A ruble?" said Froyim. "Heaven forbid. No. I won't sell it for money."

"Then what would you take?"

"No money, that's for sure," said Froyim firmly. "Just think of it! Part of an inheritance that has come down to me through generations. Still, who knows . . . perhaps . . . if you'll give me that freshly killed hen in addition to the ruble, I'll make you a present of the stick."

Well, they arrived at a trade, though Froyim hesitated for a moment. But finally he gave her the stick and returned home carrying a fat hen for the Sabbath and a ruble into the bargain.

96

What Makes Tea Sweet: An Exercise in Logic

A yeshiva student said to one of his fellows, "The sages ask: What makes the glass of tea sweet? If I reply that it is because of the sugar, then I must ask: What is the teaspoon's purpose? The answer: To sweeten the tea, for which the proof is as follows: When you put sugar into the tea, it does not turn sweet until you have stirred it with the teaspoon. In which case, why do we need the sugar at all?"

The second student replied, "Indeed, it is true that the tea is sweetened by the spoon. Now, why do we need the sugar? My reply is that sugar is necessary because it's only when the sugar dissolves that we know it's time to stop stirring."

97

The Visitor from the World Beyond

An innkeeper bought his family meat and fish and told his simpleton wife to get them ready for *shabes nakhmu,* the Sabbath of Consolation.

On Friday evening just before the meal, a visitor appeared at the innkeeper's house. "A good Sabbath to you," he said. As it happened, the innkeeper was not at home just then, so the innkeeper's wife said, "Are you *Shabes Nakhmu?*" The visitor, sensing an opportunity of some kind, said, "Yes, I am."

The innkeeper's wife said, "I have everything ready for you. There's fish, and meat, and so on." Then she served him all the good things she had prepared.

When he had done eating and drinking, she asked, "Where are you from?"

"From the world beyond," he replied.

"How are my parents doing there?" she asked.

"Quite well," he said, "but they suffer a little from the cold. You wouldn't perhaps be able to send them some clothing?"

So she gathered up her husband's suits and her dresses and gave them to the stranger.

When the innkeeper came home, she told him that *Shabes Nakhmo* had been there and that she had given him food and drink, as well as all their suits and dresses.

"What have you done?" he shouted. "How in the world could *shabes nakhmu* be here?"

Quickly the innkeeper harnessed the horses to his wagon and drove off in pursuit of the stranger. But that sly fellow, suspecting that he might be followed, went into a forest, stripped himself naked, and put his arms around a tree.

Driving through the forest and seeing a naked man embracing a tree, the innkeeper stopped his wagon. "Did a man carrying a bundle go by here?" he asked.

"Yes," said the naked man. "I saw him."

The innkeeper said, "Will you be good enough to chase him and bring him back here?"

"I'm sorry, I can't," said the thief. "As you see, I'm holding up this tree, which happens to be the tree that holds up the world. If I go away the tree will fall, and then, of course, the whole world will. Although if you' like, you can take your clothes off and hold up the tree in my place. Then I'll be glad to chase the fellow with the bundle."

The innkeeper took all his clothes off and put his arms around the tree while the thief, jumping into the wagon, drove off.

9 8

The Ten Women

Once upon a time women decided that they, too, wanted to form a *minyen*, a prayer quorum of ten, and pray together as a group, just like the men. So they sent a deputation to the Lord of the Universe.

"*Reboyne shel oylem*," they said, "why are we any worse than the men? Why can't ten women get together and pray as a group?"

The Lord of the Universe replied, "If you can manage to count to ten, you have my promise that you too can form a *minyen*."

So the rabbi's wife hurriedly gathered together the worthiest women of the town and told them what the Lord had said.

She led the women to the synagogue, and once they were inside, she started to count them. But she included herself in the count, so there turned out to be eleven. Seeing that, she asked one of the women to step out of the group and counted once more. But this time she forgot to count herself, so now she counted nine women. Well, she asked the woman who had stepped aside to rejoin the group. This time when the rabbi's wife counted, she included herself, so once again there were eleven.

When she saw that she continually miscounted, she decided that it would be better if she got each of them to make a figure of clay and poke a hole in it with her finger. Then by counting the holes, she would know how many women there were.

But one of the women in the group was a snuff sniffer. When she worked with her clay, she put two fingers into it, as if taking a pinch of snuff. So when the rabbi's wife counted the holes, she came up with the number eleven again.

Then, seeing that using fingers had produced a miscount, she got the idea of telling the women to make the holes in the clay with their tongues. After all, each person has only one tongue.

So the clay figures were re-formed and each woman made a hole with her tongue. But one of the women had such a long nose, that when she bent to make a hole with her tongue, she poked another hole with her nose. When the rabbi's wife counted the holes, she was dismayed to come out with eleven once more. Feeling at an impasse, and unable to think what to do, she ran helter-skelter to the rabbi and asked his advice.

"How can I help you," he said, "if you insist on poking your noses where they don't belong?"

And the moral of this tale is: Women! Don't poke your noses into the affairs of men.

The Congregation Loves Jam

One Sabbath before the reading of the Torah, Motke Khabad went up to the reader's table, brought his hand down on it with a bang, and announced, "Congregation! Those of you who love jam are invited to my house after the service. Come at three o'clock."

When the service was over, Motke went home. He ate his *tsholnt,* then lay down for his nap. When he woke at three, a considerable crowd had gathered in his courtyard. Motke went up to the people and asked, "Are you all here?"

"Yes," came the reply, "we're all here."

"In that case, you can all turn around and go home. Now I know how many of you love jam."

1 0 0
Motke Khabad Needs a Place to Live

One day while out walking, Motke Khabad stopped on a street to look at a house. Someone passing by said, "Would you like to buy that place?"

"Yes," replied Motke. "Yes."

"Have you got the money for it?" asked the passerby.

"Oh, I've got the money for the building. The rub is that I haven't got the money for the loaf of bread you're supposed to carry across the threshold when you buy a new house."

1 0 1
Why the Head Turns Gray before the Beard

One day a king rode out into the countryside, where he met a poor Jewish farmer who was working in his field. The farmer's head was gray and his beard was black. This struck the king as strange, so he called the man to him and said, "How is it that your head is gray and your beard is black?"

The man replied, "It's because my head is older than my beard. And that's why it turned gray first." This reply pleased the king, and he commanded the man not to tell anyone what he had said. "You may tell it," he said, "only after you have seen me a hundred times." The man promised to obey the king's command and the king rode away.

When he returned home, the king put the same question to his ministers: "Why does the head turn gray before the beard?" When none of them could come up with the right answer, he gave them a month to think the matter over, after which they were to bring him their replies.

The month passed quickly and the allotted time had nearly arrived, and still no one had found the right answer. It was then that one of the ministers remembered that the king had been riding in a certain district on the day when he had put his question. And so he too rode out in that district, and sure enough, he came upon the same Jewish farmer whose head was gray and whose beard was black. He approached the man and said, "Tell me, why is your hair gray and your beard black?"

"I'm sorry, but I'm not allowed to tell you."

The minister said, "I'll pay you well if you tell me."

"All right," said the man. "I'll tell you after you've given me one hundred silver rubles."

The minister immediately brought him one hundred silver rubles, and the man told him the answer to the riddle. The minister promptly reported it to the king.

The king, however, guessed at once that the Jewish farmer had divulged the answer. So he sent for the man and said, "Are you aware that you have earned a severe punishment for revealing the secret I commanded you to keep?"

The man replied, "Do you remember that you said I could reveal it only after I had seen you a hundred times?" Here, the man took the hundred silver rubles from his pocket and showed the king his likeness on each coin. "At first," he said, "I refused to tell the secret. It was only after the minister had brought me the hundred rubles and I had seen your face on each of them that I felt I had a right to tell."

The king, seeing that he was dealing with an astute man, decided not to punish him. Instead he asked the Jewish farmer to stay with him and be his advisor. From that time on, the king kept the man beside him and consulted him before he made any decision.

This caused jealousy among the king's other ministers, and they concocted a plot to destroy him.

Now, the custom was that when the king summoned his ministers together to tell him stories, the first story was always told by the minister who sat on the king's right. When he was done, he would tap the minister to his right with a stick. That official in turn would tell his story and then tap the minister to his right with the stick. And so on around the circle until the last minister, who sat at the king's left, told the last story and the storytelling session was done.

Now, what the ministers plotted was to seat the Jewish farmer at the king's left and then, against tradition, to start the storytelling in the middle of the circle. Thus when the Jew received the stick and finished telling his story, he, not being the last one to tell a tale, would have to strike the king with his stick. And striking the king was a crime punishable by death.

Well, the plot went as planned, and when the farmer received the stick, he suddenly understood what the ministers had in mind. So he turned to the king and said, "Before I tell my story, I'd like to ask your advice."

"What is it?" said the king.

"Tell me what I ought to have done in the following situation: I was traveling along one day when I saw a great fire at a distance, and in that fire a number of people were trapped."

"You ought to have rescued the people," said the king.

"Very well, then. But as I hurried to rescue them, I came upon a deep pond that stood between me and the fire. If I entered the water, I would surely drown because I can't swim, and that would be no help to the people in the fire. So I was brought to a dead stop. Now, my question to you is, "What should I have done?"

"You should certainly not have entered the pond. Your death would have been of no help to the people who were trapped."

When the farmer heard the king's reply, he handed the stick to the other ministers, saying, "If I used the stick to strike the king, it would be for me like drowning in the pond, and my death would have done you no good."

The ministers, seeing that he had more wisdom than they, decided to patch up their quarrel and became his good friends from then on. And that was the end of that.

102
The Love Potion

I know another little tale, not quite proper, but it is amusing. If you like, I'll tell it to you.

Once upon a time there was a husband and wife, very poor folk. To make it worse, they had a great many children, all girls. And it happened that the wife, as was not unusual with her, was pregnant again. Her husband thought, "Who knows, perhaps God will send us a son this time, and I haven't even got the wherewithal for a circumcision feast." He concluded that, what with one thing and another, he would do better to go out into the wide world begging for alms so that he'd be able to pay for the circumcision feast. So that's what he did, and it wasn't long before his family lost all track of him.

Meanwhile his wife came to her time and was, with God's help, delivered of a boy. But her house was very cold and she had nothing to heat it with. Lying in bed, she remembered that there were a few pieces of coal somewhere in an attic corner. She turned to her daughters and said, "Children, go to the attic, where you'll find a few bits of coal. Bring them down so we can warm up the house a little. I'm very cold." So her daughters went up to the attic and found the coal. But they noticed that there was something bright and gleaming among the coal scraps, and they ran down to their mother and told her so.

"Well," she said, "bring me a couple of pieces of whatever it is that's glittering there." So they fetched down two pieces of the bright stone. When their mother saw what they had, she knew at once that it was something valuable. She said to her oldest daughter, "Carry one of these to the goldsmith and ask him what it's worth."

The goldsmith took one look and knew that it was no ordinary stone but a diamond. He bought it from the girl for a great deal of money, which she took home to her mother. Well, it wasn't long before there were all sorts of good things in the house, and more than enough money to pay for a fine circumcision feast.

Now that she was prosperous, the woman felt that it wasn't suitable to keep living in her village. She and her daughters moved to a large town where they bought a fine house, and soon she became well known for her charitable gifts to the poor.

All sorts of poor people from all corners of the world visited her, drawn by her reputation for generosity. Among those who came was her own husband, who was still trying to gather enough money to pay for a circumcision feast.

The woman knew him at once, but he didn't recognize her because her appearance had changed with prosperity. Well, she handed him a substantial sum of money. When he saw it he stood amazed; no one had ever given him so much before. The woman said, "Don't be so surprised, sir. Take this and buy yourself some fine clothes; then come back and help us celebrate the Sabbath."

And that's what he did. When he returned, she welcomed him, seated him at the head of her table, and asked him to bless the wine.

Her children looked on, wondering, but they said nothing. When the stranger had finished blessing the wine, the woman served him two large pieces of fish, well peppered and salted, and then other fine dishes: soup, meat, stew. The poor man downed everything and relished every bite.

When the meal was over, she showed him to a room where he could spend the night. Then she made up her own bed and went to sleep. But in the middle of the night the poor man awakened with a powerful thirst, so he left his room and stumbled about in the dark, searching for water.

The woman called to him, "Sir, what are you looking for?"

"For something to drink," he replied.

"Come here," she said. "I'll give you something to drink."

So he went into her room, where she poured a glass of wine and handed it to him. He drank and smacked his lips. Then he said, "That's a mighty tasty drink. What is it?"

She replied,

> *"The drink is wine*
> *And you are mine,*
> *And I am thine."*

And in the morning she told her children, "This is your father."

103

Skotsl Kumt: Skotsl's Here

You know that among Yiddish speakers, the expression *Skotsl kumt,* "Skotsl's here," is used by women to greet another woman when she comes into the house. Would you like to know its origin? I'll tell you a story that will explain it.

Once upon a time the women complained that everything in the world belonged to men. Men got to perform the *mitsves,* the religious commandments; they got called to read from the Torah. In short, they got to do everything. As for the women, they got nothing. No one paid them any attention at all. So they decided to form a deputation that would take their complaint to the Lord of the Universe.

But how was it to be done? Well, they decided that they would heap women up in a pile, one on top of the other, until the woman at the very tip could pull herself into heaven.

The first thing they did, then, was to dig a pit in which one of the woman knelt. Then other women climbed on her, one on top of the other. At the top of the pile was Skotsl. Because she was both very clever and a skillful speaker, she was chosen as the one to talk with the Lord of the Universe.

Everything went well as the women were climbing onto each other. But just as Skotsl reached the top, the hunchbacked woman at the base of the pile twisted about, and the women came tumbling down. Well, of course there was nothing but noise and confusion, with everyone trying to locate everyone else. But Skotsl was nowhere to be found, though they searched for her everywhere. And so there was no one who could be counted on to talk with God, and the situation of the women remained unchanged. Everything still belonged to the men.

But from that time on, women have not lost their hope that one day Skotsl will come. And that's why, whenever a woman comes into a house, they call out joyfully, *"Skotsl kumt,* Here comes Skotsl," because who knows—one day she might really be there.

104
The Clever Little Tailor

Once upon a time in a small town there lived a tailor who wanted to be a singer—and not just a singer, but a cantor. One day his employer said, "I'll tell you what. If you can beguile the animals of the forest with your fine singing, I'll see to it that you become a cantor."

"All right," said the tailor, and off he went into the forest, singing. He sang and sang but not one animal responded. So he thought the matter over and decided to build a little wooden hut. A round hut with an attic. And when he had finished, he set out a great heap of meat in the downstairs room while he hid in the attic. As it happened, a passing hungry wolf smelled the meat. Approaching the hut, he saw that no one was there, so he went in and ate meat to his heart's content. When he was full, he lay down to rest.

Then the tailor came down from the attic and said, "Wolf, wolf, how would you like to become a porter?"

"I'd like that very much," said the wolf, "but I don't know how."

"Come," said the tailor. "I'll show you." He led the wolf outside and then up to a pile of stones. "Wolf," he said, "turn around with your shoulders toward me and I'll show you how to become a porter." The wolf did as he was told. He turned around with his shoulders toward the tailor. The tailor filled a sack with the stones and then, when he had tied the sack to the wolf's shoulders, he ran off. The wolf tried to follow but couldn't and began a dreadful howling.

Well, the tailor left him there howling and ran back to his attic, where he lay down and waited. As he lay there, a hungry bear came by and smelled the meat. Approaching the hut, he saw that no one was there, so he went in and ate meat to his heart's content. When he was full, he lay down to rest.

Then the tailor came down from the attic and said, "Bear, how would you like to become a musician?"

"I'd like that," said the bear, "but I have crooked fingers so I can't hold a fiddle properly."

"Come with me," said the tailor. He led the bear to a village near a mill where there were huge round stones with clamps screwed into them. "Put your hands into the clamps," he said to the bear, "and I'll straighten your fingers so you can become a musician." The bear did what he was told, and the tailor turned the screws until the bear's paws were held tight. Then the tailor ran away. The bear tried to run after him, but he couldn't get his paws loose. So he set up a dreadful yowling.

Well, the tailor left him there yowling and ran back to his attic, where he hid and waited. As it happened, a hungry fox passed by and smelled the meat. Approaching the hut, he saw that no one was there. But a fox is very sly, and so he thought, "Shall I go in or not?" Still considering the matter, he opened the door and went in. He saw that there was no meat left, though he could still smell it, and started to leave. But the tailor hurried down and grabbed his tail. "Fox," he said, "how would you like to be a cantor?"

The fox replied, "No, I wouldn't. What kind of a fool do you take me for?" And with that he yanked himself away so hard that his tail came off in the tailor's hands. The fox, now without a tail and in pain, ran off, planning revenge against the tailor. "Well," he thought, "I can't do much by myself, but I'll get all my animal friends together and we'll teach him."

The fox met a bird that said, "Why are you so unhappy?"

The fox replied, "Because the tailor tore my tail off when I said I didn't want to become a cantor."

The bird said, "Never mind. There's a remedy near at hand. Dip yourself in that nearby stream, and your tail will grow again." The fox did as he was told and his tail grew out again. Then he ran off to call his friends together so that they could get even with the tailor. As he ran, he came upon the wolf who was unable to move because his back was loaded with stones. The fox said, "What's the matter with you?"

The wolf replied, "The tailor has turned me into a porter."

The fox laughed, "Ah, fool that you are. The tailor is a cruel fellow, and this was his way to keep you from eating him up." With that he untied the sack of stones and took them off the wolf's shoulders, after which they ran along together. As they ran, they came upon the bear who stood with both of his forepaws clamped between the millstones.

"What's the matter with you?" they asked.

"The tailor has turned me into a musician," replied the bear.

"Ah, what a fool you are," they laughed. "The tailor was simply afraid you would scratch him with your claws, and so he clamped your paws between the stones." They released the bear, and then all three of them ran to find the tailor.

The tailor, seeing the animals running angrily toward him, thought of a way to fool them once again. He unbuckled his belt and dropped his trousers. Then he tied the torn-off fox's tail to his own naked bottom. He turned around with his bottom toward the animals and began to wiggle the tail. The animals, who had never seen a creature like that before, were frightened and took to their heels until they were back in the forest.

When the tailor saw that, he returned to his employer and told him everything he had done. The employer laughed and laughed, and then saw to it that the tailor became a cantor, in a peasant village named Mara Tiara. And that's that.

Two Tunes for Three Hundred Rubles

In a small town once, there was a man who had a daughter for whom he wanted to make a match. When a young scholar was proposed to him, he offered three hundred rubles as dowry and three years of *kest,* room and board. The terms of the marriage contract were agreed to and the marriage took place.

After the wedding, the young husband lived with his wife at his in-laws' home and continued his studies. When the three years were over, the wife said, "We can't keep living in my parents' house. Why don't you go into some sort of business?"

"What sort of business?" asked the husband.

"My father has a horse and wagon," said his wife. "He'll let you have them and you can be a trader in the villages."

The young man took the three hundred rubles, harnessed the wagon, and went off to buy and sell things in the villages. On the outskirts of town he saw a shepherd tending his sheep. The shepherd was singing a little melody:

The young husband listened to the tune and thought, "If I buy that melody, I'll be able to sell it to the cantor in town for three times what I will have to pay for it." So he got down from his wagon and said, "Shepherd, how much do you want for that melody?"

"A hundred and fifty rubles," was the reply.

The scholar paid the money without hesitation. Then he got back into his wagon, took the reins in his hands, and called out, "Giddyap."

And so he went on his way.

As he drove along, he met a cowherd who was pasturing oxen. The cowherd was piping a lovely melody on his flute:

The young husband reined in his horse and thought, "If I put the two melodies together, I'll make three times whatever they cost me." So he asked the cowherd, "How much do you want for that melody?" And the cowherd replied, "I want a hundred and fifty rubles."

The young man slapped his hand against his forehead and cried, "Oh dear, I'll spend all of my wife's dowry and have to return empty-handed."

Just the same, he paid over the money, took the melody, got back on his wagon, and drove off, crying "Giddyap."

When he got home it was almost dawn. As he drove along, he remembered that a man named Berish the Tailor lived nearby. "Hmm," he thought. "I know what I'll do. I'll go to Berish the Tailor and get him to stitch the two melodies together. Then I'll sell them to the town cantor for twice as much money."

He went to the tailor's window and knocked. "Reb Berish," he called, "Open up."

The tailor cried, "Who's that knocking at my window?"

"It's me, Moyshe," he said.

"What do you want?" asked the tailor.

"I want you to do some stitching for me." And he sang:

"Is that it?" asked the tailor.

"No," he said, "I have more."

"What else?"

And so he sang:

Reb Berish unwound his measuring tape and heated his pressing iron. Then he cut and stitched and ironed the two melodies. The young man paid him a few groshn, got back on his wagon, and drove home.

When he came to the house, he knocked at the door and called, "Get up, Sorele. It's me, your husband, I'm back."

So she got up and came running to the wagon to see what sort of merchandise he had bought. Finding the wagon empty, she asked "Where is the merchandise?"

"I have it," he said.

"Where is it?" she asked.

And so he sang:

"That's what you bought?" she cried.
"No," he said. "There's more."
And so he sang:

Hearing that, she ran wailing to her father. "I've got to divorce that husband you gave me," she cried. "He took the three hundred rubles of my dowry and gave them away for a couple of melodies."

Her father ran to the rabbi, who sent for the young man and his wife. The rabbi asked the young man, "What did you do with the money?"

"Dear Rabbi, I made a purchase."

"What did you buy?"

And so he sang:

The rabbi said, "That's all you bought?"

"No," said the young man, "there's more."

"What else?"

And so he sang:

And so the rabbi gave her the divorce.

Some True Miracles of God

Once there was a poor *melamed* whose shrewish wife made life miserable for him. One day when he came back from reciting evening prayers at the synagogue, his wife poured out a torrent of abuse while she was serving his dinner. Finally he could take it no longer. "I can't stand your howling!" he cried, and made up a bundle containing his *talis,* his *tfiln,* his gaberdine, and a couple of shirts. He put the bundle in a sack and took up his walking stick. When his wife had fallen asleep, he turned down the lamp, banked the fire in the hearth, kissed the *mezuze* on the door, and left home.

During the night his wife woke and saw that the door was unlatched and her unfortunate husband was gone. She concluded that he had left to bathe before saying his midnight prayers.

As the *melamed* went on his way, a snowstorm blew in on a strong wind. With the snow and wind in his face, he began to freeze. After a while it was impossible to go on, so he sat down to rest for half an hour, but the wind blew colder and colder. Finally he got up and went on his way, praying to God that he might come upon a settlement soon.

This time as he walked, he lost his bearings and reversed his direction. He thought he was going forward, but in fact he was retracing his steps. Since the wind now blew at his back, the *melamed* was grateful to God for coming to his help. But he continued to wish with all his heart that he might come to a village.

Walking quickly with the wind's help, he did arrive at a settlement. All the houses were dark except one, in whose windows a gleam of light showed. And that house was his own home, but the *melamed* didn't know it. He went up to the window and knocked, calling, "Please, please. Won't you let me in? I'm a poor man, frozen through." His wife recognized his voice at once, but she pretended she didn't know him. She let him in and made up a bed with a warm feather comforter near the stove.

The poor fellow undressed and thanked God for His mercy. His wife put out the lamp. An hour or so later, she took her place beside him and before he knew it, the *melamed* felt himself to be truly fortunate. He had a good bed and more besides.

When he woke in the morning and looked around, and saw that he was in his own home in bed with his own shrew of a wife, he laughed out loud and said, "Blessed are the ways of the Lord."

· · ·

PART SIX

Sages,
Tsadikim,
and
Villains:
Legends

My grandfather and I would sit in the old synagogue in the interval between early and late evening prayers, and we'd talk quietly. It was then that he would tell me legends about the ancient sages and later heroes, about important events that happened long ago and in more recent times.

        —Memoir from Berestetshke, Poland, 1925

The children of Hasidim would repeat the legends their fathers brought back from the rebbe's court, legends about the miracles wrought by these wonder-workers.

        —Memoir from Eastern Europe, ca. 1930

𝒯he stories in this section are all legends. Since they are mainly religious stories, it is not always easy to make a sharp distinction between them and the pious tales. Traditions that were once strongly attached to particular persons or places have tended to wander so that it is difficult to determine their original contexts. The characteristic difference between the two kinds of tales, however, is that while the pious tales were perceived as fiction, the style and tone of the legends clearly indicates that the tellers and their audiences believed that the tales were true.

The first group of legends in this section is centered on the wonder-working *tsadikim,* the saintly spiritual leaders of the Hasidic community. Hasidism is a pietistic mystical movement that emerged in the middle of the eighteenth century in the Ukrainian provinces of

Podolia and Volhynia. Later it spread into Polish Galicia, Rumania, Hungary, and throughout Eastern and Central Europe. Today its centers are in the United States and Israel. Numerous dynastic *hoyfn* (courts) were formed in Eastern Europe, and each court had as its central figure a disciple, or a descendant of a disciple, of the Baal Shem Tov (literally, Master of the Good Name), the founder of the movement. It was believed that through the extraordinary mystical powers of the *tsadek,* the charismatic spiritual leader, ordinary men could be brought closer to God. The central focus of Hasidic belief concerns God's omnipresence in all things and a wish to achieve unity with the divine by intense concentration and the abandonment of self.

Each court nourished legends that testified to the wondrous powers of the rebbes of its particular dynastic line, as well as to their special personal and philosophical characteristics. The mere telling of these legends was viewed as a mystical experience. It was not only a means of glorifying the *tsadikim* but also of sharing in their piety and power. The Baal Shem Tov is said to have claimed that recounting tales in praise of the *tsadikim* was like engaging in *ma'aseh merkava*— the mysteries of the heavenly throne and chariot. To tell a legend about a Hasidic rebbe became itself a religious act, a meritorious deed.[1]

For over two hundred years a rich oral storytelling tradition flourished in Hasidic courts. It became, and continues to be, part of the Sabbath ritual: Hasidic men still meet three times on the Sabbath to pray and attend communal meals. At the *melave malke,* the fourth meal, they gather at the rebbe's table to hear stories of Hasidic saints and sages. The *yortsayt,* anniversary, of the death of a rebbe, is another occasion for retelling the legends of his deeds. Of course the legends are also exchanged informally and casually in daily conversation and at the *shtibl,* the small Hasidic House of Prayer.

Typically, Hasidic legends are short. They contain only one episode, which is related in a linear fashion with no suspense. Some are told as eyewitness accounts, as "true" hagiography. For example, "A Modern Miracle" begins: "My father, may he rest in the light of paradise, loved to tell this tale about the Rebbe of Nizkhizh. Though it wasn't really a tale, but something that actually happened to him." Other legends, like "The Baal Shem Tov and the Herdsman," may tell more about the Hasidic worldview than about actual events. Some are told in the "enigmatic mode," like "Rebbe Malkiel and the 702 Candles," so that the truth will be veiled from the eyes of scoffers.

As a group, the legends offer a garland of praise to these revered spiritual leaders. In some the tellers express awe at a rebbe's superior faculties and unusual powers, ranging from mystic capacities to sympathetic magic. The rebbe is depicted as behaving in mysterious ways. In "The Boy Who Put Two Socks on One Foot," for example, he can foresee the outcome of future events and has power to influence them. Like "The Fleet-Footed Tomeshef Rebbe," he can traverse huge distances in the wink of an eye. He can be in two places at once; he can even ascend to heaven while remaining on earth.

These narratives also serve to give comfort. They catalogue the ordinary requests of the plain folk who traditionally came to the rebbe for help, as well as the fantasies they developed about how the rebbe might reverse their fortunes through a miracle. Like the pious tales, these legends deal most often with the mundane concerns of the adult world: a mean landlord, a well that goes dry, the hope for a child. The rebbe acts as helper and intermediary between God and men in these everyday trials. He hears the pleas of childless couples and prays for their fertility; he helps a woman in childbirth, and a child left alone. As in "The Curious Disciple," he gives aid to troubled petitioners in their dealings with local squires and landlords.[2] Curiously, it was not only the Hasidim who believed in the magical powers of the rebbes. According to An-ski, "In many villages, gentile peasants adopted the beliefs in wonder-working rebbes. It frequently happened that peasants would come to a rebbe with a *pidyen,* a petition for children . . . for good crops."[3] Thus, in "Rain and the Rebbe of Stolin," peasants seek the rebbe's help in a drought.

Hasidic rebbes are teachers of religious precepts and proper conduct, and some Hasidic legends contain motifs found in pious tales.

A rebbe can, for example, be an admonisher, or a punisher, of the greedy, the stingy, the skeptics, disciples who go astray, or those who engage in scholarly nitpicking. He is not above being punished himself if he insists on satisfying his curiosity when that is forbidden.

From the anti-Hasidic camps come tales that poke fun at the so-called miracle workers. Both the traditionalist anti-Hasidic *misnagdim* as well as the modern enlightened *maskilim* scoffed at the supernatural powers attributed to the Hasidic rebbes. Amusing as such tales might be, the collectors of Yiddish oral legends tended to concentrate more on the Hasidic than the anti-Hasidic tales.

In the second group of legends presented in this section, the typical hero is a Biblical or post-Biblical rabbinic figure, a man who excels in scholarship and piety.[4] Our sampler includes legends about Moses; Judah Halevi, the twelfth-century religious philosopher and poet; Rabbi Isaiah Horowitz, the seventeenth-century Cabalist; the Vilna Gaon, an eighteenth-century spiritual and intellectual leader; Jonathan Eybeschuetz, an eighteenth-century Talmudist; and Moses Schreiber, a nineteenth-century religious scholar.

Such legends may open with an attribution like: "This is the story that Rabbi Joshua ben Levi tells," or "I heard this from my father when I was a boy." This sort of opening serves to authenticate the veracity of the legend. There are numerous descriptions in the memoir literature of the *kheyder*-teacher who tells legends to the children about figures of the Bible "as if he had known them personally."[5] Among the favorite themes are disputes over matters of faith, unjust acts followed by penance, and Messianic longings. Some of the tales tell of the hero's humility, or his exceptional kindness and humaneness; others treat his awesome wisdom or his ability to deal directly with the supernatural.

Such tales had a rich resonance both for rabbinic traditionalists as well as for Hasidim. In these tales, as Abraham Joshua Heschel puts it, "The present moment overflowed its bounds, since people lived not chronologically, but in a fusion of past and present. They lived with the great men of the past, not only in narrating tales about them, but also in their emotions and dreams. Jews studying the Talmud felt a kinship with its sages. . . . In their souls, simple Jews were always prepared to welcome the Messiah."[6]

Our section closes with several Yiddish legends about secular historical figures. The heroes and villains are the politically and economically mighty: czars, emperors, and financiers. Often they appear unexpectedly and in disguise, not unlike Elijah the Prophet in the pious tales. Some of these legends reflect the actuality of East European Jewish life: the edicts that restricted legal rights, residence, and choice of occupation; the conscription laws which forced many Jewish soldiers to give up their religion.

The two legends about Czar Nicholas the First, "The Cantonist's Mother and Czar Nicholas the First" and "Czar Nicholas Decrees the Burning of the Talmud," show him as beneficent in one case and villainous in the second. History tells us that this nineteenth-century despot should not have been a positive figure in any Jewish legend. But legends, like tales told as fiction, may reveal fantasies. A mother whose son was inducted into the army at the age of twelve for twenty-five years of service may well have hoped for a miracle. She may have dreamed that the very czar who signed the inhumane conscription edict would take pity on her and free her son—if only he got to know her personally.

Legends about the much-loved Emperor Franz Josef of Austria, on the other hand, were always positive. Not only did his 1849 Constitution grant Jews civil and political rights, but his refusal to confirm the appointment of an anti-Semitic mayor in Vienna in 1895 was remembered with appreciation.

Yiddish lore about Napoleon Bonaparte was also current into the twentieth century. One memoirist from Gordz in Lithuania writes: "Some of the children of the higher grades in *kheyder* were proficient in telling wonderful legends about Napoleon which they had heard from their fathers and brothers."[7] As late as 1939, ethnographers collected numerous items of Jewish folklore—some favorable, some unfavorable—about Napoleon, including legends, jokes, games, and songs.[8]

The financier Rothschild was another subject of both legend and folksong. As suggested by the three short pieces included here, he did not fare too well in either genre. In fact, the last tale in this section cheerfully kills him off in his countinghouse.

Sabbath in Paradise

Once there was a *tsadek,* who was on a journey somewhere. I think his name was Reb Elimeylekh. Well, he traveled and traveled but couldn't seem to get anywhere. Since the Sabbath was creeping up on him, Reb Elimeylekh sent his *shames,* his assistant, to look for the right road. Several hours went by, and still the *shames* had not returned. It was getting dark, so Reb Elimeylekh began to pray with great passion, the way such a *tsadek* does. His prayers resounded to the heavens.

Just then he saw a man coming and felt a bit better, because it meant that he must be near a settlement. The man approached and asked him if he wanted to spend the Sabbath with him. To which Reb Elimeylekh replied, "Well, why not?"

The man warned Reb Elimeylekh that when they got where they were going, he must not ask questions. In fact no matter what he might see, he must not make the slightest sound. Well, as you can imagine, he had no choice but to agree. They went on their way, and Reb Elimeylekh saw a wonderful palace in the distance.

The man took him up to its door and opened it. The room inside was so beautiful that Reb Elimeylekh's eyes were dazzled. Then he heard music that seemed to be played by a fine band of *klezmer* musicians, and it was so lovely it almost overwhelmed him. The door opened, and several prayer quorums came in and began to sing with radiant faces.

An old man whose gray beard reached to his chest moved forward and recited the Sabbath service in such sweet tones that he seemed to be entirely transformed. Reb Elimeylekh was sorely tempted to ask him who all the people were, but remembering what his guide had told him, he said nothing. As they finished their prayers, the old man was given a golden goblet of wine. With smiling eyes he received the wine and blessed it. When he was done with the blessing, a woman's voice was heard to say, "Amen."

Later Reb Elimeylekh was led into a room even more beautiful than the first. He was seated beside other men at a table that had sparkling place settings. As for the food, his first bite sent a rush of pleasure coursing through his limbs.

When the meal was done, everyone at the table sang once more. Reb Elimeylekh was tempted again and again to ask what sort of place this was, but always he stopped himself, remembering what he had been told.

A while later his guide came over and said, "Follow me. I'll show you where to sleep." As he walked after the man, Reb Elimeylekh wondered whether he ought to say something now, but he restrained himself. The room into which he was led was so fragrant that he fell asleep at once.

It seemed that only a few hours had passed when he heard, as if in a dream, the singing of many birds. It was morning, and his guide soon appeared. Handing him a long shirt, he told Reb Elimeylekh that it was time to go to the bath. There he saw the men with whom he had eaten the night before. When Reb Elimeylekh descended into the bath, he couldn't feel the water's touch, that's how blissful it was.

Later he went back to pray, and heard the same melodies he had heard the day before. Then it was time to read from the sacred Book, and it occurred to Reb Elimeylekh that now, since Torah readers are called up by name, he would learn who his guide was. But when he heard them calling out "*Moyreynu Moyshe bar Amram,* Our Teacher, Moses, son of Amram, the sixth portion," he felt himself trembling. The next name he heard was *Dovid hameylekh,* King David. Then *Shloyme hameylekh,* King Solomon. When he heard *Avrom ovinu,* Our Father Abraham, being called to read the portion of the week, he was completely nonplussed. He wanted to say a few words to *Avrom ovinu,* but he restrained himself.

Later in the dining room they ate and sang. After that, Moses discoursed on the Torah, revealing such secrets as Reb Elimeylekh had never even dreamed of. The assembled company listened attentively, their faces bathed in light.

At dusk Reb Elimeylekh went to say his first evening prayers. When night fell, the old man, who was the Patriarch Abraham, made the *havdole* blessing marking the close of the Sabbath, and King David accompanied him with exquisite melodies on his violin.

After that several beautiful women entered and danced so well that everyone joined in. Then a voice called, "Quiet. The celestial council of justice is about to convene." Hearing that, Reb Elimeylekh was unable to contain himself any longer and cried out "Ah!"

At once everything disappeared. He found himself standing in an open field.

108
The Baal Shem Tov and the Herdsman

The Baal Shem Tov, of blessed memory, was very anxious to know who would be his neighbor in paradise. One Sabbath evening when, as usual, he experienced an ascension of the soul, he learned that it would be a man named So-and-So, the son of Such-and-Such, a complete unknown who lived in a small *shtetl* somewhere. The Baal Shem wondered what was the nature of the man's good deeds, that he was assured the kind of place in the World of Truth which he, the Baal Shem, had been able to earn only by an entire lifetime of sanctity.

Soon after the *havdole* service, he ordered Alexey, his coachman, to harness his horse. He rode off to the town where the man lived and inquired about him everywhere. But it seemed that no one knew him; Later, however, someone did remember that there was a person in town by that name. Still, the Baal Shem wouldn't be interested in him; he was a herdsman of some sort. A crude fellow. Hardly an observant Jew, though he was decent enough.

The Baal Shem disguised himself in ragged old clothes. That evening at the outskirts of town, on a street where Gentiles lived, he knocked at the door that had been pointed out to him. A woman opened it and asked what he wanted. The Baal Shem replied that he was a beggar on a long journey, and that he wanted a night's lodging.

When he was admitted, the Baal Shem saw a peasant's house, complete with white doors and doorposts to which no *mezuzes* were attached. Not the sort of place that would make a good impression on the Baal Shem. "Where is your husband?" he asked.

"Busy with the cattle," she replied irritably, then flung him a bit of black bread and pointed out a corner where he could sleep.

The Baal Shem leaned against a wall but found that he could not sleep. A little while later a rough fellow came in dressed like a peasant, with a coat made of pelts that was bound at the waist by a string. He carried a rude stick and a sack over his shoulder from which a peasant's flute protruded. "Evidently the man of the house," the Baal Shem thought.

Without so much as a "Good evening," the herdsman flung down his sack and stick. Then he sat on the floor and demanded his supper.

When he was done, he nodded toward the Baal Shem and asked his wife, "Who's that?"

The Baal Shem waited to see what would happen. When the man had eaten his bread and some groats—without washing his hands, without reciting a blessing—he took out his flute and played a melody. Then he flung himself down on the floor and went to sleep. Again without a blessing. Don't even ask whether he recited the bedtime prayer.

The Baal Shem watched him with amazement. "Well," he thought, "who knows? He may be a *lamedvovnik*. Perhaps he performs his holy work at night when everyone else is asleep."

That night, the Baal Shem didn't sleep a wink, afraid that he might miss the herdsman's holy labors. But the herdsman slept like a log and never left off snoring.

At dawn the herdsman got up and tied on his rope belt. He put a piece of bread into his sack and went off to drive his cattle to pasture. Did he wash his hands or recite any benediction? What a ridiculous question.

The Baal Shem was more and more perplexed. Just the same, he dressed and stole after the herdsman. In the field the herdsman sat down, opened his sack, and took out his bread. Raising his eyes to the heavens, he said, "Lord, I want to eat." Then he broke off a morsel of bread and ate it. That done, he lifted up his eyes again and said, "Dear Father in Heaven, thank You for giving me food. I wish there was some way I could serve You, but what can I do? I'm poor and untaught. Well, at least I can play You a little tune."

When he had played his flute for a while, the man lay down and slept until noon. Then he woke and said again, "Lord, I want to eat." He ate and played the flute some more.

At the end of that day the Baal Shem, in a very cheerful mood, returned to Mezhibuzh. There he told his disciples the story of the man who couldn't take a bite without acknowledging the Creator of the Universe. And later he added, "Well for the man who is destined to be his neighbor in Paradise."

1 0 9

Yisroel, the Child Rebbe

When the old Rebbe of Stolin, the grandfather of the present Rebbe, passed away, his son, Reb Yisroel of blessed memory, was still a little boy. Both are now in the world to come. Reb Yisroel died a few years back in Frankfurt-am-Main, which is why he was known as the Rebbe of Frankfurt.

He was (may he forgive these words from where he is now) something of a scamp. Though he had become the Rebbe, he used to chase about all day with other children, making mud pies and playing hide-and-seek and other such games. But all that to one side, people used to come from all over the world to consult him. He was, after all, the son of the Rebbe of Stolin. However hard they tried, though, they could never find him at home. He was always off somewhere—in the courtyard, in the garden, or God alone knows where.

One day a village innkeeper who was very unhappy came to consult the little Rebbe. Moved by some mad whim, his landlord, the local squire, had given the innkeeper three days to clear out of his domain. And neither tears nor such lamentations as would raise the dead would move him.

And so the innkeeper had come to the young Rebbe—who was nowhere to be found. Whenever they thought they had him, he just laughed and disappeared again. Well, the innkeeper hung around for two days without being able to talk to the Rebbe. Then heaven itself took pity on him and the Rebbe showed up in the garden, making mud pies.

The innkeeper approached and began to pour out his grief. "Woe is me, Rebbe. Advise me!" he cried. The boy did not answer, but dug holes in the ground and set sticks into them. "Dear Rebbe, what counsel shall I take away with me?" the innkeeper demanded. "You fool," the Rebbe said angrily, "don't you see these holes I'm digging?" The innkeeper caught an inkling of his meaning and went back home. There his wife ran to greet him, crying, "The wicked squire is dead, may his bones be scattered! He was careless as he was hunting and shot himself. We're saved."

110
The Disciple Who Went Astray

A former disciple paid a visit once to the Rebbe of Ostrovets. The Rebbe observed that the young man had changed in some way—something was amiss with him. The Rebbe asked him what had gone wrong. The disciple explained that while studying for his rabbinical examination he had begun to read secular books, and that they so absorbed him that he was neglecting his studies.

The Rebbe inquired, "Have you read one of those books today?"

"Yes," the disciple replied.

The Rebbe said, "Tell me what the story was about."

The disciple said, "Why should I trouble the Rebbe with an old wives' tale?"

But the Rebbe insisted, and so the disciple told the story. It was about a man on a journey who was terribly hungry because he had nothing to eat. He found a lump of iron that was as round as a head and covered with mud. He picked it up, but he couldn't eat it. He went on his way and came upon a man who was carrying a horse's head. And of course the head could be eaten. So he said, "Give me the horse's head, because I'm dying of hunger."

The other man said, "Let me have the lump of iron and I'll give you the horse's head."

And so the hungry man gave him the lump of iron and got the horse's head to eat.

The other man took the lump of iron home with him. After he scraped the mud off, he discovered that it was a lump of gold. He said, "If the other fellow had known that it was a lump of gold, he never would have made the trade."

The Rebbe said, "Do you know who that story is meant for? It's meant for you. You had a golden head, and you've traded it for the head of a horse."

111

The Rebbe's Melody

The Hasidim held that deep secrets of the Torah could be found hidden in melodies. According to the teller of this tale, it was said of Reb Shneyer Zalmen, the founder of Habad Hasidism, that before he sat down to his studies he would sing the following song:

> *All the angels, all the seraphim*
> *Ask who God may be.*
> *Ah woe, what can we reply?*
> *"No thought can be attached to Him."*
>
> *All the peoples—every nation—*
> *Ask where God may be.*
> *Ah woe, what can we reply?*
> *"No place is without Him."*

There is a third stanza, said the storyteller, but he could not remember it. Tradition has it that Reb Shneyer Zalmen wrote ten songs to accompany each of the ten mystical sfires, *the divine emanations in which God's creative power unfolds, according to Cabalistic doctrine. One of those melodies, widespread among the Hasidim, was known as "The Rebbe's Melody." And about it, the storyteller told the following tale.*

One Sabbath day Reb Shneyer Zalmen was explicating Torah to his disciples. As he spoke, he noticed an old man, a stranger to him, sitting tensely opposite him. The man was staring into the Rebbe's eyes and seemed to be trying desperately to understand what was being said, but it was clear from the grieving look on his face that he could not.

When the Rebbe retired into his study, he sent for the stranger and asked him if he had comprehended the day's discourse. The man wept as he replied that he had been unable to follow the holy words. He explained that he had been orphaned at an early age. And his mother had been too poor to keep him in primary school, because she needed his help in supporting the family. So he became a workingman, and later, when he married, he did not have time for Torah study because he was supporting his wife and children. "All I can do," he said, "is to recite the Psalms. And though I recite them daily, I don't understand them too well.

"Now in my later years, with my children grown and out of the house, I find myself drawn to the study of Torah, but the scholars in the synagogue laugh at me.

"And so, having heard that you befriend all men, I've come to sit at your table to study along with the others. It's made me very happy to be a man among men at last. But when you begin to explain the Torah and I can't understand what you're saying, my happiness curdles and my joy turns to grief.

"Rebbe, Holy Rebbe, tell me how to become worthy of studying with you. What must I do to understand the Torah?"

The man bowed his head and the tears streamed down his face. Reb Shneyer Zalmen put his hand on the man's shoulder and said gently, "No more tears. Today is the Sabbath and one may not be sad on the Sabbath.

"What you heard me explaining today was the Baal Shem Tov's conception of Hasidism. And if you haven't understood what I said in words, I'll help you by singing a song. Listen, for all of the Baal Shem's thought is hidden in it."

And here Reb Shneyer Zalmen began to sing a sweet melody, one phrase after another. The man listened as if he had been turned into a pillar of attention. Not so much as an eyebrow moved. And the more the Rebbe sang, the brighter was the glow in the man's face. He felt his soul being transported. A warm flush of happiness surged through him. When the Rebbe finished singing, the man cried out, "Rebbe, I understand, I understand. Ah, Rebbe, I feel worthy now to be your student."

And from then on, it was the Rebbe's custom to sing that melody at the conclusion of his discourses as a way of clarifying them, just in case there was someone at his table who could not fully understand his words.

And the melody is known to this day as "The Rebbe's Melody."

112

Don't Go into the Mud in the First Place

When the Rebbe of Radzin was still quite a young man, he came into his *shtibl* one day and found a couple of Hasidim engaged in an intense scholarly debate, which they could not bring to a conclusion. Because the Rebbe of Radzin was famous for his scholarship, they asked him to decide between them. Instead, he told the following tale:

Once a group of wagon drivers sat talking at an inn. As often happens, the oldest of them presided over the conversation. And now he pointed at a young man and asked, "Who is that young fellow?"

"He's a young wagon driver," was the reply.

"Come here, my son," the old driver said. "Tell me, what do you do when your horses draw your wagon into the mud?"

"You put a lever under the rear axle and lift the wagon out," replied the young man.

"Oho, clever lad," said the oldest driver. "But what happens if the lever sinks into the mud as well?"

"You take a beam and put it under the lever."

"Clever. Oh, very clever. And you call yourself a wagon driver? If you've got a lever and a beam, there's no problem. But what if you don't have either?"

The young man stood silent, unable to reply.

"I'll tell you what," the old wagon driver said. "A good driver doesn't let his horses pull the wagon into the mud in the first place."

And with that the Radzin Rebbe showed the two scholars how deeply they had sunk into the mire.

1 1 3
The Missed Moment of Redemption

The Rebbe of Kaliv was one of the greatest of the Hungarian Rebbes. On the anniversary of his death Jews were granted the privilege of traveling to Kaliv by train free of charge. All they had to do was show a certificate from the city council.

It happened once that the Rebbe of Vizhnits sent three of his disciples to Kaliv for the Passover holiday. When they arrived and made their way to the Rebbe's house, they found him outside chopping wood. They greeted him in the usual fashion, and the Rebbe honored them with the task of carrying in the wood. That, he said, would make them worthy of sharing his Passover meal.

They carried in the wood and waited impatiently for the holiday celebration to begin. Certainly the Vizhnits Rebbe would not have sent them such a great distance on Passover evening for nothing. They sat around the *seyder* table expectantly. The Rebbe, smiling the same sort of enigmatic smile as when he had bidden them carry wood, sat down with them. Then a Gentile boy and girl arrived and helped themselves to the Passover wine, after which all three, the Rebbe and the boy and girl, danced a cheerful dance, a *freylekhs,* together. They danced off into another room while the Vizhnits disciples looked at each other in dismay. What had they fallen into? "It must be that we have stumbled into the company of Satan. May the Merciful One help us to survive this holiday."

The Rebbe came back and, looking pleased, inquired, "Well, how did you like them? Not a bad couple, eh? Do you approve of their betrothal?"

When they replied that they had not come to arrange any betrothals, the Rebbe became disconsolate and the service proceeded in silence.

After the first days of Passover, the disciples traveled home discontentedly. It goes without saying that they were also somewhat irritated with the Rebbe of Vizhnits, to whom they promptly reported the disturbing Passover they had had. "Ah," groaned the Rebbe, "fools that you are. Had you but approved of the betrothal, then the Redemption would have come. Because the two Gentiles, the boy and the girl, were actually the angels Michael and Gabriel."

114

The Mekarev Rebbe Gets Even with a Stingy Woman

Well, let me tell you a story that I myself heard some time ago from the old Rebbe of Mekarev, may he rest in peace. When it was time for me to do my military service, my mother, may she rest in peace, who was a follower of the Mekarev Rebbe, begged me to go with her to visit him. Well, at first I was reluctant, but finally she persuaded me. We came to the Rebbe's house and spent the Sabbath there. On Sabbath night the Rebbe presided over a large and densely packed company. I pushed my way through the crowd hoping to hear a few of the Rebbe's good words. And the Rebbe was telling some sort of tale—what it was illustrating, I can't remember. But what I'm going to tell you is word for word what I heard the Rebbe say.

"Gentlemen," said the Rebbe of Mekarev, "listen. This happened a few years ago. My *shames* and I were traveling and came to a nearby village." (The Rebbe gave the name of the village, but I can't remember it just now.) "We stayed at an inn for a few days. The innkeeper's wife, a mother of six daughters, asked me to pray that she might bear a son. If she had a son there would be someone to say *kadesh,* the mourner's prayer, for her and her husband when the time came. Well, I agreed to pray for her and she promised me eighteen rubles in payment for my help.*

"A year went by and Czar Nicholas issued an edict which, you may remember, forbade Jews to travel. Well! A royal decree. Several years went by and, of course, we did not travel. But then the decree was canceled. During the period when we were not permitted to travel, I learned that the innkeeper's wife had, with God's help, given birth to a son. So I sent my *shames* to the village to ask for the eighteen rubles. The innkeeper's wife carried on at a great rate and absolutely refused to pay. 'These are hard times,' she said. 'We can't pay. I'll send the money when things get better.'

"Well, what can you do? Curse her? After all, she's the mother of small children. Curse the child? Why? What have I got against the child? So I prayed that God would send her twins the following year. And the good Lord complied. Miraculously, she gave birth to twins. Not a month later, the innkeeper's wife hurried in to see me, crying, 'Rebbe! Be good enough to pray for me. Ask the good Lord not to send me any more sons—or daughters either. Here,' she said, with tears in her eyes, 'here are the eighteen rubles I promised you. Take them.' "

And that's the sort of holy men there were in those times. Where do you find their like today?

* Eighteen is considered a lucky number in Jewish lore. The letter value of the number eighteen can be represented in Hebrew as the word *khay,* meaning "life."

115

The Happy Pair and the Baal Shem Tov

A stingy tavern keeper who leased his tavern and a mill from the local nobleman had a manservant and a maidservant who were in love. The young couple could not marry because they did not have enough money. The maidservant had fifty rubles all told; and the manservant had fifty rubles all told. Each of them was saving the money for when they would marry.

In a nearby village there was a Jew who could not pay the rent on his house, and the nobleman decreed that he must hang. The man appealed to the Jewish community, crying, "Will you see me hanged for fifty rubles?"

No one came forward to save him, however, and the day came when the poor man was to die. Minutes before the hanging, the two servants cried, "Stop! We'll pay the fifty rubles." And thus the man was rescued from certain death.

Someone went to the Baal Shem Tov and told him the story, but he said, "I know about it. I'm going to see them tomorrow."

The next day the Baal Shem Tov arrived in the village and had himself driven to the tavern where the two servants worked. When he had eaten and drunk, the Baal Shem turned to the young couple and asked them why they were still unmarried. The maidservant said, "We don't have enough money." And she started to tell him the story of the fifty rubles.

The Baal Shem said, "I know all about that. But do you still want to marry this young man?"

She replied, "What's the good of saying I want to, if we haven't got the wherewithal?"

The Baal Shem Tov said, "I'll see to it that you're married." And he took them into town and saw to it that they were properly clothed, and then bought them whatever else they might need for their marriage.

At the wedding the Baal Shem asked the stingy tavern keeper what he would give the couple as a wedding present. The tavern keeper replied, "I can't give them anything. I have children of my own, and who knows what will happen to me later in life? I can't deprive my children of their inheritance."

"In that case," said the Baal Shem to the tavern keeper, *I'll* give them wedding presents in your name. I'll give them the tavern and the mill."

This remark struck the man as so farfetched that he simply ignored it and walked off.

After the wedding the Baal Shem Tov invited the couple to come home with him. He told them to take a good deal of food with them. Then, just as they started out, the Baal Shem Tov suddenly disappeared, and the young couple were left alone in the countryside.

They walked and walked until they were in the middle of a forest. There they heard someone groaning. They went closer and the groaning got louder and louder. Suddenly, they came upon a pit and there in the pit lay a man and a horse. When the man saw the couple he said very weakly, "I'm hungry." So the couple threw food down to him until he had eaten his fill and grown strong enough to climb out of the pit.

Well, how was it that the man and the horse happened to be there? As it turned out, he was the son of the nobleman who owned the tavern run by the stingy tavern keeper. The nobleman's son had been missing for three days and was being sought everywhere. He had been on his way someplace when he fell into the pit, and if it had not been for the young couple, he would certainly have died of hunger.

Well, they all rode together to the nobleman's house, and what celebration there was! The young nobleman told the whole story of how the couple had rescued him from death. In the evening, there was a great banquet, and the young nobleman's mother called to the assembled company, "Let me have your advice. What shall I give the couple who rescued my son from death?"

All the people shouted, "Let them have the mill and the tavern!"

And so the stingy tavern keeper and his family had to leave their home and become beggars, while the former servants took over the tavern and the mill and became very rich.

But that's not the end of the story. The Baal Shem Tov wanted to test whether they still had any memory of their earlier lives as poor folk. So he came to their village, but before entering their house he lay down in a puddle and got himself thoroughly dirty.

When he came into the house, a servant girl cried, "Get out of here. Just look at you, what a filthy mess you are." The former maidservant, hearing this, came running in and scolded the servant girl and asked the man to come inside and brought him food at once.

Then the disguised Baal Shem said that he wanted a place to sleep, and the former maidservant prepared a bed for him. The Baal Shem said, "I'm not going to undress; I'm going to get into bed wrapped in my coat."

"Well," said the innkeeper's wife, "never mind, just go to sleep. If the sheets get dirty, we'll wash them."

The next morning, after the Baal Shem Tov had eaten the breakfast the innkeeper's wife served him, he told the couple who he was. He blessed them with happiness and abundance, then disappeared.

That's the sort of thing the Baal Shem Tov used to do.

1 1 6

The Fleet-Footed Tomeshef Rebbe

The butchers of Tomeshef were traveling homeward on a certain Friday evening. When night began to fall, they calculated how much farther they still had to go, and they realized that even if they had horses fleeter than winged serpents, they would not arrive until after the lighting of the Sabbath candles.

As they rode through the forest some seven kilometers from Tomeshef, they saw Reb Yisrulishl, the Rebbe of Tomeshef, making his way home. They introduced themselves and offered him a seat in their wagon. But he refused, saying, "Go on, go on. I won't ride with you, but you'd better go swiftly or you'll not arrive until after the blessing of the Sabbath candles."

The butchers were loath to leave him there, knowing that if it became known in Tomeshef that they had left the Rebbe in the woods, the people might be angry enough to stone them. But the Rebbe stubbornly refused to ride with them. The butchers, seeing that nothing they said made any impression, had to drive off without him.

They had traveled hardly half a kilometer when remorse overwhelmed them, so they rode back to the Rebbe and tried once again to persuade him.

But all for nothing. And this time they drove off as fast as they could, meaning to report in Tomeshef that they had seen the Rebbe in the woods. Perhaps someone else would ride out to get him.

When they reached Tomeshef, they found the Sabbath candles burning everywhere. And when they neared the Rebbe's house, they were stunned by the sight of him pacing back and forth on his footbridge.

117
The Right Order Is Important

There was a certain rich man named Shimen Goldtsvayg whose children all died. Once Reb Shmelke came to Rusmoldavi, where he stayed in the home of Goldtsvayg's father-in-law. Goldtsvayg too came there for the Sabbath. Reb Shmelke received Goldtsvayg's petition and asked him, "What is it you want?" "Rebbe, I'd like to have children that will live." "I understand. The problem is this: you've committed a sin. You married the younger of two sisters before the older one was married, and that's forbidden. But you can resolve the problem. Let your wife's older sister move in with the two of you, give her a dowry, and see that she gets married. Then you'll have children that survive." The rich man did everything the Rebbe told him to do, and his wife gave birth to children that lived.

118

Reb Khaim Urbakh Rocks a Cradle on Yom Kippur

Some eighty years ago Reb Khaim Urbakh was the Rebbe of Lentshits. People said that he used to rise at midnight to study and pray with Elijah the Prophet. There was also a story told about him:

Once, on Yom Kippur eve, as he was on his way to recite the *kolnidre* prayer, he heard weeping from a home on the Jewish street. He went into the house and found a child crying while a girl slept nearby. The Rebbe sat down and rocked the cradle.

Meanwhile at the synagogue people were getting worried because the Rebbe had not been seen. The *shames* ran out to look for him. After hunting for a long while, he finally found him beside the child whom the Rebbe had rocked to sleep.

It was from that time that the Rebbe forbade women to go to *kolnidre*.

119

Rain and the Rebbe of Stolin

Yisroel Perlov of blessed memory, the Rebbe of Stolin, went out one fine morning to take a drive in his carriage. As he was riding along, he passed through a village. When the Gentiles in the place realized that it was the Rebbe, a huge crowd gathered, a crowd so dense it became dangerous. The whole village was there, and the people prostrated themselves before the Rebbe's carriage and would not let him pass.

The Rebbe was astonished, "For heaven's sake," he said, "what is it you want?"

"Holy Rabbi," came the tumultuous answer from the crowd, "we will not let you pass until you promise us rain. It's nearly three months since we saw any rain. We're exhausted for lack of water. Everything has dried out: the grain in the fields, our cattle in their stalls. And we have turned gaunt watching them."

The Rebbe stood, quietly thoughtful, then he looked up at the sky, after which he gestured toward the crowd. "You may go back to your homes. Tomorrow there will be rain." Then he drove off. When people got up the following morning, they looked at the sky—not even a cloud. It was bright, clear. The sun was blazing. Eleven o'clock came; then twelve. It was nearly one, and still not the slightest trace of rain. What did it mean? What about the Rebbe's promise?

Suddenly around two o'clock a cloud appeared. The sky grew dark and it began to rain—a veritable deluge. For three days and three nights it poured, filling every lake and river and creek.

1 2 0
The Miracle of the Dry Well

The Rebbe of Vizhnits, Reb Mendele of blessed memory, was being driven out of his mind by a man who complained that he had built a house and bricked in a well, and it had all cost him a great deal of money, but there was no water in the well. One day the Rebbe said to him, "When I travel to Kosev to visit Reb Khaim, the route I take will be near your house. Remind me then."

When the time came for the journey, the Rebbe passed near the man's house at about the time of early evening prayers. The Rebbe interrupted his journey and said to the man, "I want to wash my hands. Dip up a ladle of water from your well for me."

"But Rebbe, the well is dry," said the man.

"Don't be a fool. Have you ever seen a well without water? Take your ladle and dip." Since it was the Rebbe's command, the man did as he was told, and indeed he drew up a ladle of water. The Rebbe washed his hands. "Now dip up a cup of water; I want a drink, too." The man drew up a full cup of water. The Rebbe drank—and from that time on there was always water in the well.

121

The Reincarnation of Queen Esther

The following took place in Khentshin at the court of the Rebbe of Khentshin, of blessed memory. It happened like this: There was for many years an idiot wandering about Khentshin who was called Mordkhe Mendl, the town fool. Like all such souls, he made his living by begging, and slept at night in the synagogue beside the stove. Then one night the news spread through the town that the idiot had died.

It goes without saying that nobody made much of a fuss over his death. Indeed, it occurred to no one to go to the funeral. But then a strange thing happened. The old Rebbe of Khentshin put on his *zhupitse,* his long satin coat, took his tall hat and his cane, and attended the funeral. All the while that the idiot was being buried, the Rebbe stood beside the grave with huge tears rolling down his face. His disciples, seeing him weep, were awestruck, but no one ventured to ask why he was crying. Not until several days later, when the Rebbe was presiding over his table, did any of them dare ask why he had wept at the grave of Mordkhe Mendl the fool.

The Rebbe gave a brief sigh and replied, "Let me tell you the story of what happened to my grandfather of blessed memory.

"A poor teacher, a very pious Jew, once lived in Khentshin. This Reb Borekh had a pale, sickly wife and a sweet little daughter named Esther. Reb Borekh was afflicted with a cough, and from time to time he brought up blood. But was there ever a poverty-stricken teacher who had time to devote to his own health? Well, our Reb Borekh's cough got continually worse, with more and more blood, and then one day he took to his bed, where he lay for several weeks getting progressively weaker, until the end finally came and Reb Borekh died. He left his wife and twelve-year-old daughter Esther to struggle for their bits of dry bread.

"Well, one misfortune after another overtook them. First Esther contracted smallpox. Over the months that the child's illness lasted, her mother spent the last of her few groshn and succeeded in rescuing her daughter from the Angel of Death. So Esther recovered, but her mother, as the result of long, sleepless nights, and days without food, became sick. At first she was not seriously ill, but later one of her lungs gave out and her situation became steadily worse. Good neighbors called the doctor, but God had something else in mind for her. After the mother had lain unconscious for a couple of weeks, she died.

"For the fully orphaned Esther a life of pain and grief began. At first people pitied her, but then they forgot her entirely. Well, hunger is a powerful force, and Esther was forced to beg for bread. Wherever she went she was given a few groshn, and that's how she lived.

"But when it was Friday night, the night before the Sabbath, Esther would light the candles she bought with the money she had collected begging. And this began to irritate various prosperous people: how is it that one who lives by begging does not buy herself a dress, or shoes? Instead, she lights finer-looking Sabbath candles than many well-to-do women.

"The wrath of the women was so great that they began to scant the money they gave her. But no matter how little Esther got, she bought candles for the Sabbath, even if it meant giving up food.

"Finally the prosperous women were so angry that they gave her no money at all. They decided to donate bits of bread or Sabbath *khale* instead. 'Now,' they said, 'let's see where the child gets her candles.' That Friday night, Esther's window was indeed dark. On Sabbath morning it seemed to them that her door had been closed for much too long. Because her windows were covered, no one could look in, but finally the neighbors decided to break the door down. And this is what they found: Esther the orphan lay dead. From all appearances, she had been dead for several hours."

Here the Rebbe paused. He sighed and went on: "And at the funeral on Sunday morning, my grandfather of blessed memory picked her grave plot out himself. And when she was buried, he delivered a fiery sermon that was part homily and part funeral oration. Whatever it was, my grandfather of blessed memory had never wept so much before in the course of a sermon. His disciples stood by, amazed, with tears in their eyes.

"Later when the Rebbe came home from the funeral, he told his intimates, 'Know that the biblical Queen Esther experienced no deprivation in this life. For that reason, the Celestial Council of Justice decreed that she must be reincarnated as the daughter of a poor man and endure hunger and die, so that her portion in the world to come might not, God forbid, be diminished in any way.' The Rebbe was silent, and there was silence in the room as well."

"After an interval he said, 'Do you see, my dear friends, how careful one must be of any soul? Because the very greatest of souls may find itself incarnated in the body of the most abject fool.' "

122

The Penitent and the Rebbe of Tshekhenove

A beautiful young woman from a good family hanged herself in a certain town one day. When she was cut down, people were unwilling to carry her home to her parents. So she was left lying before the gates of the cemetery, and the burial society was asked to appoint someone to sit with the body. It sent a young man who, sitting there all alone with her, was seized with lust and possessed the body. When he realized what he had done, he was overwhelmed with grief. He could find no peace. And the more he thought of what he had done, the more heavy-hearted he became. Unable to rest, he went to the great Rebbe of Tshekhenove and told him what he had done. The Rebbe said, "Step out of the house." The man went out and stood in the vestibule.

There he sank into a trance of some sort—a waking sleep—in which it seemed to him that he was running past towns and forests, mountains and valleys. He saw beasts and wondrous other things. And it seemed to him that he ran and ran, and the sweat poured down his face.

All at once he ran toward a city. And there, in that place, was a beautiful young woman hanging before the city gate. And the man who was on watch before the gate started toward the suicide to do what the young man himself had done. So the young man killed the watchman to keep him from violating the body.

He was terrified and wept, because he had committed one great sin and now he had committed a second.

Just then the door of the Rebbe's house opened and the young man was called back in. "Look at the clock," the Rebbe said. The young man looked. No more than an hour and a quarter had passed since he had left the Rebbe's chamber. "Well," said the Rebbe, "what did you see?" The young man told him everything and then wept. "Now, Rebbe, I've killed a human being."

"Console yourself," said the Rebbe. "It was not a man you killed. What you killed was the *yeytser-hore,* the evil passion that led you to your sin."

1 2 3
The Boy Who Put Two Socks on One Foot

There once was a tenant innkeeper who had no children. He used to go to his Rebbe and pester him again and again for a blessing that would produce a child. Finally the Rebbe said that in a year's time a son would be born. And the Rebbe added that he wanted to be informed when the child came.

And that's how it was. A year later the innkeeper's wife gave birth to a son, and on the same day the innkeeper went to the Rebbe and invited him to the circumcision ceremony. But the news made the Rebbe so unhappy that he wept. The innkeeper insisted on knowing why. The Rebbe replied, "Your son will have many virtues and will become a great Talmudic scholar, but on the day he learns to put on *tfiln* he will drown—unless you watch him very carefully. You will receive a warning sign on the day that he puts two socks on the same foot and then hunts for the second sock."

And that's how it was. When the boy was thirteen years old, he started to put on *tfiln*. His father went to the synagogue with him, and when they got home, the boy became confused and had to lie down. He took his clothes off and went to sleep. When he awoke, he put two socks on the same foot and started to search for the second sock. His parents, seeing this, were very frightened. So they locked him into a room, but he broke a window and got out.

When the parents saw the open window, they ran to find their son. He was on his way to the river, but they brought him home and locked him up again. It was a very hot day and he kept wailing and begging to be let out to go bathe—or at least to be given something to drink, because he was burning up with heat. But his parents were adamant and kept him in the room until nightfall.

At dusk when people went to the river to bathe, they saw two human, double-headed creatures emerge from the water wringing their hands. "Oh woe," they cried out, "it's already so late, and still he hasn't come." Then they vanished.

The bathers told the story in the village, and there they learned that the two-headed creatures were waiting for the innkeeper's son.

And that's how the innkeeper and his wife saved their son from drowning.

1 2 4
The Power of the Mourner's Prayer

Two young friends from the same town traveled to see the old Rebbe of Alexander, Reb Henekh of blessed memory. They arrived just as it was getting dark. The Rebbe greeted them, but ordered them to take the road to Lodz at once. He said that when they came to a fork in the road, they were to separate and each go a different way.

Both of the young men were frightened. The whole thing seemed very strange to them, especially the command to travel at night on an unknown road. But what could they do? They had the Rebbe's instructions.

They were even more afraid when they came to the fork and parted company. In order to make things a bit more cheerful, they agreed to call out to each other as they went their ways. And so they did, until neither of them could hear the other.

One of the young men went on for a couple of hours until he came to a village, where he spent the night. The other, however, lost his way in a forest. After a couple of hours he caught a glimpse of a light and went toward it. He found that it came from a hut, which he entered. But no one was there, and he sat down in a corner of the room and dozed off. He woke when he heard an old man and a peasant woman come in, and as he watched, they began to dance. They danced for a considerable time; then the old man brought in a bundle of straw, which he lighted, and burned himself and the woman up. When they were consumed, they reappeared and began to dance again. Then they burned themselves up once more. And this happened several times. Watching, the young man was so terrified that he fell asleep from sheer fright.

When he woke in the morning, he found that he was lying in the forest and that there was no sign of the hut. He went at once to the Rebbe and told him all that had happened.

The Rebbe said, "My son, I sent you on your journey so that you would learn what you need to know: that old man you saw dancing was your father. When he was alive, he used to sin with that peasant woman. You were a small child when he died, and before his death he asked me to do him a kindness and arrange that a pious act be performed on his behalf. Now, this scene you witnessed last night is repeated every night. And you are permitted to see it so you would understand why you must say the mourners' prayer, the *kadesh,* for him, and study a chapter of commentary from the Mishnah every day. Your acts of piety will help him.

From that time on, the young man performed those acts of piety.

1 2 5
The Curious Disciple

One of the disciples of Reb Khaskele came to Kozmir and complained bitterly that the local squire, the *porets,* was tormenting him about a debt. That he was threatening to drive him from his home unless the money was paid immediately. Reb Khaskele gave his disciple a letter addressed to the squire, and the Hasid rode away. On the journey he opened the letter and found nothing but blank sheets of paper. The minute he arrived home, he took the letter to the squire and watched as the squire opened it, looked at its contents, turned pale, and said, "Very well, I'll wait another month." At the end of the month, the Hasid paid the debt in full. Later the Hasid came to Reb Khaskele again, and the Rebbe said, "If you hadn't opened the letter, he would have forgiven you the entire debt."

1 2 6
A Common Piece of Earth

Reb Avrom HaMalekh, called "The Angel," had a number of opponents, *misnagdim.* Once an entire group of them arrived at his house to make fun of him. He knew what they were up to, so he stood at his window and looked out. They came in, but he did not turn around. Some hours passed before he greeted them. They asked, "Why were you looking out the window that way?" He replied, "I was looking at the mountain over there, wondering how a piece of common earth like that can give itself such airs."

1 2 7

Reb Malkiel and the 702 Candles

Reb Alter of Shtutsin used to tell the following story about Reb Malkiel the Rebbe of Lomzhe, the author of the *Divrey-Malkiel*.

One day Reb Malkiel lost his way on a journey. Because the Sabbath was rapidly approaching, it appeared that he would have to stop somewhere for the night. He noticed a hut some distance away and, drawing near, he was delighted to see a *mezuze* nailed to the doorpost. God had sent him to a Jewish home where he could spend the Sabbath.

He went into the hut and found a little boy playing on the floor and an old woman salting meat in preparation for the Sabbath meal. He said, "Tell me, may I spend the Sabbath here?"

The woman said loudly, "Yes."

"Where is your husband?" he asked.

"He is pasturing the cattle in the woods," she said.

In a while her husband came in, nodded at the woman, and greeted Reb Malkiel.

Sometime later, the woman blessed the Sabbath candles and they all seated themselves at the table. The man of the house made the prayer over the wine, as is the devout custom. He ate a bit of fish and a bit of meat and an olive-sized bit of the bread. After the meal he recited the blessings like a man of learning and then left the hut.

Reb Malkiel asked, "Where has your husband gone?"

The wife replied, "He's spending the night in the woods with the cattle." This struck Reb Malkiel as mysterious, and in general the husband gave him a strange feeling. In appearance his host seemed to be an unlettered workingman, but he had spoken his prayers and the blessing over the wine very much like a man of learning.

When the household was asleep, Reb Malkiel went to the bedside of the couple's little boy and gave him a chain, a button, and other such shiny things that attract children. Then he said, "Show me where your father has gone."

"All right," the boy replied and led him to the woods. There they came to a cellar. The boy said, "In that cellar you'll find a little door. If you open the door, you'll see a room. My father is inside it."

Reb Malkiel took the boy home and then returned to the cellar. When he opened the door, he was startled to see a number of people sitting around a table on which were 702 lighted candles. And every sort of good food was on the table, and at its head sat the man who had been Reb Malkiel's Sabbath host. When the company saw Reb Malkiel, everyone stood up.

Reb Malkiel's host, looking at him, opened a sacred text and pointed to it. He said "You see where it is written, 'It is forbidden to inquire too deeply.' "

Reb Malkiel stayed with that company for the whole of the Sabbath, and on Sunday he went home. In Lomzhe he made inquiries about his host and was told that in winter the man sold bundles of logs and in summer he sold sand. But poor as he was, when he went to buy an *esreg,* a citron, before the Succos holiday, he always said, "Give me the best *esreg* you have and I'll pay whatever you ask."

The more Reb Malkiel discovered about the man whose guest he had been for the Sabbath, the clearer it became that he had been in the home of a *lamedvovnik,* one of the thirty-six hidden saintly men without whose merits the world could not continue to exist.

128

A Modern Miracle

My father, may he rest in the light of paradise, loved to tell this tale about the Rebbe of Nizkhizh. Though it wasn't really a tale, but something that actually happened to him.

It occurred soon after my grandfather was married, when he was perhaps thirteen years old and still living in his father-in-law's home. One day his father-in-law, who was a disciple of the Rebbe of Nizkhizh, decided to take a trip to visit his Rebbe. He took his son-in-law along, so that he might introduce him.

Off they went. Well, they arrived in Nizkhizh, settled into a rooming house, rested a while, and then went to see the Rebbe. The warden of the synagogue, seeing them, ushered them right in.

Oh yes . . . I nearly forgot the main thing. My father was wearing a new pair of lacquered boots, made to order. Now, lacquered boots were not considered Jewish dress, but something aristocratic, *daytsh-merish*—that is, strictly for westernized moderns. But as an only son my father was much indulged; nothing was too good for him.

Well then, they walked in to see the Rebbe, and the boots went squeak, squeak, squeak. Step, squeak. Step, squeak. Well, never mind. They approached the Rebbe: my grandfather greeted him first, then introduced my father so that he too might greet him.

"You've a fine son-in-law," the Rebbe said, and pinched my father's cheek. "And he has fine boots," the Rebbe added. "They go squeak, squeak, squeak, squeak."

Later my grandfather said that he would have preferred for the Rebbe to slap him ten times than to say what he did. Well, what's done is done. They stayed and joined the Rebbe's circle over the Sabbath, and everything was fine. On Sunday just before they were to start home, they went to say their goodbyes to the Rebbe.

"No," said the Rebbe, "what's your hurry? If one can afford lacquered boots, one can afford to follow me too." My father and my grandfather, blessed be his memory, felt their hearts sink, but if the Rebbe expressed a wish, who would object?

So they stayed. The next day, Monday, the Rebbe made his rounds in the district, and my father and his father-in-law followed him. They went first to one town, then to another. Perhaps, they thought at each place, the Rebbe would send them home from there. But no. Not on your life.

The Rebbe feigned ignorance of their discomfort. They followed after him for another week and a half, but still he didn't let them out of his sight. Finally he said he wanted nine rubles, and then they could go home. "On your way," the Rebbe remarked as they were making their farewells, "you will pass such-and-such a squire's place, where there will be a hundred oxen for sale. You must go to him and buy fifty."

Finally, and after much difficulty, they left the Rebbe. Altogether they had half a ruble in their pockets. How could they even consider following the Rebbe's instructions? The real question was how they were going to make the long journey home with fifty kopecks.

But now listen. As they were passing some squire's compound, the squire himself came out to greet them. "Hey, Jews. Do you want to buy something?" he cried cheerfully. "I have a hundred oxen to sell."

"Pardon me, lord, but I have no money just now," my grandfather replied.

"Who's talking about money?" said the squire. "Go on, take the ones that please you, and you can pay some other time. I trust you."

Well, to make a long story short, they picked out fifty of the oxen. The squire even lent them two herdsmen, and they went off with the cattle. Later they made a tidy profit from the resale, and that was the beginning of an important business relationship with the squire.

Clearly it was a miracle. This much I know.

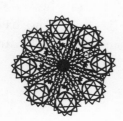

129

How Judah Halevi Entered Heaven Alive

In heaven, in paradise, there was a space available for the soul of a *tsadek* among the seats in the Celestial Council of Justice, right next to the Holy One, blessed be He. The *tsadikim,* the saintly ones in heaven, were asked, "Who is worthy to be seated in that most honorable place?" They divided into two camps: One group proposed the great poet and religious philosopher Judah Halevi; the second group objected. But the first group prevailed, so God sent for the Angel of Death and said, "Go bring me the soul of Judah Halevi. Do not come back without it."

The Angel of Death descended to earth and, disguised as a short man with a pointed beard, went to Judah Halevi. He found the rabbi studying *gemore,* a commentary on the Mishnah. Now, that was bad for the Angel of Death, who could do nothing while the rabbi was at his pious work. Judah Halevi saw something in the man's eyes that made him suspicious. He said, "What do you want?"

The Angel of Death replied, "I am the Angel of Death. God has sent me for your soul." And he told him everything that had happened up in heaven.

"Stop. You're not going to get what you came for. Your stories don't fool me; you can't have my soul," said Judah Halevi.

The Angel of Death realized that he was in trouble. "What's to be done?" he wondered. He couldn't possibly go back without Judah Halevi's soul. Then he had an idea. He said, "Climb up on my shoulders and I'll take you up to the gates of paradise for a moment, where you can see what's happening on your account."

So Judah Halevi seated himself on the angel's shoulders. And when they approached the gates of paradise, he saw heaven's spacious hall —larger even than the synagogue in Koyl! The hall was empty because the saintly ones had gone out for a stroll with God. Judah

Halevi leaped down from the shoulders of the Angel of Death and went into the hall, where he instantly made a vow: "No matter what, I'm not going to leave this place."

When the saintly ones came back from their walk, they saw that there was a man from the world below wandering about. "We had to pass through seven sections of hell before we got in here, and look at him: not dead, and in heaven."

But God, aware of the vow that Judah Halevi had made, commanded that the Book of Memories be brought before Him. Then He said, "If we find it written that there is even one vow that Judah Halevi did not keep in the world below, then this latest vow of his will be null and void." But there was no record of such an unkept vow. And that is how Judah Halevi was allowed to stay in heaven, without having died.

130
Rabbi Joshua and the Emperor of Rome

The Emperor of Rome once said to Rabbi Joshua, "If you have a God, show Him to me. Then I'll know that He's real." Rabbi Joshua said, "Come with me and I'll show you." They went out into the street. Rabbi Joshua told the emperor to look up at the sky, but the emperor could not because the sun was shining so brightly. So Rabbi Joshua said, "The sun is but a servant of God, and you are unable to look at it. Then how do you expect to see God Himself?" The emperor was embarrassed and went home.

131
A Wonderful Legend of a Cave

A rich Arab nobleman owned a cave in which a saintly Jew was
buried. And the nobleman was one of the friendliest of the Gentiles.
Understanding the nature of the man who lay there, he kept a light
always burning over the grave, adding oil every day as needed.

The nobleman also kept his sheep in the cave, as people used to
do in those days. His shepherd drove the flock out every morning,
pastured them all day, and drove them back into the cave in the
evening. And that had been his custom for many years.

One day the shepherd forgot to lock the door to the cave. All
night he worried for fear someone would steal something, and at
daybreak he quickly dressed and hurried to the cave. There he was
astonished to find a wild animal standing immobile near the eternal
light. The shepherd understood at once what had happened. The
animal had meant to lick the oil in the light, but the spiritual power
of the saintly man was so great that it had paralyzed the beast. So
the shepherd killed the creature and from that time always left the
door of the cave open. He no longer worried about thieves.

Early one day the nobleman went to the cave and to his surprise
found the door unlocked. He was very angry with the shepherd and
beat him, though the shepherd insisted that no one could possibly
steal anything from the cave.

Finally the nobleman decided to test the shepherd's claim, so he
too left the cave unlocked. One night thieves sneaked in and filled
their sacks with the goods that were stored there. Then they started
to leave, but at once paralysis seized them. The cleverer of the thieves

understood what was happening and flung their sacks away, and were thus able to escape. Those who did not think so quickly were left standing paralyzed, the sacks in their hands.

In the morning the nobleman entered the cave and found the slow-witted thieves holding the sacks. It was then that he fully appreciated the saintly man's greatness.

He called in the Jewish inhabitants of his city and told them about the wonders worked by the holy man's grave. After that, of course, he gave a banquet worthy of a king. And from then on he helped the Jews in every possible way.

1 3 2
Waiting for the Messiah

Ibn Ezra was a perpetual wanderer, traveling from village to village, from town to town. It happened once that he came to a town where he could hear no human sound, nor, as he entered, was anyone to be seen. He walked street after street, but all were empty. This struck him as so strange that he decided to enter a house to try and find a human being. As he went into the kitchen, he saw all sorts of good food on a table, but everything was cold because there was no fire in the hearth. In the second room he came upon a table laden with wines and brandies and baked goods—strudles, honey cakes, fruit-cakes, and cookies—but no one was in the room. Amazement! When he went into a second house, it was like the first. And the same was true of every house in town.

He thought it over and decided to visit the synagogue. Now, the synagogue, it turned out, was filled with people. All wore their prayer shawls, and all stood stock-still. Then Ibn Ezra, of blessed memory, asked one of the men why he never moved, but the man did not even look at him. So Ibn Ezra approached a second man and begged him to explain the mystery. Why had they been standing there for so long, and why did they stand so still?

"Many, many years ago," replied the man, "people went off to the synagogue for *kolnidre*. There the whole congregation, men, women, and children, felt a surge of power as they stood praying to God. And so they continued to stand all night long, feeling that the power was capable of changing the world. So convinced were they that this was true that they vowed, all of them, not to leave the synagogue until the Messiah came to lead them from it.

"Their decision," the man went on, "created turmoil in heaven, because it was not yet the destined time for the Messiah. And so it was decreed that, since the congregation would not leave the synagogue unless the Messiah came, they must stand in the synagogue with their prayer shawls on until his arrival.

"And so we stand here all week long, except on Friday evening, when we celebrate the coming of the Sabbath. And we have been standing in just this way for many, many years as we wait for the Messiah."

That was what the man said. And when Ibn Ezra heard it, he bade farewell and left him standing there until the coming of the Messiah which, we pray, may happen in our own days. Amen.

The Torah of My Servant Moses

This is the story that Reb Joshua ben Levi tells concerning the time when the Holy One, blessed be He, gave the Torah to Moses, peace to his memory.

As Moses was descending again from Heaven, Satan came to the Holy One, blessed be He, and said, "Lord of the Universe, where have You hidden the Torah?"

The Holy One, blessed be He, replied, "I gave it to the Earth."

Satan went to the Earth and said, "Earth, where did you hide God's Torah?"

The Earth replied, "God knows everything. But as for me, I don't have the Torah."

So Satan went to the Sea and said, "Sea, where have you hidden the Torah?"

The Sea replied, "I don't have it."

So Satan went to the Abyss and said, "Where have you hidden the Torah that God gave you?"

The Abyss replied, "It's not in my depths."

Then Satan went to the dead and to those who are lost and asked them, "Where have you hidden the Torah?"

They replied, "It's true that we have heard of it, but we don't know where it is."

So Satan went to God and said, "I've searched the entire world over and have not found the Torah."

The Holy One, blessed be He, said, "Go to Ben Amram—to Moses, son of Amram. I gave it to him."

So Satan went to Moses and said, "Moses, where is the Torah that God gave you?"

Moses replied, "Who or what am I that the Holy One, blessed be He, should have given the Torah to me?"

When God heard about this, He said, "Moses, why did you deny that I gave you the Torah?"

Moses replied, "Lord of the Universe, how can I take it upon myself to boast that it is I who have received the Torah, an instrument which produces such joy that studying it makes all humankind happy every day?"

God said, "Moses, Moses, it is not well to belittle oneself. Still, because you would not boast of having the Torah, let your reward be that it will henceforth be named after you."

And so it is written, "Remember the Torah of My servant, Moses . . ."

1 3 4
Rabbi Jonathan and the Minister: A Disputation

As everyone knows, Rabbi Jonathan, the author of *Urim ve Tummim,* was constantly engaged in debate with the greatest people in the nation over matters of faith.

And there were those who were not fond of him. It was, for example, said of him that in the intermediary days between the first two and last two days of Passover, he prayed using *tfiln* that did not contain parchment slips with the appropriate verses from the Bible.

The rabbi had a keen intelligence and he was a God-fearing man, as everyone knew. A story is told about a minister who, meaning to test Rabbi Jonathan's intelligence, sent a messenger inviting him for a visit. However, the minister instructed his servants not to tell the rabbi where in the palace he was to be found.

Reb Jonathan came to the palace and asked to be shown to the minister's room. One guard replied that he was in such-and-such a room; another guard gave the rabbi quite different directions. And so with all the guards: they gave him contradictory answers and directions. Finally the rabbi paused and, thinking the matter over, decided that the minister must be in a particular room. He went to it and, indeed, there was the minister.

When the rabbi presented himself, the minister was amazed. "Ha! How did you know I would be in this room? Who told you?"

"How could anyone have told me, since all your Swiss guards gave me contradictory directions? Now, we Jews have a saying, 'Follow the majority.' And that's what I did. I thought through everything they told me and counted up the replies. It was clear that this was the room, so I went to it."

"In that case," said the minister, "why is it that you Jews don't follow the majority in today's world? Why do you insist on being a minority among the nations?"

The rabbi thought for a while, then he said, "In the palace, I followed the majority because I knew that you were here. What was in doubt was which room you were in. But we Jews have no doubts about where we are in the world. And that's why we don't accept conversion and remain a separate people."

1 3 5
He Has Only One Weakness

The *Ksav-soyfer,* a son of the *Khsam-soyfer,* was, like his father, the head of a large yeshiva.

One day a father came to the *Ksav-soyfer* to get some information about a young man who had been proposed as a husband for his daughter. The *Ksav-soyfer* said, "Yes, he's a fine young fellow. He has only one weakness. He doesn't know how to play cards."

The man was astonished. "Rabbi," he asked, "is that a weakness?"

The rabbi replied, "Yes. If one who doesn't play cards doesn't know how to play, it's not a weakness. But when one who does play doesn't know how, then that's a weakness."

1 3 6
The Rabbi Shows Respect for His Shoemaker

The story is told that the humble Rabbi Akiba Eyger once sent a note to his shoemaker asking him to return the boots he had been given for repair. He addressed the shoemaker as follows: "To the Most Holy Revered Great Scholar . . ." The shoemaker, thinking the rabbi was mocking him, was offended and hurried to him to complain. The rabbi's reply was of the utmost simplicity: "How can you think I meant to mock you? Letters to me are addressed that way all the time."

1 3 7

Evening the Score

Once upon a time there was a great famine in the land of Israel. Three men were sent abroad to raise funds for the needy. One was the Holy Shelah, Rabbi Isaiah Horowitz; the other was his assistant; and the third was a *shoykhet,* a ritual slaughterer of cattle and poultry.

When they arrived on this side of the sea, they rented a horse and wagon and traveled from town to town and from city to city, gathering alms for the starving. In order to keep the wagon driver from knowing where they kept the money, two of them—the Shelah and the *shoykhet*—drilled a hole in a floorboard of the wagon and poured the coins into it. But they drilled too deep, so that the money went in on one side of the floorboard and fell through the other side.

At last they had gathered a goodly sum and were planning to return home. As they approached the border, they went to take the money from its hiding place. To their horror they found not so much as a single coin left.

Suspicion immediately fell on the *shoykhet.* Well, there was no way for him to go back and begin collecting again, so with a heavy heart the poor man made his way home. There the case was investigated, and it was concluded that it must have been he who took the money. And so he was condemned to have an ear cut off and was barred from his profession. And it was done.

So he became a homeless wanderer. One day in the course of his travels he went into a store where the shopkeeper was already waiting on a customer. The *shoykhet* did not want to disturb them, so he took a chair near the wall to wait his turn. As he sat, he heard them making a mistake in the bill. He went up to the shopkeeper and his customer and, apologizing for his interference, pointed out that such-and-such a mistake had been made in the bill. They added it up once more, and it turned out that he was right.

The owner of the shop was a widow, so she asked the *shoykhet* to work for her as a bookkeeper. And that's what happened. He settled down there.

When some time had passed, the shopkeeper came in one day all dressed in her holiday finery and said, "I'm a widow and you please me. I'd like for us to be married." He thought she was making fun of him—after all, she was a very rich woman.

To make a long story short, they were married. Of course, now everything changed for him. Now he was well fed and well dressed, and he had a gold watch and chain like a rich man.

It turned out that the Shelah went once again on a fund-gathering trip. On the evening before Passover, he asked people in the town where he happened to be staying to recommend a household that strictly observed the dietary laws—in which he could spend the holiday. Everyone said he should go to the house of such-and-such a man, that is, to the former *shoykhet,* because no one was more pious or kept a more kosher home.

The Shelah inquired at the house if he might stay there over the holiday. "We would be honored to have you," said the former *shoykhet*, whom the Shelah did not recognize. The *shoykhet*, on the other hand, recognized the Shelah. He set aside a room for the holy man and furnished it with everything needful.

On the night before Passover, the *shoykhet* bought a bottle of smelling salts and sharpened his slaughtering knife. Then he went into the Shelah's room and said in a commanding voice, "Now, come and lie down." The Shelah was terribly frightened, but the *shoykhet* shouted, "There's no help for it. You can't possibly fight me. Lie down; I'm going to tie you up." The Shelah begged for a little time so he could say *vide,* his final confession of sins, and the *shoykhet* agreed. Then he tied him, one hand to one foot, the way one binds cattle, and so tightly that the Shelah fainted dead away. With that the *shoykhet* let him sniff the smelling salts, and the Shelah slowly came back to consciousness. He said to the *shoykhet*, "I see that you didn't kill me. So what was the point of all that?" The *shoykhet* reminded him of all that had happened. And he had worried, said the *shoykhet,* that a man as holy as the Shelah might come before the Seat of Judgment having committed the great sin of defaming an innocent man. And so he had contrived for the Shelah to do penance in this world.

138
Reb Leybele of Mir Goes to the Marketplace

In the town of Mir, once a famous center of Torah scholarship, there lived Reb Leybele Mirkes, a naïve soul who studied Torah day and night and knew nothing at all about business. It happened one day that as he was studying in his chamber, the door opened and his wife said angrily, "Why don't you become a businessman? We're getting poorer with every passing day." Reb Leybele tried to reason with her, explaining, "You can't teach this old dog new tricks." But she wouldn't listen. Seeing that he could not pacify her, he had no choice but to do what she wanted. He made one condition, however: "I'll travel to buy the goods, but you'll have to sell them." She agreed to his proposal.

The town seethed with excitement when they learned that Reb Leybele had decided to go traveling on business. No one could believe that a man who had never been anything but a scholar, and who hardly knew what a coin looked like, would be able to conduct business.

Since there were no trains in those days, Reb Leybele bought a horse and wagon and hired a driver. He took a packet containing ten thousand rubles and started off one morning. He had spent the night in prayer and Torah study, and had asked the Lord to make his journey prosper. In the morning at dawn he had gone to pray with the congregation, and after reciting his prayers, he had spent half the day studying various texts, as was his usual habit. Then he ate breakfast, after which he recited blessings. Finally, and with great difficulty, he got into his wagon which, as if it were teasing him, moved ever so slowly out of the town.

As he traveled, Reb Leybele interrupted his journey at every prayer time so that he could join whatever congregation was near. And he studied Torah texts as well, which of course doubled the time he spent in each village.

When he came at last to the great fair in the town of Zeleve where he was to buy goods, he went to the home of the local rabbi. There he wanted to discuss a difficult passage in a volume by the Rambam, Maimonides. The rabbi, seeing that Reb Leybele had come to Zeleve on business, interrupted to tell him that the fair had closed down long ago. Reb Leybele was not at all disturbed. "Ah well," he said, "there'll still be goods to buy." Wondering what sort of man this was, the rabbi bade him farewell.

Reb Leybele went into town and called on various brokers. Since the particular cloth he asked for had sold out at the fair, they all urged him to buy red cloth of the sort used to trim hats and the seams of officers' trousers. No more than nine ells of that cloth were ever used during a year in Reb Leybele's town of Mir. But the brokers talked fast and hard, and in the end he bought ten thousand rubles' worth of red cloth. His business done, he climbed into his wagon and started back to Mir.

When he got home and displayed his bargain cloth, his wife scolded him bitterly. "What have you bought?" she shouted. "Have you gone completely out of your mind?" Reb Leybele replied, "Do you think there's only a black god in heaven? There's a red god as well."

Everyone was surprised when Reb Leybele was summoned to nearby Neshviezh, to the home of Count Radzivil. There the servants told him that the count, having read a minister's report regarding troops, had ordered the minister to buy red uniforms for the whole regiment, soldiers as well as officers. That is a lot of red cloth, and the entire order was indeed filled by Reb Leybele Mirkes. This transaction made him rich for the rest of his days.

1 3 9

Napoleon the First and the Jewish Officer

At the Battle of Austerlitz, where Napoleon acquired his great fame, he sat on his horse and watched through his field glasses while the Austrian troops died like flies. So he commanded that a white flag be run up as a sign of truce, and he called for any of his officers who could speak German to be brought before him. Naturally most of those who presented themselves were Jews, who, knowing Yiddish, felt confident they could speak German.

The officer whom Napoleon selected was a middle-aged man with a son serving with him in the same regiment. Napoleon sent all the others back to the battlefront and told the officer to sit down. He himself sat at a table and wrote a letter to the Austrian general reproving him for letting his soldiers die in such numbers instead of surrendering.

When the letter was done, he put it into an envelope which he did not seal. "I know you'll read the letter on the way," he said to the officer, "so go ahead—you might as well do it now."

The officer took the letter and read it, then said to the emperor, "Your majesty, my son is serving with me. Permit me to say farewell to him before I leave."

"What's this?" Napoleon rose from his desk. "Are you afraid that you won't return from the mission?"

The officer replied, "I'm certain the Austrian general will have me beheaded."

Napoleon said, "Mark my words: if he beheads you, I'll mass my full army, take Vienna, and behead the whole population."

For a moment the officer was silent. Then he said, "I'm amazed at the concern you have for a Jewish officer. But I must say that no matter how many heads you lop off in Vienna, you won't find a single one that fits back on my shoulders."

140

Napoleon in Vilna

It is said that Napoleon happened to pass through Vilna on *Tisha b'Av,* the ninth day of the Jewish month of Ab, a day of fasting and mourning. There he visited a synagogue, where he saw Jews seated on the floor and weeping. Curious, he inquired why. Of course he was told that they were mourning for the destruction of the Temple and praying for it to be rebuilt in Palestine.

Napoleon laughed. "And is this the way you mean to retake Palestine? Here," he said, pointing to his sword, "this is the way to retake Palestine."

141

Nafol tipol: Napoleon, You Will Fall

When Napoleon drove through Kozhenits, he heard that the town had a pious man who was known as the Preacher of Kozhenits. Napoleon was curious to meet this saintly figure and to question him about his war with Russia. He consulted his officers, and it was decided that he should disguise himself as an ordinary person. If the Preacher of Kozhenits recognized him, it would be proof that he had extraordinary powers.

So Napoleon disguised himself as an ordinary general and went to visit the Preacher of Kozhenits. The Preacher, of blessed memory, was the child of his parents' old age and had been sickly all his days. He was so weak that he studied Torah lying in bed, but the moment Napoleon came into the house, the Preacher got to his feet and recited the blessing one makes over royalty. The emperor was amazed and said, "It's true I am the emperor. But how did you recognize me in the uniform of an ordinary general?"

The Kozhenits Preacher replied, "It's because your guardian angel came in with you, and I recognized him at once."

So Napoleon questioned the Preacher regarding his war with Russia. The holy man said, "You'd do well to harness your carriage and head toward Paris at once, because soon it will be too late."

Napoleon said, "If it happens that I am triumphant in my war against Russia, I'll have you hanged over the town gate." Then he left in a rage. No sooner had he gone than the Preacher took down the Book of Esther and, chanting the text, read the words *Nafol tipol,* "Thou shalt surely fall," from which he deduced the meaning, *"Napoleon tipol,* Napoleon, you will fall."

142

The Cantonist's Mother and Nicholas the First

When I was a boy of ten or eleven, my greatest delight in the winter season was to sit with the graybeards near the warm stove in the study and prayer house as the Eyn Yankev *[a popular collection of Talmudic stories and commentaries] was being read. This occurred in the interval between late afternoon and evening prayers, and sometimes it happened that the reader did not come, or came late. Then and on some Saturday nights, the graybeards would tell tales. One of these old men was fascinated by Czar Nicholas the First, and his cronies teased him for constantly telling stories about Nicholas. Still, when he started on one of his tales, like this one, they listened with pleasure.*

Nicholas used to enjoy disguising himself in peasant's clothing or worn military uniforms and wandering about to see what was going on and hear what was being said about him. Many an unwary person was ruined because he didn't guard his tongue in the presence of the disguised czar.

On one of these excursions through his villages in the Jewish Pale of Settlement, the czar and his entourage entered a forest to hunt. Nicholas, dressed like a common soldier in a ragged coat, took a wrong turning and lost his way. It was evening. A light snow had begun to fall which grew heavier and heavier until it turned into a true blizzard. Fortunately for Nicholas, he noticed a gleam of light and followed it until he arrived at an inn run by an old Jewish widow. When the woman saw the exhausted, frozen soldier, she snatched up a broom and brushed the snow off him, removed his torn greatcoat, and settled him at a place on the stove to warm himself. Then she turned to brew him a cup of chicory. All the while that she was cleaning him up and cooking for him, she repeated, "Oh, my boy. You're absolutely frozen."

There were peasants already sitting in the room. When they saw the ragged, shivering soldier, they began to call down fire and brimstone on the czar—Czar Nicholas. Their complaints were the old ones: that all the czar ever did was skin them alive, enslave them, draft them into the army forever. And so on, and so on.

The widow, however, defended the czar and made excuses for him. She argued that peasants weren't smart enough to know who was the one truly responsible. She pointed out that even if the czar were an angel, he wouldn't be able to help them because his noblemen kept him ignorant. "I can't believe," she insisted, "that one chosen by God to be czar is a bad man. Just don't forget—he's God's annointed."

The peasants didn't agree with her and became increasingly excited. They used her own case as an example: Whoever heard, they asked, of taking away the only son of a woman as old as she was? But she held stubbornly to her view that the czar was absolutely not responsible for drafting her son into the army. She felt sure that if the czar knew what her situation was, he would send her son home. As she talked, she handed food and drink to her "little boy," as she called the frozen soldier.

When all the peasants had left the inn, she prepared a soft place for Nicholas to sleep and gave him a warm quilt. And so it was her amazing luck to have Nicholas the First himself spend the night as her guest. In the morning when her "boy" had had a bit of herring for his breakfast and washed it down with a cup of chicory, he said, "Granny, how did it happen that your one and only son was taken away?"

"It's because I'm a poor widow and I have no one to take my part. The rich pay to keep their sons out of the army. So when the czar's *khapers** come to our villages, they pay no attention to the cries of the poor. They grab even such sons as mine—even an only son. It does no good to complain."

"Granny," said the czar, "why didn't you go to the provincial capital and complain to the governor?"

She replied, "Ah, my dear, I went there. It was very, very hard for me to get to him. But at last I succeeded in presenting my petition and the rural district's certificate of judgment that my son was an only child. I begged him to give my son back to me. And he promised to do it. But, my boy, you see how it is. It's been more than half a year and my son isn't back yet."

She heaved a sigh, shook her aged head, and said, "No, my boy, it's hard to get justice if you're poor and old."

Nicholas asked her for a piece of paper, but she had none. So he tore out the endpaper of the Book of Psalms he found on one of her shelves and wrote a few words on it. He handed her the sheet and told her to take it to town and give it to the bailiff. He would send it where it ought to go, and her son would certainly be returned to her.

She looked at him, amazed. "Ah, my boy, what good is your bit of paper? If the governor himself, though he promised, didn't help me, then certainly you can't. At the most, the bailiff will laugh at your note and at me for bringing it." But Nicholas insisted that his paper would help. He said that if she got a horse and sleigh, he would ride part of the way with her to the bailiff.

Once in the sleigh, Nicholas cautioned the old woman not to show his note to anyone but the bailiff. Then he bade her a warm farewell

---

* Under the "cantonist laws," boys were forced to serve in the Russian army for twenty-five years. Jewish communities in Russia had special officers, dubbed *khapers* (snatchers), for seizing male children—ages 12 to 25, and in exceptional cases as young as 8 or 10—who were incarcerated in a communal building and handed over to the military authorities to fill the cantonist quota. Russian authorities hoped also to alienate Jewish children from their own people and religion by means of this long army service.

and promised that he would see her again after she and her son were reunited.

In town the old woman, following Nicholas's instructions, went directly to the bailiff's house and gave him the paper. The bailiff read it and immediately invited her to sit down. Then he asked her to describe the man she called "this little boy." She told him what the soldier looked like and how he had stumbled, frozen and snow-covered, into her inn. She told him too that she hadn't wanted to bring the note, but that the soldier had forced her to.

The bailiff observed that she had done well to follow the soldier's advice, because her son would shortly be returned to her. Then he accompanied her to the sled, helped to settle her into it, and once again assured her that her son would be home very soon.

And indeed, not long after that her dear son, wearing new woolen clothes, came home in a sleigh drawn by post-horses. Plenty of happy tears were shed by both of them. After they calmed down, her son related all the hardships he had endured from the time the *khapers* took him until he finally came home. And the old woman told him everything that had happened to her: how a poor soldier had sent her to the bailiff with a note ordering her son discharged. And how she had not wanted to go, and how the soldier had insisted.

A little while later, the old woman and her son heard from the peasants in the village what had happened in the town where the *khapers* lived. Cossacks had surrounded the town at night, and early in the morning the authorities rounded up all the *khapers* and all the rich people of the town, put them in chains, and took them away—no one knew why or where.

Later still, the governor himself came to the town and drafted every rich young man into the army. The old woman and her son were beginning to wonder who that soldier might have been, and what danger they might be in since she had, at first, refused to follow his instructions.

Not long after these events, an expensive carriage bearing several officials pulled up before their inn. The mother and son watched in fear as the officials made their way inside, but one of them told the woman not to be frightened, since they had come only to take her and her son to visit a good friend. At their urging, mother and son took their places in the carriage, though they were afraid to move a muscle lest, God forbid, they inadvertently damage it.

The carriage drew up before a palace, where beautifully dressed servants hastened to greet them. They were taken to baths and washed clean, then dressed in fine clothes. Later they were escorted to a second palace and shown the rooms in which they would sleep. The servants brought them food, as well as a certificate that the food was kosher.

They stayed in the palace for a week, eating and drinking the best of everything. Then an official led them to an even finer palace and into a large, richly decorated hall. There they sat and waited, until a side door opened and Nicholas the First entered. Thinking that he had come to lead them to another hall, they rose. Nicholas drew nearer to the old woman and said with a smile, "Granny, take a good look at me. Maybe you'll know who I am." She looked him over for a while, then shook her head. So Nicholas removed his uniform and stood before her in the ragged overcoat that he had worn when he first stumbled to her inn. The old woman had just time to cry, "Oh, my little boy!" before she fainted.

When she opened her eyes, she found herself lying in a royal bed. Beside it stood her son and a physician. She whispered "My little boy," over and over again. "My little boy."

A few days later when she had recovered, Nicholas sent for her once more and thanked her for her herring and chicory with such generous gifts that her son was later considered one of the wealthiest men in Russia.

"And that's how it is in the world," the gray old storyteller used to say, *shaking his head. "It all depends on fate. For some people Nicholas's excursions brought disaster, for others great happiness."*

1 4 3
Czar Nicholas Decrees the Burning of the Talmud

Czar Nicholas issued an edict to have the whole of the Talmud burned. The chief rabbi then disguised himself as the czar and, preceding the czar to the chancellery, he tore up and burned the papers on which the edict was printed. When the czar came to the chancellery to sign his decree, he saw that all the copies had been destroyed. "Who did this?" he asked. "You yourself," came the reply. "You were here earlier, and that's when you did it."

"Ah," said the czar, "when Elijah the Prophet meddles in the matter, there's nothing I can do."

And the decree was cancelled.

1 4 4
Emperor Franz Josef and the Innkeeper's Infant

Emperor Franz Josef, disguised as a beggar, came once to Mieditsov, a village near Bitershtayn. There he spent the night at an inn run by a Jew.

The innkeeper had an infant who was lying in its cradle. During the night the baby cried a great deal. The emperor could not endure the poor child's crying, so he spent the entire night rocking the cradle. In the morning as he was leaving, he turned to the innkeeper and said, "It was the emperor who rocked your cradle." Then he gave the man a gift and went on his way.

1 4 5
The Poor Man and Rothschild

There was a poor beggar who went to ask Rothschild for alms. He was met at the door by someone who asked what he wanted. "I have to see the baron," he replied.

He was led into a room where, shortly, Rothschild's secretary came in and said, "How can I help you?"

The beggar replied, "I have an important business matter to conduct with the baron." Well, the long and the short of it was that in spite of the secretary's insistence that he could help him, the beggar refused to talk with anyone but the baron. Finally there was no help for it; the baron came in and asked the man what he wanted.

"Nothing, really," said the man. "I simply wanted to ask you for alms."

"What? Is it for alms that you insisted on seeing me personally? Why couldn't you have asked my secretary?"

"Dear baron," said the man, "maybe you're the world's greatest financier, but don't try to give me advice on how to beg."

146
Rothschild's Shoes

"What kind of shoes does Rothschild wear?"
  "Probably golden shoes."
  "Then what does he do when it rains?"
  "He puts on galoshes."
  "Then nobody can see the golden shoes."
  "So he makes holes in the galoshes."
  "But then the shoes get wet."
  "So he stuffs the holes with straw."

147
Rothschild's End

The Vienna Rothschild went one day into his strong room, but he forgot to take his keys. The minute he walked in, the door slammed shut so he could not open it. Since the room had no window, there was no way he could get out. He shouted and shouted, but nobody heard him. A few days later when people began to wonder where he was, they organized a search. Eventually his servants opened the strong room and found the Baron Rothschild lying dead on the floor. He had starved to death.

PART SEVEN

Elves and Dibbuks, Ghosts and Golems: Supernatural Tales

Reb Ayzik, a forest overseer, loved to carve in his spare time. And while he carved ritual spice boxes with little towers and doors, and tobacco boxes and toys for us children, he would tell us tales of little elves, of *shretelekh.*

—Memoir from Kolomey, Poland, the early part of this century

And in *kheyder* when the *melamed* was away in *shul* for afternoon and evening prayers, we would sit in darkness, huddle near the oven for warmth, and tell scary stories about the spirits who throng the *shul* after midnight, and the tricks they play on anyone who has to sleep there—so that a beggar would rather sleep on the floor of the humblest house than enjoy the honor of a bench in *shul.* We would tell stories about *sheydim,* dibbuks, Lilith.

—Memoir from interbellum Eastern Europe

𝔐edieval fears and superstitious beliefs survived well into twentieth-century Europe, particularly among tradition-bound villagers and small-town dwellers. Demons, dibbuks, and golems were as vivid a part of village life as the miracles and wonders that were an integral part of received religion. For examples of how these rogue traditions affected Yiddish folklore, we turn now to East European *mesoyres,* local legends—called "memorats" by folklorists.

The memorat is an account of an extraordinary event purported to have actually occurred in a specific place at a specific time. The Yiddish memorat may tell of an encounter with supernatural creatures—with a malignant *shed,* demon, or with a mischievous but kind *shretele,* an elflike household familiar. It may also explain local lore: how a synagogue came to be built in a certain location, or how it was miraculously saved during a fire; the history of a curious grave marker, and the mystery within a cave.

The range of supernatural creatures includes the *shretele,* the *lantekh,* and the *kapelyushnikl.* The kindly *shretele* may well have been brought along by Jews from Alsace and southern Germany, where an elf with the same name has been popular among non-Jews for centuries, and may also bear some relation to the *skrzat,* the house elf, which made its appearance in Polish folklore around 1500. The naughty bridge hobgoblin, *lantekh,* appears to be none other than the French *lutin,* who was brought to Eastern Europe by Jews in the course of their migration. The teasing *kapelyushnikl,* who likes to pester horses, on the other hand, is apparently native to Slavic soil and may be an original East European Jewish creation. In Polish, *kapelyushnikl* means "hat maker," and indeed the little creatures wear hats.

Lilith, the Assyrian *lilitu,* was a more formidable adversary. Originally a wind spirit, in Talmudic times Lilith became an evil and erotic night spirit, while in medieval and modern Jewish folklore she was seen as a demoness who attacked newborn children and their mothers.

Other supernatural interventions described in memorats challenge the very limits of the human condition. They may signal a soul returning after death, or one entering the body of a living person. In some of the tales the transmigrated soul is called a *gilgl*—though a *gilgl* can also be an animal's soul. The term *dibbuk* seems to be restricted to the restless spirit of a deceased person. Supernatural tales may also involve a golem, a man-made creature of enormous physical strength, like the one said to have been created in the sixteenth century by Rabbi Loew to protect the Jewish community of Prague. It was believed that a holy man, possessed of the power of the Holy Name, could exorcise a transmigrated soul, could cast a demon out into uninhabitable places, could create a golem and turn it back into dust again. Even Satan could be foiled by absolute devotion and intense prayer.

Memorats are nearly always simple in structure, usually containing a single narrative motif. They are often told as eyewitness accounts or contain a personal testimonial: "I heard this myself from an old man who lived there." Some of them plunge right in: "One night a sick man was walking near the synagogue." Occasionally the teller will say, "This happened in the old days," with the implication that such things no longer happen.

Needless to say, there were many who sneered at these spooky local legends. After all, they were beyond proof, and founded on medieval superstitions. In "A *Balshem* Drives Out a Dibbuk" a rationalist has a good laugh with a pseudo-holy man. The powerful final story in this section, "The Last Dibbuk," recreates a dramatic and decisive confrontation between those who believed in spirits and those who did not.

148

The Shoemaker and the Shretelekh

Some *shretelekh*, small elflike creatures, slipped into the home of a shoemaker and made themselves cozy there. At the time, the shoemaker was so poor that he had only enough leather to make a single pair of shoes. He cut the leather to the pattern and laid it on his worktable. Then, in confidence that the Lord would come to his aid somehow, he went to sleep. When he rose the next morning, imagine his astonishment at finding a completed pair of shoes! He examined the workmanship and saw that it was of the highest quality. He sold the shoes for enough money to buy leather for two more pairs. And the next morning there were two finished pairs of shoes on the table. When he sold them, he had enough money for four pairs. After he had cut out the leather this time, he and his wife decided that they would hide to discover who was making the shoes. And in the middle of the night they saw four tiny, handsome, raggedly dressed little men who sat down and began, each of them, to make a pair of shoes. The shoemaker was amazed at their speed. When they were finished, they put the shoes on the table and ran away. In the morning the shoemaker's wife said, "Those little people have made us rich, and we must thank them. See how ragged they are; they must be cold. So let's make them some clothes."

When the couple had finished sewing four tiny suits of clothes, they hid once again to see what the little people would do. The *shretelekh* were astonished to find clothes instead of leather waiting for them. One of the little men, when he had put on a suit, began to clap his hands, and he sang,

"Hey, don't we look glorious.
No more shoemaking for us!"

With that all four began to sing. Then, dancing on the table and chairs, they danced their way out of the house and into the street and were never seen again.

But the shoemaker and his wife continued to prosper right down to the last day of their lives.

1 4 9

The Synagogue, the Church, and the Town Hall

For a long while the Jews of Alik had been begging their nobleman to build them a synagogue, and the Christians had been pleading for a church. He, for his part, wanted to build a town hall.

Well, a day came when the nobleman was taken so ill that it seemed no one could cure him. So he made a vow to build a large and beautiful church. But he stayed as sick as ever; indeed, he grew weaker by the day. When he felt himself at his last gasp, he made a vow to build a large and beautiful synagogue. Lo and behold, he felt himself growing better at once.

After he was fully recovered, he began to think about which of his vows to keep first. If he built the church first, the Jews would take offense. If he built the synagogue first, he would provoke the Christians. If he followed his own wishes and built the town hall, the Jews and the Christians would both be angry. So he decided to have all three structures built simultaneously and to make them identical.

He hired a famous foreign architect and instructed him to erect the three buildings at exactly the same time, stone for stone. The architect drove three posts into the ground to indicate where the church, the synagogue, and the town hall were to be built. Then he stretched a rope from post to post and, balancing himself on it, went from one point to the other, laying brick after brick in sequence. As the buildings rose, he tied the rope higher and higher up the posts. And that was how he was able to build the three structures simultaneously.

They were the most beautiful buildings in the world, so beautiful that the nobleman, worried lest the architect construct others as wonderful somewhere else, had the posts cut down just as all three were finished. As a result the architect fell from the ropes and died.

When I visited Alik, I came upon an old church with remarkable architecture, but I did not see either a synagogue or a town hall. I was told that they had burned down some while ago.

150

The Transmigrating Soul

My grandfather bought the forest in Paluzh and ordered the peasants to cut down some trees. One day a group of children went to the forest to gather mushrooms. When they finished they ran off, having forgotten about one little girl so that they left her behind. The girl sat down to rest on the stump of a tree—and at that moment she began to cough, because a *gilgl* had entered into her.

At last she got home, and her family noticed that she coughed with the sound of a dog barking. When she was silent, the *gilgl* spoke; and when the *gilgl* spoke, she developed a goiter. The *gilgl* used to call the girl's mother "Mother," and they had to give him whatever he wanted. One day when he wanted milk, he said, "Mother, unless

you give me milk, I'll strangle your daughter. So bring me milk."
Another time when the girl's mother was baking *khale,* the braided
Sabbath bread, he said, "Mother, make *khale* for me, too. I want to
eat some."

One of my uncles told him one day, "You've got an awfully big
mouth. You want everything." This made the *gilgl* cry. Whenever
they ordered him to leave the girl, he would say, "If you want me to
leave, you'll have to bring ten rabbis. But if you bring the Rabbi of
Oshmen, one will be enough."

My grandfather disguised himself and said, "I'm the Oshmen
Rabbi, and I order you to leave this girl."

The *gilgl* replied, "Some rabbi you are! You're the one who bought
the forest and sent a couple of huge peasants with axes into it to
chop down trees. And they cut down the one I lived in so that I had
to enter the girl."

The *gilgl* told them that he had once transmigrated into a dog, a
very quiet yellow dog that my father himself had seen. Then Gentile
boys killed the dog, so the *gilgl* entered into a horse, but the horse
died, so he entered into a tree. Then Shmuel-Yoysef of Paluzh bought
the forest and had the tree cut down, after which the *gilgl* entered
into the girl.

He tormented the girl so severely that finally they went to the
Rabbi of Oshmen. And the rabbi quarreled with the *gilgl,* because the
gilgl wanted to leave by the girl's throat and the rabbi wanted him to
leave through one of her little fingers. At last he did leave, and a
great shot was heard. The story is told that before he went, he asked
that candles be distributed for the sake of his soul. After that, the
rabbi advised the family to sell the house and leave the town. They
followed the rabbi's advice and emigrated to America.

151

Who's Milking the Cows?

There was a dairyman who had several cows that gave a great deal of milk. When they suddenly went dry, he realized that someone must be milking them. He watched them carefully all day but saw no one, yet when he tried to milk them the next morning, he couldn't get even a glassful from them. That night at nine o'clock, the man went into the cow barn. He lighted a candle and set it under a great barrel, hid himself in a corner, and settled down for the night. At two in the morning he heard footsteps; then a tiny man and a tiny woman came into the barn. They both wore little caps, and the woman's hair was braided and tied with pretty ribbons. He watched as they seated themselves on milking stools, set buckets under the cows, and started in to milk. At that the man upended the barrel, and when his candle lit up the barn the *kapelyushniklekh,* the little cap-wearers, started running. The male got away, but the dairyman was able to catch the female, and he beat her severely. She pleaded with him, saying, "If you spare my life we'll never come back, and your cows will give double the amount of milk they used to."

And that's exactly what happened.

152
The Passover Elf Helps
Great-Grandmother

One Saturday evening in fall, after the holidays, my great-grand-mother was standing beside the stove rendering down goose fat. She was all alone in the kitchen; the house was hushed and still. Suddenly in the chimney corner, she saw a tiny hand stretched out, palm up, as if it were asking for something. She felt terribly frightened but forced herself to remain calm while she put a piece of crackling into the little hand. Then she started to pour the rendered fat from the frying pan into containers. But no matter how often she poured from the pan, it stayed full. She poured and poured until every vessel in the house was brimming with fat. Every pot, every pitcher, every tub. And the fat continued to flow as from a spring.

About midnight my great-grandfather woke up and saw that the kitchen was brightly lighted and his wife was still standing at the stove. He got out of bed and said irritably, "Why are you fussing with the fat at this hour? It's almost dawn."

"Well," said my great-grandmother, "there went that. Too bad. Our household was being blessed: we had an elf, a *shretele,* in the house, and now you've chased it away."

153
The Old Shul in Motele

In the town of Motele there is a synagogue about which tales of wonder are told. I have heard them myself from an old man who lived there. Listen now to what they say about that synagogue:

There was once a rabbi in the town who was a great genius and a saintly man, a *tsadek*, may his memory be blessed. Even the Gentiles greatly respected him.

One day it happened that the lord of a nearby castle got sick (God keep us from the same) and the doctors despaired of his life. The nobleman decided to send a servant to the holy man to ask him for a blessing. As it happened, the nobleman was actually a great anti-Semite but, because he was in such trouble, the rabbi was willing to give him a blessing.

And afterward the nobleman did indeed recover. Since the town of Motele did not have a synagogue, the lord had the idea of donating lumber to the Jewish community so it could build one. He gave the Jews twelve of the largest trees in his woods, and from those twelve trees they built a synagogue so large that today it holds a congregation of two hundred.

A considerable time has passed since its construction, but the synagogue still looks practically new. And to this day, when a misfortune (God forbid) happens in the town—when someone is sick, for instance, or a disaster threatens the community, people gather to pray at the grave of the holy rabbi, may his memory be blessed.

154

The Blacksmith and the Horses with Human Hands

In 1904 I arrived in Dorohobuzh, and in May I traveled from Horets to the station. We passed through a village called Visokoye, where there was a blacksmith who lived in a beautiful two-story house with a balcony and an orchard. Astonished by all this, I asked, "How did a blacksmith get to be so rich?" So they told me the following tale:

Once on a Shrovetide evening, there was a knocking on the smith's door at midnight. He came out and a group of men asked him to shoe four horses. He didn't want to, but they pleaded with him and promised that he would be well paid. He finally agreed, fired up his forge, and went to work.

When he took up one of the horses' feet, it turned out not to be a hoof, but a human foot. Human feet and human hands! He was too terrified to go on, but the men stood over him and threatened him with whips as they ordered him to shoe the horses.

Trembling, he obeyed. When his work was done, they poured out a great pile of golden coins for him. He let the coins fall from one hand into the other, and the money was transformed into hot coals.

Just then it turned three in the morning and all the roosters began to crow. He looked around and saw nothing: no money, no coals, no people, no horses. He was so frightened that he fainted dead away.

In the blacksmith's house the family noticed that the smithy had gone dark and silent. They too were afraid and, taking up torches, went out to see what was wrong. In the smithy they found the blacksmith lying unconscious. There was a pot filled with gold rubles by his side.

He has been a rich man from that time to this. The story is well known in Dorohobuzh, and when the peasants drink with the blacksmith, they always say, "The devil's tricks don't bother you!"

1 5 5
The Mysterious Gold Chain

In the old days people used to celebrate the end of the Sabbath with a third meal, a considerable gathering. Just as if they were in the homes of the rich, they served many dishes: borsht, potatoes . . . Once, just as the Sabbath ended, Khane was sent to bring wood from the shed. As she entered it, a glittering chain dropped from the ceiling and lay upon her neck. A heavy gold chain. Without a moment's hesitation Khane spread the skirt of her dress and began to gather the chain into it. She pulled and pulled and pulled, as if she were milking a cow.

Inside the house they waited for the wood so they could begin cooking the meal. Khane didn't come. "Khane," they called, but there was no reply because she couldn't interrupt what she was doing. Finally someone opened the door of the shed and called, "Khane," at which the chain broke with a clang and half of it flew up and disappeared. What was left was worth a fortune, and so all the children were well married.

Things like that don't happen nowadays. And generally, these miracles used to take place only at the close of the Sabbath.

156

The Unquiet Grave

The grave of the great Rabbi Moses ben Israel Isserles, who was called the Rema, is in Cracow. Once there was a poor young man who went to the caretaker of the cemetery and asked to buy a plot near the Rema's grave. At first the caretaker refused to sell him one because he thought these should be reserved for dignitaries, but then he began to think: "I'm an old man, after all, and I'm sure to die before him. So who'll know whether I ever sold him the plot?" Reasoning thus, he finally accepted the man's money for a plot near the Rema.

The very next day a death was reported—and it was that of the young man who had bought the plot. The caretaker was afraid to tell anyone what he had done, so he simply had the man buried in a different plot. Soon afterward the dead man's ghost began to appear in the caretaker's dreams, demanding the plot he had bought. Night after night the ghost disturbed the caretaker's rest. Finally the caretaker decided to go to the rabbi with the whole story and to get his advice.

The rabbi said, "Tell the ghost that he can move to the other plot. A promise should not be broken." So that's what the caretaker told the ghost when it paid its next visit.

The following day it was observed that there was a new grave near the place where the Rema was buried. Meanwhile the grave of the recently buried man collapsed in on itself. Soon afterward a gravestone was placed on the unidentified new grave, reading, "Here lies a person unknown."

It's said that the gravestone can be seen there to this day.

157

The Large Stone Synagogue
of Berditshev

In Berditshev—I believe it was in the days of Reb Levi Yitskhok of Berditshev—there lived a rabbi, a very holy man. Reb Liber was his name. He was a quiet, inward person fond of going out into the fields to pray. One day the nobleman of the town went by as Reb Liber was saying his prayers near a tree. Seeing someone standing rigidly under a tree in an open field, the count sent a guard to ask what he was doing. The rabbi made no response to the question. The count then ordered that the man be brought to him. The guard took the rabbi and escorted him forcibly to the carriage, but the rabbi did not reply no matter how often he was addressed. This so angered the nobleman that he ordered his men to give the rabbi thirty lashes. Reb Liber bore the punishment without so much as a sigh. When he was released, he went back to the tree and resumed his prayers. This astonished the nobleman, and he decided to wait in order to see what would come of it all. When Reb Liber finished his prayers, he went up to the count and said quietly, "Tell me, brother, what was it you wanted to ask? I'm ready to answer your question."

Surprised, the nobleman said, "I want to ask two questions: First, why did you refuse to answer when I spoke to you before? And second, why do you call me 'brother,' since I've had you so cruelly beaten?"

Reb Liber replied, "I was unable to answer you because when you asked your questions, I was in the presence of the Lord of all Lords, and I was making an accounting to Him of my life in this world. So you see, I could not be interrupted. And I called you brother because all men are God's children, and as children of the same Father they are then brothers."

"But weren't you inclined to hate me for having you beaten?"

"No. In fact, I pitied you."

"Why?"

"Because it was not you who was beating me. It was God who was punishing me. And I pitied you because God had chosen you to be His instrument in a matter as dreadful as beating a fellow human."

These words made a deep impression on the nobleman. He said, "I see that you are a pious man and I'm sorry I had you beaten. I beg you to pardon me and to give me a penance."

"I pardon you freely. As for a penance, pledge that you will never henceforth raise a hand against a brother."

"Does that include my peasants? Can't I even beat them?"

"They too are the children of God, and your brothers."

The nobleman gave his word. Then, to console Reb Liber for having had him beaten, he made this promise: "I will cause a synagogue to be built here on this spot where you prayed and where I had you beaten."

And he kept his word. He had a great stone synagogue built, and when the town of Berditshev grew, that synagogue turned out to be in the very heart of the town.

1 5 8

The Golem of Vilna

If you know the secret Name of God, you can build worlds and you can destroy them. You can move mountains. You can also make a human being—a living person—out of clay. A golem.

One such golem was made by a great rabbi, a gaon, a genius. Oh, what marvelous consolation that golem was for the Jews! The rabbi created him so that he could provide the Jews with fish for the Sabbath. He would send the golem into the depths of the river, where the golem, using the language of fish, called them together, trapped them in a net, and distributed them to the Jews.

The Vilna Gaon formed this golem out of sand and clay and water. And since the Gaon, may heaven be radiant for him, was a scholar and knew the five Books of Moses and the Commentaries all by heart, as well as all the secrets of the Cabala—since he knew all that, he also knew the blessed Lord's secret Name of Names and had written it down on a piece of paper. This he put into the golem's ear, and it was the writing on the paper that turned the clay into a living human being.

The golem could leap from roof to roof, like a bird, and he could disguise himself so that nobody knew who he was. He could drift through the air like a breeze on a cold day. Ah, what was there he couldn't do?

He was at once human and inhuman. For instance, the Gaon could send him to the synagogue to extinguish the Sabbath candles, because, though he had the appearance of a human being, he was not really human and therefore not required to fulfill all the prescriptions of the Torah. He was allowed to violate the Sabbath.

But his most important work was to defend the faithful on holidays and market days, when drunken peasants turned ugly and started to beat Jews. It was then that the Gaon turned the golem loose. Ah, how the golem used to crack their heads and break their arms and legs! There was no way they could escape from him. Sometimes he was on the rooftop, sometimes underwater in the river, sticking out his long stone tongue. When the governor heard about him . . . ah Lord, Lord . . . the golem, I mean the Gaon, sent the golem to slap the governor around a bit.

When the Gaon decided that he did not want the golem to be a golem any longer, he simply removed the bit of paper with the Name of Names on it from the golem's ear. He did so because, may the good Lord be thanked, there are now plenty of fish in the market-place. Even such poor folk as we are can afford a bit of carp for the Sabbath. Besides (and I hope never to see the day), should the time come when we do need the golem again, there will be someone to revive him. A new gaon will arise who will put the terrifying bit of paper into his ear. But I trust God will protect us from that. It will be much better if we never have need of the golem again.

The Baal Shem Tov and the Gilgl

In a prophetic vision, the Baal Shem foresaw that a certain young woman would die on a Friday on her way to the wedding canopy. So he ordered his horses to be harnessed and started off to her town. When was it he made the journey? Three or four days before the wedding.

Arriving at the town, he went to the home of a tenant innkeeper and said, "May I spend the night?"

"Of course," was the reply. "You're welcome to spend the Sabbath with us. There's going to be a wedding on Friday."

Friday came and the bride died. The town was in an uproar. The groom wept and wailed. The mother wept and wailed. Just think, a bride dead before her wedding.

People brought the news to the Baal Shem. "Don't be disturbed," he said, "I'll be there soon. Meanwhile, gather the burial society together."

When he got there, he saw that the bride was dead. "Carry her to the cemetery," he said, "but take her bridal dress with you. Who knows what may yet happen?"

They dug her grave and put her in it, face up. Then the Baal Shem asked them to select two strong men and told them to get into the grave, one on one side of the bride, one on the other. He cautioned them not to get any earth on themselves. "And be sure to watch her," he said. "Never lose sight of her. Don't look at anyone but her. Just stand there. If you see the Eternal One looking down on her, or if you see an expression on her face, don't be frightened. Soon she will turn pale, then color will come into her face. If you see her eyes opening, lift her out of the grave at once."

And that's what happened. And when they took her out of the grave, the groom was there and the Baal Shem too, leaning on his stick, looking down. "Dress her in her bridal dress," he said. "Set up four poles and this sheet, and get ready to lead her to the canopy."

They did everything he told them to. Then the bride and groom were led to the *khupe* and the ceremony took place as if she had not died.

Well, how was all that possible? The answer is this: a *gilgl* had taken possession of the young woman sometime before. A *gilgl* is the transmigrating soul of someone who has died. And the time had come for this *gilgl* to leave her body, and in order for him to do that, she had to die. And so she did. But when the Baal Shem said to the *gilgl*, "I order you to leave her," the *gilgl* fled and the bride's soul returned to her body.

And so she was led to the wedding canopy, after which they all rode away.

1 6 0
The Shretele That Took a Little Nip

Reb Shiye Heshl, a bookbinder, tells this story:

"My grandmother used to tell all sorts of tales, but I have to say that she never told any lies. Once she told us that one day when she was lying in bed, she saw an elf, a *shretele*, crawl out from under it. Her baby was also lying in the bed and crying. The *shretele* went up to it and rocked it for a while, then gave the baby a light slap which made it stop crying. After that the *shretele* trotted up to a cupboard where a flask of brandy was stored. It took out the brandy, had a few nips, and ran back under the bed.

"Well, from that time on, my grandmother never had to buy brandy, because no matter how much you poured out of the flask the *shretele* had sipped from, it always remained full."

1 6 1

The Lost Hat and the Pile of Gold

A wagon driver coming to harness his gray horse one morning noticed that it was exhausted and sweating. He remembered hearing that *kapelyushniklekh* liked gray horses and often spent the night riding them. He had heard too that if anyone snatched the caps off their heads, they would go away and not return—and moreover, they would pay a lot of money to get their caps back. He knew also that they were afraid of light, and so one night he took a lantern and hid in the barn. As he lay there, he heard his horse whinnying and the sound of running. He stood up and raised his lantern high. The *kapelyushniklekh,* seeing the light, scattered in all directions, and one of them, in his haste, left his cap behind.

The wagon driver took the cap home with him. The next night a couple of *kapelyushniklekh* came to ask for it and promised to give him a great deal of gold in return. He consented, but demanded the gold first. Hardly a moment passed before a heap of gold appeared in front of him, so he gave them the cap. He stood wondering where to hide the gold and which of his debts to pay first—when dawn came, and in the light of day he saw that instead of a heap of gold, there was a pile of rocks lying there.

The Miracle of the Beer Keg

My Shiye managed to save up sixty gildn. From time to time he would withdraw five or ten gildn, and I would keep track of how much was left. One day I took out twenty gildn, but when I counted what was left a few moments later, the whole amount was there. I counted once, I counted twice, and there they were: sixty gildn. So I told Shiye that he must have made a mistake. He counted the money once more. Still sixty gildn! "We've both made mistakes in counting," I said, "or else you don't remember how much money you put in."

"Don't be crazy," he said.

"Come on," I said, "I know how much I took out." Well, what do you think? It was only after we mulled it over that we realized the money had been blessed. Evidently the good Lord on high had done a miraculous thing, and if the Lord wills it, prosperity comes in the door unbidden.

Yes, yes. Such things did happen. Wait. Would you like another instance? Didn't something like it happen to me just before the war? You know, of course, that the holiday season is good for business. I manage to sell several barrels of beer and, with God's help, some brandy. Good enough! One day I noticed that the cashbox was full and the beer and brandy barrels were filled to the top—though we had been drawing from one of them all day long. So I said to Shiye, "What's going on? Usually the barrels are empty by now, yet you've been drawing from the same barrel all day long."

It was then that I went up to the barrel to draw myself some beer. I said to Shiye, "I don't believe it. Look, it's still full." Then I shook the barrel and—slap, slap. It was empty. Who knows? If I had kept my mouth shut and pretended not to notice, it might still—ah well. Would that the good Lord would do the same thing again.

1 6 3

How Doves Saved a Synagogue from Fire

Some forty-five years ago, the whole town of Gorlits was destroyed in a great fire. People fled to the safety of the fields from the all-consuming flames. The Jews of Gorlits were truly in despair when the flames began to approach the old synagogue. But just as the fire drew near it, a flock of white doves appeared and held the flames back with the breeze they created by flapping their wings.

1 6 4

The Calf That Turned to Gold

There was this widow who had many children. She had to go to work every morning, so she prepared food for the children and then locked them in the house. Every day when she came home, her children told her that a calf had darted out from behind the oven and eaten the meal of the youngest child, Sorele. Each day when their mother started to leave for work, the children would weep because they were afraid of the calf. But since she had to go, there was no help for them. Then one day as the children were eating, the calf darted out once more from behind the oven and began to eat Sorele's meal. This time the child grew angry and struck the animal on the head with her spoon. In that instant the calf was transformed into a heap of gold. When the widow came home, she could see at once that the gold was worth a fortune.

165

A Cave That Leads to the Land of Israel

The road that leads to a certain village in the district of Shebershin passes between two mountains through such a steep valley that the traveler feels as if he has entered a pit. There is a cave in that valley which the local peasants call the "Synagogue." The story is told that when the Jews found their way into Poland after their expulsion from Spain, they stopped in the cave to rest and study and pray. And in nearby trees there are still to be found carved Hebrew words which read as follows: "This is where we completed the reading of the Talmud tractate 'Shabbat.' " And the brook running past the cave is called the Brook of the Prophet Samuel.

Another cave in that region is reputed to lead to the land of Israel. A story is told about a holy man clothed in white who lived some hundred years ago. He was called the White Rebbe and is still widely known for his miracles. He was very anxious to provoke the coming of the Messiah. One day, saying that he was on his way to the land of Israel, he went into the forest. He was followed all the way to the cave by a few pious women and a crowd of pranksters. At the entrance to the cave, he sent a kid in and settled down to wait for three days. When the kid had not returned at the end of that time, he said it proved that this was indeed the road to the land of Israel. Then he himself entered the cave and was never seen again.

166

Late-Night Spooks

One winter evening a number of men were sitting around in the synagogue telling stories. One of them, a workingman who sat a little apart from the others, fell asleep. Later the synagogue caretaker, not noticing he was there, locked him in the building. In the middle of the night the man awoke and saw a number of white-clad people dancing to the sound of music. He tried to get to the window to call for help, but someone gripped him from behind. Giving a wrench, he pulled away and ran to the window, where he began shouting. A crowd gathered. At last the rabbi, together with a *minyen,* a prayer quorum of ten men, went into the synagogue and escorted him out.

And that's why, in the Great Jassy Synagogue in Rumania, they recite their prayers early and avoid prolonging them into the night.

167

The Demon Sheep

A Jew was traveling from his village to town. On the way he noticed a bound sheep lying in the road, bleating. The villager jumped down to load the sheep into his wagon. Though the animal was very heavy, the man was not willing to untie it, so he heaved and hauled and labored until at last he got it stowed away. Then he had to crack the whip because the horses could not pull the wagon unless they stretched and strained. As they drew near town, the man felt the wagon moving more easily. Looking back, he saw the sheep standing on its hind legs, exposing its rear end to him. "Ha, ha, ha!" it cried. "I sure made you heave and haul and sweat, didn't I?" Then it leaped from the wagon and disappeared.

1 6 8
The Dibbuk Melody of Tolne

In the town of Vishnevits the cantor was an older Jew and a disciple of the Rebbe of Tolne. Now, because his voice was beginning to fail, some of the congregation argued that it was time to get a new cantor. But they were opposed by the disciples of the Tolne Rebbe, and the result was that a small war developed over the issue.

It happened one day that the cantor's voice turned very hoarse. And when his hoarseness persisted, even the disciples of the Tolne Rebbe conceded that it might be time to look for a new cantor.

As is the custom among Jews, they came to terms with the old cantor. They got his permission (given grudgingly, you may be sure, but what else could he do?) to hire another cantor, a young man who was pious as well as a fine musician. The whole town was delighted by the sweetness of his voice when he sang the prayers, and they respected him for his piety and his good character.

The deposed cantor, who could hardly bear to acknowledge the talent of his younger rival, regarded him with envy and hatred. At last, just at the time of the high holidays, grief made the old cantor desperately ill, and just before Rosh Hashana he was carried to his eternal rest.

Everyone mourned his passing. Some people, even those who most opposed him, felt that they had had some share in bringing on his death. As for the young cantor, he went about depressed and restless, like a man stumbling in the World of Chaos. He too felt that he had hastened the old cantor's death.

Then misfortune struck him. On the beginning of the Jewish New Year, just as he was about to sing the *musef* prayers beginning with *hineni heoni mimaas,* "Here I stand poor in deeds," he stood suddenly stock still, unable to remember the melody he had prepared for the words. He shut his eyes and searched his memory, without success. Not a trace of recall. Then the shade of the old cantor rose before his eyes, and the words *hineni heoni mimaas* rose from his throat. But not in his own voice, and not in the melody he had prepared; no, it was the melody the old cantor had sung for years. The congregation recognized the voice at once and knew, too, that the melody of the *hineni* was the old man's.

The new cantor fainted away. Just as his assistants were lifting him, he came to. With uncanny strength he tore himself out of their grasp and rushed to the *bime,* where the angry voice of the old cantor came from his throat, crying, "I am still the town cantor. This is my pulpit and I will sing the *hineni* according to my melody."

The young cantor, pale and faint, was led home and the *musef* service was conducted by a member of the congregation.

Soon after Rosh Hashana the young man was brought to Rebbe Dovidl in Tolne. Reb Dovidl took the cantor into his study and shut the door so they could be alone. "Now," he said, "sing me the *hineni* with your melody." The cantor sang, but what came out was the hoarse voice of the dead man, the old cantor.

Reb Dovidl said angrily, "A melody must be sweet and pleasant, and prayer too must be sweet, especially in the Days of Awe when one prays, 'May it be Thy will, O mighty Lord, that my voice may neither falter nor turn hoarse; may it grow steadily stronger until it is like the clear sound of the *shoyfer.*' He who leads the prayers must use his voice to persuade the Lord of the Universe. And to persuade Him one needs a better, a lovelier voice than yours is now. Go, then, back to your rest, and let this man, who stands in your place, pray to the Lord in his own fine voice so that he can plead with Him for the salvation of his people."

There followed a long silence. Then Reb Dovidl spoke once more, this time without anger, in a gentle voice: "The two of you are both cantors. Now pay close attention to the *hineni,* which I will sing according to my own melody. Listen hard and learn it by heart, for your own good."

With that Reb Dovidl began to sing the *hineni* in a clear voice and with a new melody which rose higher and clearer at every note he sang. Higher and higher, a song from the heart, at once sweet and ecstatic. And when Reb Dovidl finished with the words *shomeya tfile,* "Hear my prayer," he lifted his tear-stained eyes, and with his hands outstretched said tenderly, "Now you, who are one of the purified dead, go back to your rest. The melody I've taught you will unbolt every door and open every gate for you, and you will achieve your soul's repair. And I assure you that you will be found worthy to sing this very melody to the *tsadikim* in the Garden of Eden."

Then Reb Dovidl went up to the young cantor and embraced him. Looking deep into his eyes, he said, "Now let's both try to sing the *hineni* according to my melody. The old cantor is no longer here, and he will never again appear in your synagogue."

Reb Dovidl began to sing his *hineni,* and the young cantor, his voice fully restored, and clearer, purer than it had ever been, sang along with him.

And this was the melody that for many years was sung by the Hasidim of Tolne. The melody they called the Dibbuk Melody of Tolne.

The Missing Bridegroom

There were two boys who were friends, and who always studied the Talmud together. Then it happened that one of them died. So the other was left to study alone. In time he grew up, and a marriage was arranged for him. Now, the custom is that the groom is not permitted to be alone on the day before the wedding, but since everyone was very busy, he slipped out of the house for a minute. He was no sooner outside than his childhood friend came up to him and said, "What are you doing?"

At first the groom was frightened, but then his fear left him and he replied that he was about to be married. His friend said, "Come with me and I'll show you where I live."

"How can I?" replied the groom. "I'm to be married tomorrow."

"You can come for a moment," replied the friend. He led the groom to the outskirts of town and into a very fine house. On a table lay a volume of the *gemore*. "Let's see," said the friend, "which of us is better at remembering our lessons." And so they sat down to study, and they studied together for a hundred and fifty years.

When the hundred and fifty years were up, the groom left the house and headed back to the home of his prospective father-in-law. Everything was changed, however, and when he came to what had been the father-in-law's house, he saw that it was altogether differently constructed. The people of the town, seeing him dressed in the style of a hundred and fifty years ago, laughed at him. When he went into the house and inquired for his bride, the occupants thought he was insane. But there was an old woman keeping warm near the oven who heard his questions and the names he gave. She told him that a hundred and fifty years ago, a young man had disappeared the day before his wedding. The groom, hearing that, understood what had happened and uttered a prayer to the Lord. And then he died.

170
Two Hrubeshoyv Legends

In Hrubeshoyv there was a *minyen*, a prayer quorum of Jews that was known as the Great *Minyen*. Its members were all holy men living in concealment. All were workingmen: a tailor, a shoemaker, a porter, a carpenter, a smith, and so on. They used to meet after midnight in the small synagogue, where they immersed themselves in the holy Torah. One day they decided to force the Messiah to come.

There are two stories about what happened then: one is that a member of the *Minyen* made a mistake in the names they used to invoke Him and instead invoked the evil Samael, and so they were all consumed by fire. The other version is that the Baal Shem Tov, when he heard what they were up to, dispersed them because it was not yet time for the Messiah. To this day it is said that their grave-stones are visible only once a year, on the first day of the month of Elul.

There are all sorts of stories about these holy men. It happened once that the *menoyre*, the seven-branched candelstick, the hanging candelabrum, and various other things were stolen from the syn-agogue. In spite of an intensive search, the thief could not be found. The Jews of Hrubeshoyv were very unhappy. Then a member of the Great *Minyen* came to the synagogue. It was the carpenter, who took out a large drill and started to bore a hole in the place where the *mezuze* was nailed to the doorpost. Immediately afterward a man with a hole in his head came running, bringing the stolen things.

171

Why the Rebbe's Pipe Must Be Kept Lighted

One day a Hasid was on his way to see his rebbe. As he walked along, a woman came up to him and said that he would have to marry her. "I can't possibly do that," said the Hasid. "I have a wife and children at home." But she replied, "If you don't marry me, I'll kill you." The Hasid pleaded with her, saying he couldn't give an immediate answer, he needed a little time to think it over.

"All right," said the woman, "you have a year to think about it. After that you'll have to marry me." And with these words she disappeared.

The man went to his rebbe and told him what had happened. The rebbe said, "Don't worry, I'll help you. Come back to see me before the year is out."

Six days before the year was out, the Hasid returned to the rebbe. The rebbe seated him at the head of his table and said to the other Hasidim he had called in, "No matter what you see, don't be frightened." No sooner had he spoken than a woman came in. At her entrance darkness fell, but when the rebbe concentrated his mind, the room brightened once more. "What is it you want?" asked the rebbe.

"I want my husband," she replied, "the one who is sitting at the head of the table. He belongs to me."

"He can't possibly marry you, because he has a wife and children at home," said the rebbe. Then, lighting his pipe, he said, "I'll tell you what. You can marry him when I have finished smoking my pipe. But so long as this pipe stays lighted, you will have no power over him." He had no sooner spoken than the woman disappeared. And the Hasid went home to his wife and children.

For his part the rebbe took care to keep his pipe lit, and years later on his deathbed he gave orders that it must never be allowed to go out and that it must be kept well hidden. "Because if it ever goes out, she will have power over the Hasid even after his death. She can draw his soul down and force it into the body of some other man, who then must marry her." And ever since, from generation to generation, the rebbe's descendants have kept his pipe lighted and hidden.

172
Luckily, the Rooster Crowed Late

It was twelve o'clock midnight. Suddenly Reb Moyshe heard someone dancing near his window. Since it was summer, he went out of the house wearing only his trousers. All at once he felt himself being grabbed by demons, and the next thing he knew, he was flying through the air. Though he tried, he was unable to cry out for help.

Well, they tormented him all night long until a rooster crowed and he found himself standing in the meadow on the other side of the mill stream. It was still an hour and a half before dawn. When he saw someone he knew, he begged the man to bring him his clothes so he could dress and walk back to town. The man fetched his things, and Reb Moyshe went home.

My grandmother, who told me this story, used to say, "And if the rooster had crowed a little bit earlier, the demons would have dropped him in the middle of the stream."

Neither Eat nor Drink
What a Demon Offers

It once happened that a number of Hasidim, driving in a carriage, came to a town and asked the local *moyel*, the ritual circumciser, to accompany them to a village for a few hours. The unsuspecting *moyel* went with them. They drove on and on, on and on. The trip seemed endless. At last they drove into a dense and very dark forest. In its midst stood a fine house into which they led the *moyel*. As he was examining the child to be circumcised, the newly delivered mother said, in a whisper: "Whatever you do, don't eat or drink anything here or you'll be lost. These people are demons, and everything you see here is meant to deceive you. Long ago I was traveling when they handed me a drink of water, and from that time on they had such power over me that I could not escape."

Well, he circumcised the child, after which he was led into a grand hall royally furnished and decorated, with a table full of good things to eat. But when the *moyel* refused to eat or drink anything, the house suddenly disappeared. It was weeks until, footsore and weary, he found his way back to his home town.

174

A Balshem Drives Out a Dibbuk

This is a true story about a *balshem,* a wonder-worker. The eighty-year-old taleteller from whom I got it gave me the *balshem*'s family name—it was Zhuravitser.

There was a young man in our village who was very clever, but an idler. One day he disappeared, and no one knew what had become of him.

Five or six years later, my father had to travel to a *shtetl* in Volhynia on business. There he wanted to go to an inn, but the place was packed and the street outside was jammed with people trying to push their way in.

"What's going on?" my father asked.

"There's a *balshem* inside," was the reply. "He's giving out talismans against all sorts of sickness, and amulets to help women get pregnant."

Just then the door of the inn opened and someone ran out right in front of my father. He was wearing a white satin coat, a waistband, and a fur-trimmed hat. My father looked closely at him and cried, "Moyshele, is that you? Are you the *balshem?*"

"Hush," said the *balshem.* "Come with me. I'll let you in on something."

He seated my father on his wagon and they rode off to the home of a rich villager. The *balshem* had been summoned to drive a dibbuk out of this villager's daughter, who was unable to sleep at night and kept shrieking that there was a demon in her featherbed.

When they arrived, the *balshem* asked to be taken to the young woman's room. Then he sent everyone out so that, as he said, he could practice the discipline of seclusion. Those who eavesdropped at the door could hear him chanting phrases from the Cabala.

Suddenly all was silent. The door opened and there stood the *balshem.* He asked the rich villager to bring him a yellow cat and a small container of pitch. After much searching, a yellow cat and some pitch were found and given to him. Then he shut himself into the room once more, but this time he had my father with him.

He took the cat and smeared it with the pitch. Then he cut open one end of the featherbed and inserted the cat. That done, he opened the door and ordered that the young woman's bed be carried to the edge of a nearby wood.

When his instructions had been followed, he said, "Wait. Very soon I'll drive the demon out of your daughter." Taking a glass of water into which he had poured effervescent powders, he began to mutter incantations, all the while making faces, spitting and whispering. The water in the glass fizzed and bubbled. The Volhynia bystanders, who had never seen such powders, trembled at the dreadful signs.

It was then that the *balshem* took his stick and began to beat on the feather bed. There was a terrible screeching and out sprang the cat. At the sight of the strange black creature, feathered all over, that leaped yowling out of the featherbed, the awed bystanders cried, "Hear, O Israel."

The young woman, seeing that the demon had fled, grew calm and from then on was able to sleep at night. Soon she recovered her health. Of course, the *balshem* was well rewarded and stood generous treat to my father, who confessed that no real *balshem* could have invented a more effective way of driving out a demon than Moyshele.

At which both he and Moyshele doubled over with laughter.

175

Lantekh, the Bridge Hobgoblin

When the old rebbe, Shneyer Zalmen, was a young man, he lived with his parents-in-law in Vitebsk. Displeased with what they saw as his strange religious behavior, they urged their daughter to divorce him. But despite the problems he created in her life, she was not willing to part from him. She said that her husband was a great man.

In Vitebsk a small river sets off a district called Zadunove from the rest of the town. To get there, one had to cross a footbridge, and for a while, the way across the bridge was barred by a hobgoblin, a *lantekh*. Now, the rebbe's mother-in-law deliberately sent the rebbe to get her something from Zadunove. As the rebbe started across the bridge, it began to tremble and he felt that someone was trying to tear his fur hat from his head. Understanding at once that this was the hobgoblin's work, he cursed it and drove it away to the most distant of deserts, saying, "You belong in uninhabited places."

And from that time on, the *lantekh* was never heard from again.

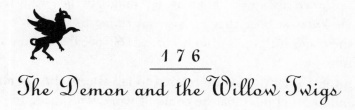

176

The Demon and the Willow Twigs

One Hoshana Rabba night, a member of the Great *Minyen* of Hrubeshoyv was returning home from a village carrying a *heshayne,* a sheaf of hallowed willow twigs.* He was on his way to the synagogue to recite the Psalms. As he went along, he met a demon disguised as a woman who had an infant in her arms. The woman stopped him and said, "What is it you're carrying?"

---

* During Succos it is customary to beat a bunch of willow twigs against the reading desk of the synagogue as an accompaniment to prayer.

"A sheaf of hallowed willow twigs."

"No," she said, "that's a broom."

"A sheaf of hallowed willow twigs," said he.

"A broom," said she. And round and round this way they went several times. She wanted him to say that the sheaf of hallowed willow twigs was a broom so that they would lose their sanctity and she would have power over him. Finally he struck her across the face with his sheaf of twigs, and she disappeared. The child she had been holding fell to the ground. He took it into town to the home of a woman who had just given birth. He said to her, "Here is your child." The people looked in her bed, and there they found a bundle of straw tied up to look like a child.

177
The Sleepy Tailor and the Zmore

Once there was a tailor who was sewing for the peasants at Christmastime. Since he still had a great deal to do, and it was Christmas eve, he planned to work all night. At midnight he grew terribly sleepy. He knew at once that a *zmore* was trying to put him to sleep so that she could suck milk from his breast. He decided to stay awake at all costs.

When the *zmore* saw that he refused to fall asleep, she got into his thread and knotted it so that he couldn't work. This made the tailor very angry, and he grabbed his scissors and cut the thread in two. In the morning the severed body of an old hag was found outside the tailor's window.

From that time on, the *zmore* never bothered the tailor again.

178

The Last Dibbuk

The town of Lashkovits had never, absolutely never, had a day like
that Yom Kippur.

In the synagogue the congregation was finishing the *musef* prayers,
though in fact most of the assembly had already dispersed, leaving
only the pious old men.

The Rebbe of Lashkovits, the last descendant of Reb Meyerl of
Premishlan, stood before the Holy Ark. Wearing his prayer shawl
and his white linen overgarment, he prayed passionately, imploring
the Lord to come to his aid for the sake of his holy grandfather, Reb
Meyerl.

For some while now a murmur like the lapping of waves had been
audible from the town square behind the synagogue. Hundreds of
people, adults and children, from Tshortkev, Butshatsh, Otenyi, Pro-
shove, and even from Tarnopol, had come to witness the duel between the holy Rebbe of Lashkovits and Mekhele Volakh of
Tshortkev, the heretic follower of Rabbi Shapira.

Today the whole world would discover whose was the greater power: that of the holy faith or that of the heretics (may the Lord have mercy on them). This, anyhow, is what the pious followers of Reb Aryele-Leyb of Lashkovits were thinking and saying.

Opposing them were the Shapiraniks, the disciples of the Enlightenment and the admirers of Mekhele Volakh, who had dared to challenge the Rebbe of Lashkovits to a duel. They maintained that the duel would reveal whether the forces of darkness and superstition or the forces of light and reason had the greater power.

But the members of those two parties were but as drops of water in the ocean compared with the mob of the simply curious. In the interval after the *musef* service and the beginning of *nile,* the crowd that had gathered in the square would see the great Rebbe attempt to drive a dibbuk out of a woman and into the mouth of the heretic, Mekhele Volakh.

The cantor finished reciting the *musef* service. Not a soul was left in the synagogue except Reb Aryele and several old men in their customary places by the East Wall, who did not want to abandon him. From the alcove in which Reb Uryele stood came the fearful sounds of his prayers, which were then echoed by the groans of the old women who were still in the women's section.

Out in the open square, the impatient thousand-headed mob waited, growing larger minute by minute. Not an infant lay in its cradle. Everyone was in the square: Jews, non-Jews, peasants of every age and sex from all the nearby towns.

Standing at the center of the square was Mekhele Volakh, a smallish man with a graying yellow beard. As usual, an ironic smile played on his lips, though now it had taken on determination as well. In his gray eyes glowed the heroic light that one sees in the eyes of someone who, certain of victory, is prepared to fling himself into bitter conflict.

Mekhele Volakh was a simple sort of man. An innkeeper. Not many years ago he had been a Hasid who made fun of Rabbi Shapira and the Shapiraniks. Then suddenly—and no one knew why—he visited Rabbi Shapira. He read his pamphlets and the journal *Hamagid,* and in time he became one of the rabbi's most devoted followers, ready to walk through fire and water for the sake of the Enlightenment.

In the pages of *Hamagid* Mekhele had read how the Lashkovits "saint" was sending out letters to all parts of the world in which he claimed to heal all sorts of illnesses. The Lashkovits Rebbe asserted, furthermore, that he had a particular talent for driving out dibbuks from the bodies of their victims. Because of his skill, hundreds and hundreds of afflicted women and maidens had recovered their health. Mekhele found what he read intensely interesting and undertook to investigate what was going on in Lashkovits.

It happened that he had relatives there, who told him that in the matter of dibbuks, the Rebbe had his hands full. Lashkovits seemed to be full of dibbuks just then. There was a regular epidemic of possessed women and maidens who came to Lashkovits from towns and villages throughout the region. The word "dibbuk" and the reports of the wonders performed by the Rebbe filled the air.

And it was then that Mekhele decided to take a hand in the matter. He went first to Rabbi Shapira and described his plan: he would challenge the Lashkovits "saint" to a duel. He would "sanctify the Name" of the Enlightenment by exposing the Lashkovits Rebbe's deceit and chicanery.

Rabbi Shapira tried to dissuade him, saying that truth did not require uproar and frenzy to prevail. It went silently and moderately about its work. In any case, deceit would not endure for much longer, because darkness must fly from the oncoming victory of light. But Mekhele refused to be guided.

Mekhele asked his relatives in Lashkovits to convey the following message to the Rebbe: "I, Mekhele, the Shapiranik, the *maskl,* have contempt for your dibbuks. I say that it is all a tissue of lies designed to mislead people and separate them from their money. And if the Rebbe holds that the tales of dibbuks are true, then let him demonstrate that truth to the world. If he can drive a dibbuk *out* of someone, he ought to be able to drive one *into* someone else. And I, Mekhele, am prepared to receive such a dibbuk. If the Rebbe believes he has the powers he claims, then let him name a day and let him show the world what he can do."

Mekhele's relatives delivered his challenge. Meanwhile, the story of what Mekhele had done spread throughout Tshortkev and Lashkovits and to all the towns and villages in the region. It was said that the court of the Tshortkev Rebbe tacitly encouraged Mekhele, perhaps because it was envious of the pomp with which the Lashkovits court was conducted, or perhaps because the Tshortkev Rebbe's followers were too aristocratic for such crude miracles as driving out dibbuks.

In either case, the truth is that the Tshortkev court warned the Lashkovits Rebbe not to embroil himself in a battle with the heretics. But it was already too late for the Rebbe to back out. He had to pick up the gauntlet that had been flung down. Meanwhile he treated the matter with the utmost seriousness, hoping thereby to frighten his foe. Indeed, the Rebbe actually consulted a lawyer to ask whether he

could be sued if the dibbuk should kill Mekhele Volakh. The lawyer replied that the law books were silent on the subject of murders committed by word of mouth.

Then, through the intercession of various persons, in particular several of Mekhele's relatives, the Rebbe sought to warn Mekhele of the dire consequences of his challenge. But Mekhele was not to be put off. He was afraid of nothing.

So the Rebbe of Lashkovits deliberately set Yom Kippur as the day for the duel. And he chose precisely the time just before *nile* when every Jew stands most in fear of the Day of Judgment, the time when everyone's fate is about to be sealed. But that did not frighten Mekhele either. And now the duel was about to take place.

In the middle of the square stood the invisible dibbuk, hidden inside a woman who howled and grimaced and flung her arms and her head about as she cast venomous glances in Mekhele's direction. From time to time she lunged at him as if she meant to tear him to bits with tooth and claw. Mekhele, however, stood unmoved. He showed her his fist and said, "Keep your hands to yourself, you shrew. You're nothing but a charlatan."

At last the Rebbe, wearing his *talis* and his *kitl,* the white linen robe worn on solemn occasions, came out of the synagogue. With his eyes wide he walked slowly, solemnly, casting stern glances in Mekhele's direction as he made his way to the middle of the square.

As the crowd parted for the Rebbe, there was a sudden mass movement, as if everyone had shuddered at the same time. The now silent crowd hardly breathed. It was as if the human wave had congealed.

The Rebbe stopped and turned his penetrating eyes on Mekhele, his mortal enemy. The Rebbe's thick, dark eyebrows rose like thunderclouds. With an intonation that was at once gentle and threatening he addressed his foe: "You! Listen. Not many minutes ago we invoked God's name as we prayed, 'Turn, turn from your wicked ways. May the evildoer turn from his path and the sinner from his vicious thoughts.' Hear me, heretic, today is a day for repentance. A day for begging pardon. Now I warn you, Mekhele, you evildoer, heretic . . . repent—repent for one day, for one hour before your death. The Lord is a God of mercy. And I too will forgive you."

But Mekhele, his stance assured and impudent, his lips twisted into a contemptuous smile, turned to face the Rebbe. After a brief glance at the crowd, he said, his voice perfectly controlled, "Do your worst. I haven't come to hear your warnings. I'm here to expose you for the fraud that you are. See, I've opened my mouth. Now, drive the dibbuk into me—if you can."

A murmur swept through the crowd. The human wave shuddered once more. Cries of "Heretic! Convert! Apostate!" were heard here and there. But a fierce hush from the majority restored silence.

For one instant the Rebbe could be seen to tremble. He lowered his head, and raised it again. Then, with a fierce gesture, he stretched his right arm out toward the possessed woman who was writhing, squealing, and lunging wildly toward him. "Silence, wicked one!" he cried. "Do you hear what I say? My decree is that you shall leave the woman through the little finger of her left hand, and enter into that man who is as wicked as you are."

Again came a murmuring, but it stopped almost immediately. The eyes of everyone turned fearfully toward Mekhele.

For his part, he seemed indifferent to the gaze of those thousands. He smiled more scornfully than ever, stuck out his tongue at the possessed woman, and called, "Well? What are you waiting for?"

One minute passed; a second; a third. Mekhele, the Rebbe, and the possessed woman maintained their poses as they exchanged looks of hatred. More minutes went by. A quarter of an hour.

The increasingly restless crowd looked toward the Rebbe, who had by now turned pale. His eyes were glazed, his hands hung at his sides.

Mekhele was the first to move. He straightened up, then, seizing his coattails, turned so that he stood with his back to the Rebbe. Bending slightly, he cried, "Let him kiss my . . ."

And left the square.

Slowly, wearily, the crowd, as if it had been whipped, crept back into the synagogue for the *nile* service. The congregation felt as if this were Tisha b'Av, and not Yom Kippur.* As for the Rebbe, he said not another word. He sat in his seat with tears streaming down his face. When the service was over, he shut himself inside his house and did not leave it or even speak to anyone for two years. He lived withdrawn and abandoned, and at the end of the two years, he died. With his death the line of Reb Meyerl of Premishlan came to its end.

And from that Yom Kippur on, no more dibbuks appeared in Galicia. Mekhele Volakh had driven them away for good.

* Yom Kippur is a day of personal as well as communal repentance. According to tradition, it is a day of anxiety, because one's fate for the coming year is then sealed. Tisha b'Av, however, is a day of mourning for the destruction of the First and Second Temples in Jerusalem. The implication in this story is that the congregation felt as if a national disaster had just occurred.

Glossary

With the exception of holiday names and a few other words which have officially recognized English spellings—e.g., Hasid, rebbe, Torah—Yiddish terms appear in this book in italics and are spelled according to the YIVO transcription of their pronunciation in standard Yiddish. In some cases where the words may also be familiar to readers by another spelling, that spelling is given in parentheses at the beginning of the definition, as is the word's literal meaning, where pertinent.

The main principle of the transcription system is that each letter (or fixed combination of two letters in the case of diphthongs and consonant clusters) represents a single sound. Consonants have roughly the same sound as they do in English; vowels, diphthongs, and consonant clusters are pronounced according to the chart below. Note that there are no "silent" letters. Thus, when you see an *e* at the end of the Yiddish word *bime,* for example, remember that the word has two syllables and does not rhyme with the English word "dime." Polysyllabic words in Yiddish are usually accented on the next-to-last syllable. When the stress falls elsewhere in a Yiddish term, it is indicated in the glossary with an accent mark.

Letter(s)	*Pronunciation*	*Example*
a	as in "tar"	*kadesh*
e	as in "get"	*gemore*

Letter(s)	Pronunciation	Example
i	as in "hit" in a closed syllable	k*i*desh
	as in "beet" in an open syllable	b*i*me
o	between the vowel sounds in "done" and "dawn"	mazlt*o*v
u	between the vowel sounds in "full" and "sure"	mez*u*ze
ay	the vowel sound in "why"	m*ay*rev
ey	as in "they"	kh*ey*der
oy	as in "boy"	m*oy*el
kh	the final sound in the German "ach"	**kh**ale
zh	like the "z" in "azure"	**zh**upitse
tsh	like the "ch" in "chew"	**tsh**olnt

arendarke   A female tenant farmer or innkeeper.

Ashmodai   The king of demons in Jewish demonology (Asmodeus).

Baal Shem Tov   (lit., "Master of the Good Name") Israel ben
   Eliezer (1700?–1760), an itinerant healer and preacher from
   Podolia, who is acknowledged as the founder of the Hasidic
   movement.

balemer   A platform in a synagogue from which the Torah is read
   during services.

balkoyre   A reader of the Torah in the synagogue.

balshém   (lit., "master of a name") An itinerant popular magician-
   healer who cures the sick, exorcises demons, writes amulets, and
   performs miracles, using the magical power of divine names.

barmitsve   (Bar Mitzvah, lit., "son of commandment") A Jewish
   boy's coming of age and assumption of religious responsibility at
   the age of thirteen; the celebration of this occasion, traditionally
   during the public reading of the Torah in the synagogue.

besmedresh   (lit., "house of study") A room or house for study and
   prayer; a small synagogue.

bime   (Heb. *bimah*) A platform in a synagogue from which the
   Torah is read during services.

Bobe Ha   A legendary witch; probably related to the Slavic Baba
   Yaga.

bobe-mayse (lit., "grandmother-story") A tall tale, an old wives' tale.

bóbetske An elaboration on the word *bobe* ("grandmother," "old woman").

bris (brith) The ritual circumcision of a Jewish infant boy, which normally takes place eight days after birth; also the festivities accompanying the circumcision ritual.

Cabala (Yid. *kabole*) Jewish mystical philosophy; also the texts of Jewish mysticism.

dáytshmerish (lit., "Germanicized") Refers to language or behavior imitating West European conventions, sometimes to the affectation of sophisticated manners.

dibbuk (Yid. *dibek*) In Jewish lore, an evil spirit or the restless soul of a dead person residing in the body of a living individual; it can be expelled only by magical means.

Elyohu Hanovi The prophet Elijah.

esreg (esroygim) (etrog) A citron; the fruit used in the ritual celebration of Succos.

farfl (farfel) A type of noodle made by chopping, plucking, or grating raw dough into small bits.

freylekhs A cheerful dance.

gabe (gabbai) A trustee or warden of a synagogue or other Jewish public institution; a manager of the affairs of a Hasidic rebbe.

gaon (Yid. *goen*) Originally the title of the head of a Jewish rabbinic academy in Babylonia between the seventh and eleventh centuries C.E.; it was later applied to an outstanding rabbinic scholar.

gehenem (Gehenna) hell; the place, in Jewish tradition, where the souls of the wicked are punished and purified.

gemore (Gemara) The discussion and interpretation of the Mishnah (q.v.), a part of the Talmud.

gildn A coin worth fifteen kopecks.

gilgl (Heb. *gilgul*) According to Jewish lore, the being (human or animal) into which the soul of a dead person may pass to continue life and atone for sins committed in the previous incarnation.

gimátrie   (gematria) Numerology; the summing up of the numerical equivalents of Hebrew letters and words to provide another level of interpretation. Very common among Cabalists and Hasidic masters.

golem   (Yid. *goylem;* lit., "shapeless mass") A creature brought to life by magical means, especially through the use of a divine name. Different Jewish communities have legends about local *golems* created to protect them against persecutions, specifically against blood-libel accusations. The best-known is connected with the *golem* created in the sixteenth century by Rabbi Judah Loew ben Bezalel, known as the Maharal of Prague.

groshn   (Ger. *groschen;* Pol. *grosz*) A small coin, used in Austria, Germany, and partitioned Poland.

hakodesh borekh hu   (lit., "The Holy One, blessed be He") A reference to God that appears frequently in liturgy.

Hasid(im)   (Yid. *khosid, khsidim*) Member of a Jewish religious movement founded in the eighteenth century in Eastern Europe, organized into groupings devoted to particular rebbes and generally stressing pious devotion and ecstasy over rabbinic scholarship.

haskole   (Haskalah) The Jewish Enlightenment movement, which flourished in Eastern Europe in the nineteenth century.

havdole   (Habdalah) The ceremony performed at the close of the Sabbath to distinguish between its holiness and the profaneness of the ensuing weekdays, consisting of prayers and songs, the lighting of a twisted candle, a blessing over wine, and the inhaling of fragrant spices.

heshayne   One of a series of prayers for salvation chanted during processions around the synagogue on Succos; also the willow twigs carried in the procession around the synagogue and beaten against the reading desk of the synagogue on Hoshana Rabba (q.v.).

hómentash   A triangular pastry, usually filled with poppyseeds, prunes or plum preserves, traditionally prepared especially for Purim.

hore khoyshekh   (lit., "mountains of darkness") A legendary remote place.

Hoshana Rabba   The seventh day of Succos (q.v.).

kadesh   (Kaddish) The prayer chanted before or after certain sections of synagogue worship. It is also recited by mourners, especially by a son for a dead parent; the term can also refer to a male heir responsible for saying the prayer.

kapelyúshnikl(ekh)   (lit., "hat maker") Little spirit(s) often found around horses.

kest   Room and board provided to a recently married couple by one or both sets of their parents.

khale   (challah, hallah) Bread, usually a braided white loaf, eaten on the Sabbath and on holidays.

khaper   (lit., "catcher") Refers to kidnappers of young Jewish boys for military service during the time of the cantonists in czarist Russia.

khazn   A cantor, a leader of prayers in the synagogue.

kheyder   (lit., "room") A school where Jewish children begin their traditional education, learning the letters of the Jewish alphabet and how to read the Bible and prayer books.

khupe   (huppah) The canopy under which the Jewish marriage ceremony traditionally takes place.

kidesh   (kiddush) The benediction over wine; a Sabbath forenoon celebration in honor of a joyous occasion at which this benediction is said.

kinder-máysele(kh)   A little tale for children.

kitl   The white linen robe worn by pious Jews on solemn occasions.

kloyz   A small synagogue or house of study, frequently restricted to some occupational or social group; the term is used especially by Hasidim.

kolnidre   (Kol Nidre) A prayer recited on Yom Kippur eve.

lamedvovnik   One of the legendary thirty-six ultra-pious men who live concealed in each generation, without whom the world could not continue to exist (from the letters *lamed-vov,* which have the numerical value of thirty-six).

lantekh   A mischievous hobgoblin.

lign-máysele(kh)   (lit., "little lying tale") A nonsense tale.

maged   (maggid) A Jewish preacher, often itinerant, whose discourse drew upon biblical texts embellished by rabbinical commentaries and folklore.

malekh An angel; a divine messenger.

maskl (maskilim) An adherent of the Jewish Enlightenment movement *(haskole),* advocating the assimilation of modern Western cultural values into Jewish life.

matse (matzah) The unleavened bread eaten during Passover.

mayrev (Ma'ariv) The evening service, recited daily after sunset.

mayse/máysele A tale, a story; a *maysele* is a little story.

mazl (mazel) Luck, personified in some folktales.

mázltov (mazel tov; lit., "good luck") An expression of congratulations.

medresh (midrash) The homiletical interpretation of Scripture; the literature of that interpretation among the early rabbis which contains legends and tales as a supplement to the Biblical narrative.

melamed A teacher of young children in *kheyder* (q.v.).

melave malke (lit., "the ushering out of the queen") The evening meal marking the conclusion of the Sabbath. This is often an occasion for Hasidim to gather with their *rebbe.*

menoyre (menorah) A multi-branched candelabrum. A seven-branched *menoyre* was erected in the Temple in Jerusalem and remains an important symbol of the Jewish people; a nine-branched *menoyre* is lit on the holiday of Hanukkah.

mesoyre A local legend, a memorat.

mezuze (mezuzah) A small case containing a strip of parchment inscribed with the text of Deuteronomy 6:4–9, which is attached to the doorposts of premises occupied by observant Jews. The *mezuze* is symbolically kissed by persons entering or leaving.

mikve (mikvah) Ritual bathhouse; pool for ritual immersion.

minkhe (Minchah) The afternoon daily prayer, recited at some time between noon and sunset.

minyen (minyonim) (minyan) Prayer quorum of ten adult males, the minimum required by tradition for certain religious services.

Mishnah (Yid. *mishne*) The core of the Oral Law, compiled by

Rabbi Judah Ha-Nasi (ca. 135–217) on the basis of previous collections and codified around the year 200, forming part of the Talmud.

misnaged (misnagdim) An opponent of Hasidism within Jewish orthodoxy.

mitsve (mitsvah) A divine commandment, one of the 613 precepts of the Torah; by extension, any good deed.

moshl (mesholim) An example, an analogy, a parable.

moyel (mohel) A ritual circumciser.

Moyshe rabeynu (lit., "Moses, our teacher") The traditional way of referring to the Biblical Moses.

múmenyu An affectionate form of *mume* (aunt); comparable to "auntie" in English.

musef (Musaf) An extension of the morning prayer, recited on the Sabbath and on holidays.

muser The literature and traditions of Jewish moral and ascetic theology.

nign (nigunim) A melody, tune, or song without words. In Hasidic tradition the creation of special *nigunim* is attributed to Hasidic leaders.

níle (Neilah) The last prayer recited on Yom Kippur.

ornkoydesh (Aron Kodesh; lit., "holy ark") The cabinet located on the eastern wall of a synagogue, in which Torah scrolls are kept.

parnes A Jewish community leader.

porets A landowner, a master of an estate.

Reb The traditional title prefixed to a man's name; comparable to "Mister" in English.

rebbe (lit., "my master") A Hasidic spiritual leader; a rebbe may or may not also be a *rov* (ordained rabbi, q.v.). A *melamed* is usually addressed by his young pupils as "Rebbe."

reboyne shel oylem "Lord of the Universe."

Rosh Hashana (Yid. *rosheshone*) The Jewish New Year.

rov A rabbi, the ordained graduate of a rabbinical academy, qualified to serve as the legal and ritual authority of a Jewish community.

sandek   The person who holds a baby boy during the circumcision ceremony. The role of *sandek* is regarded as an important honor.

seyder   (seder; lit., "order") The ceremonial meal for the celebration of Passover, during which the story of the Exodus from Egypt is told.

sfire   According to Cabalistic lore, one of the ten aspects or divine emanations in which God's creative power unfolds.

shabes   (Shabbos) The Sabbath.

shames   (shammas) A sexton in a synagogue; a rebbe's personal assistant.

shed (sheydim)   A demon, devil, ghost.

Shevuos   (Shabuoth; Yid. *shvues*) An early-summer holiday celebrating the gathering of the first fruits and the giving of the Torah to the Jews.

shoyfer   (shofar) The ram's horn blown in synagogues on Rosh Hashana and Yom Kippur.

shoykhet   (shochet) A ritual slaughterer, who kills and inspects cattle and poultry according to rabbinical principles of ritual purity.

shretele(kh)   A small, kindly, elf-like creature.

shtetl(ekh)   A small town; a market town.

shtibl(ekh)   A small Hasidic house of prayer.

shtrayml   The fur-trimmed hat worn by Hasidim on festive occasions.

shul   A synagogue.

Succos   (Sukkoth; Yid. *súkes;* lit., "tabernacles") An autumn harvest festival during which one lives in a temporary shelter, a *súke,* for a week. The holiday also commemorates the Israelites' wandering in the desert following the Exodus.

talis   (tallith) A prayer shawl with fringes at the corners, traditionally worn by men during morning prayers.

Talmud   The comprehensive designation for the *mishne* and the *gemore* (q.v.). There are two versions, the Babylonian and Jerusalem compilations, completed in the fifth and sixth centuries C.E., respectively. The Talmud contains both law and legend.

tfiln   (tefillin) Small boxes (phylacteries) containing Biblical texts (Exodus 13:1–10, 13:11–16; and Deuteronomy 6:4–9, 11:13–21) written on parchment, which are strapped to the arm and forehead during weekday morning prayers by observant male adults.

Tisha b'Av   (Yid. *tíshebov;* lit., "the ninth day of the month of *Av*") A day of fasting and mourning, observed in late summer, commemorating the destruction of the two Temples in Jerusalem.

Torah   (Yid. *toyre*) The Pentateuch, the Five Books of Moses; the scroll on which these first five books of the Bible are written. The term refers also to Jewish law in general and to the traditional study of sacred Jewish texts.

tsadek (tsadikim)   An especially pious, righteous, or spiritually pure man. A Hasidic leader (rebbe) is also often referred to as a *tsadek.*

tsholnt   (cholent) A stew, usually containing meat and beans together with potatoes or barley, prepared on Fridays and, in view of the prohibition against cooking on the Sabbath, kept warm overnight to be served as the main meal on Saturday afternoons.

Vilna Gaon   (Yid. *Vilner goen;* lit., "Sage of Vilna") Elijah ben Solomon Zalman (1720–1797), rabbinic scholar and teacher, leader of the *misnagdim,* the orthodox opponents of the Hasidic movement.

vunder-mayse   (lit., "wonder-tale") A fairy tale.

yeshive   (yeshivah) A rabbinical academy, an institution of higher Talmudic learning.

yeshuvnik   A Jewish villager.

yeytser-hore   Lust, temptation, the inclination to evil; sometimes personified.

Yom Kippur   (Yid. *yonkiper*) The Day of Atonement, observed ten days after the beginning of the Jewish year, when the fate of each Jew for the coming year is believed to be judged. The day is spent fasting and reciting prayers for the forgiveness of both communal and individual transgressions.

yortsayt   The anniversary of a person's death.

zeyde   A grandfather; an old man.

zhúpitse   A caftan; a long outer coat worn by adult Jewish men, especially in the Hasidic community.

zloty   A gold coin, equivalent to thirty groshn; used in Poland.

Annotations to the Tales

(Tales are listed by number, as in the table of contents.)

The annotations list the archival or published source of each tale, and, when known, the names of the storyteller and collector, as well as the date and place the story was recorded. The reader will also find biographical data about historical personages that appear in the legends, and short comments on selected tales.

Some of the pious tales and legends have a complex history in Jewish sources, going back to the literature of the Talmud and Midrashim, which, in turn, had their roots in oral tradition. Other tales have parallels in early Yiddish printed works such as the sixteenth-century *Mayse-bukh,* or the seventeenth-century memoirs of Glikl of Hamlen. At the other end of the time scale, we find retellings of some folktales in works of modern Yiddish and Hebrew literature. A number of such literary parallels to our stories are given in the annotations.

Folklorists Antti Aarne and Stith Thompson (*The Types of the Folktale,* 1961) devised a system for classifying fairy tales and other fictional tales, and I have indicated, where applicable, a story's international tale-type number according to their widely used index. Unfortunately, there is as yet no satisfactory index to legends (stories that purport to be true) to match the one available for fictional tales.

In many cases, the story printed is but one of several twentieth century oral Yiddish versions of a tale. Selected variants which are available in English translation are given in the comments following. Additional Yiddish variants in the YIVO Archives and in published sources will be listed in YIVO's Yiddish-language edition of the collection, forthcoming.

Certain Yiddish renditions of stories that are also told in other parts of the world contain numerous features specific to Ashkenazic Jewish culture. These have been designated in the annotations as Yiddish "oicotypes," a term folklorists use for a regional or ethnic group's own form of a tale.

With the exception of a few large, well-known cities (e.g., Warsaw, Cracow, Odessa, etc.) the names of East European towns, villages, and settlements are given in this book in their Yiddish forms, in the standard YIVO transcription. The corresponding official names of these places are supplied below, and reflect the official borders of the period between the two world wars.

Abbreviations

n.d.   no date recorded
n.p.   no place recorded
I.F.A.   Israeli Folktale Archive

The following collections are housed in the archives of the YIVO Institute for Jewish Research, New York City:

V.A.   Vilna Ethnographic Commission Archive
L.A.   Litwin (Hurwitz) Archive
C.A.   Y.-L. Cahan Archive
B.W.A.   Beatrice Weinreich Archive

1. TELLER: Father of collector, Pumpyan (Pumpenai), Lithuania, n.d. COLLECTOR: Benyomin Yankev Bialostotzky. SOURCE: Bialostotzky (1962), pp. 30–31. COMMENTS: A volume of parables entitled *Mishlei Ya'akov,* culled from the Preacher of Dubno's homilies, appeared in Cracow in 1886. Unfortunately, the contexts are lost to us.

2. TELLER: Father of collector, Pumpyan (Pumpenai), Lithuania, n.d. COLLECTOR: B. Y. Bialostotzky. SOURCE: Bialostotzky (1962), pp. 37–38, abridged.

3. TELLER: Rive, the daughter of Leye (no surname recorded), n.p. COLLECTOR: Anon., Tshernyak, ca. 1927. SOURCE: V.A. 167:8.

4. TELLER: Yosl Cutler, 32 years old, artist; heard it in Zhitomir, U.S.S.R., 1925. COLLECTOR: Y.-L. Cahan. SOURCE: Cahan (1940), no. 20, pp. 75–77. TALE TYPE: cf. 947A. COMMENTS: Poverty was rampant in Eastern Europe when these tales were recounted, and, not surprisingly, appears in every genre of Yiddish folk narrative. Pogroms, World War I, the Russian Revolution and Civil War contributed to the destruction of the economic life of Russian Jewry, particularly in the *shtetlekh.* In addition, industrialization and the · development of a market economy eliminated some of the traditional areas of small-town East European Jewish economic activity. Clearly, wish-fulfillment

folktales that banished poverty would become favorites.

5. TELLER/COLLECTOR: A. I. Kon, Gorodey (Horodziej), Poland, 1941. SOURCE: V.A. 167:6. COMMENTS: The "animal fable" genre has very few examples in the YIVO archives and in the printed sources of Yiddish tales collected from oral tradition. It would seem that this is more of a written than an oral genre. Dov Noy (1976), p. 260, corroborates this finding from his experience at the Israeli Folktale Archive. See also Dan Ben Amos (1967), p. 134, where he states that "there is no folklore genre in the Haggadah, the legendary section of the Talmud, which has so few examples and yet describes so many details of the story-telling situation as the fable."

6. SOURCE: V.A. 167:11. TALE TYPE: 200. COMMENTS: The manuscript reads: "From the Archives of the Historic Ethnographic Expedition (?)" [sic]; n.d. This may be a tale originally collected during the An-ski Expedition, 1912–1914. (See the Introduction, note 3.)

7. TELLER: Rokhl Rabin, 30 years old, heard it in Orinyen (Orinin), U.S.S.R. COLLECTOR: Y.-L. Cahan, 1928. SOURCE: Cahan (1930), no. 32, pp. 177–83; Cahan (1940), no. 43, pp. 206–12. TALE TYPE: 945.

8. TELLER/COLLECTOR: M. Tolpin, Ostre (Ostróg), Poland, n.d.

SOURCE: V.A. 69:7. TALE TYPE: cf. 1082. COMMENTS: This is an example of a tale that was both read and circulated orally, and which we know functioned in conversation to make a point, i.e., as a parable.

9. TELLER/COLLECTOR: A. I. Kon, Gorodey (Horodziej), Poland, 1941 SOURCE: V.A. 167:5. TALE TYPE: cf. 947A*.

10. SOURCE: V.A. 29:2. COMMENTS: Note that Yoshe-Ber justifies his view by referring back to a scriptural passage.

11. TELLER/COLLECTOR: Anon., from Warsaw, Poland, n.d. SOURCE: V.A. 32:9b. COMMENTS: In another variant of this popular legend (Cahan, 1938, p. 148) the hero is Reb Ayzik Yekeles of Sherbershin, who dreams of a treasure under a bridge in Leipzig and then uses the treasure he finds under his stove to build a beautiful synagogue in Shebershin. According to local legend this 950-year-old structure was designed by the architects who created the famous old Cracow synagogue.

12. COLLECTOR: Berl Verblinski, Grodne (Grodno), Poland, 1929. SOURCE: V.A. 33:1. COMMENTS: This tale has a history in Yiddish that goes back at least to the seventeenth or eighteenth century, when Glikl of Hamlen (1646–1724) included it in memoirs written for her children's edifica-

tion. In connection with the preparation of this book, I asked readers of the YIVO newsletter *Yedies fun YIVO* to put onto tape any Yiddish folktales they remembered hearing or telling. A variant of this very fable was mailed to me in 1984 in response to this request. Mr. Irving Genn taped the version he remembered hearing his mother, Elke Genn (born in Smargon [Smorgonie], Poland, 1880) tell in the 1930s in New York (B.W.A., 101). His comment: "A bitter tale. You can just imagine the sorts of tales that parents in those days—the thirties—told their children."

13. TELLER/COLLECTOR: L. Las, Shebershin (Szczebrzeszyn), Poland, n.d. SOURCE: V.A. 32:86b.

14. TELLER: Anon., from Podbrodz (Podbrodzie), Poland, n.d. SOURCE: Cahan (1938), no. 5, pp. 111–12. TALE TYPE: 735* and 947*. COMMENTS: A variant of this tale appears in the Yiddish translation of Jephta Yozpa ben Naftoli's *Maaseh Nissim,* published in Amsterdam in 1696, an English translation of which appears in Zinberg (1975), p. 200.

15. COLLECTORS: The Horodenka Folklore Collectors' Club, Poland, n.d. SOURCE: V.A. 30:12.

16. COLLECTOR: Nakhmen Libeskind, Lodz, Poland, 1926. SOURCE: V.A. 69:11.

17. COLLECTOR: Y.-L. Cahan. SOURCE: Cahan (1940), no. 17, pp. 60–67. TALE TYPE: 431 and 480.

COMMENTS: The motif of the anti-hero becoming the hero is a common one in Yiddish folktales; the seeming fool at the beginning of the tale is the successful one in the end. Cf. tale no. 22, "Clever Khashinke and Foolish Bashinke"; also V.A. 30:13.

18. TELLER/COLLECTOR: Leyb Ludnik, 31-year-old tailor, Rovne (Rowne), Poland, n.d. SOURCE: V.A. 57:1. TALE TYPE: 123.

19. TELLER/COLLECTOR: Anon., from Korets (Korzec), Poland, n.d. SOURCE: Cahan (1938), no. 12, pp. 121–22. COMMENTS: This tale has affinities with Yiddish folksongs in which a young girl bemoans her unmarried state. See, e.g., *"Yome, Yome, shpil mir a lidele,"* in Cahan (1957), pp. 252–53.

20. TELLER: A young boy who attended *kheyder* with Y.-L. Cahan in Vilna, Poland. COLLECTOR: Y.-L. Cahan, 1900. SOURCE: Cahan (1931), no. 4, pp. 16–20; Cahan (1940), no. 4, pp. 22–25. TALE TYPE: 700. COMMENTS: The teller has employed some typical Yiddish folktale markers: e.g., the childless couple praying at the cemetery, the reference to the ritually important thirteenth year, and the rhymed ending.

21. TELLER: Yankl Stepanski (b. 1903), Arishtsh, U.S.S.R.; tailor and plumber, since 1922 in the U.S. COLLECTOR: Rakhmiel Peltz, Philadelphia, 1985. SOURCE: B.W.A. no. 103.

22. TELLER: Peshe-Rive Sher (b. 1864),

Kozlovitsh (Kozlovich/Kozlovshch), U.S.S.R. COLLECTOR: Y.-L. Cahan. SOURCE: Cahan (1929), no. 12, pp. 36–37; Cahan (1940), no. 18, pp. 68–70. TALE TYPE: 480. COMMENTS: See note to no. 17, "A Tale of Two Brothers."

23. TELLER/COLLECTOR: Anon., from Warsaw, Poland, n.d. SOURCE: Cahan (1938), no. 17, p. 125. TALE TYPE: cf. 210.

24. TELLER: Rokhl Cahan, aunt of collector, Vilna, before 1928. COLLECTOR: Y.-L. Cahan. SOURCE: Cahan (1928), no. 3, pp. 223–24; Cahan (1940), no. 15, pp. 54–56. TALE TYPE: 720. COMMENTS: Most often names are not mentioned in folktales. When they are, they are common to other tales as well. Sheyndele (the generic "little girl") and Moyshele (the generic "little boy") appear to be favorites in such Yiddish tales. Cf. Cahan (1938), no. 23, p. 133.

25. TELLER: A young boy who attended *kheyder* with collector in Vilna, Poland. COLLECTOR: Y.-L. Cahan, 1900. SOURCE: Cahan (1931), no. 3, pp. 12–15; Cahan (1940), no. 3, pp. 18–21. TALE TYPE: 1696. COMMENTS: Compare this tale with the Khelm tales and the stories about Khushim the fool.

26. TELLER: Moyshe Zimnik, 36-year-old carpet salesman, whose grandmother told him this tale in Belz (Balti/Beltsy), Rumania, c. 1898. COLLECTOR: Y.-L. Cahan,

1928. SOURCE: Cahan (1931), no. 11, pp. 48–50; Cahan (1940), no. 22, pp. 84–85. TALE TYPE: 210.

27. TELLER/COLLECTOR: S. Verite, U.S.S.R., 1940. SOURCE: V.A. 154:15. TALE TYPE: 567 (with motifs from 461 II/III; 921; and 922). COMMENTS: One of the favorite ways for ending a Yiddish wonder tale is the recognition of the hero upon returning home not by his physical appearance but through his telling the story of his life. Cf. also no. 30, "Of Nettles and Roses," and V.A. 154:27. "Why the Head Turns Gray Before the Beard," "The Clever Girl" and "The Bishop and Moshke" (nos. 101, 71, and 75) are additional examples of Yiddish riddle tales.

28. TELLER: Anon., from Bender (Tighina/Bendery), Rumania, n.d. COLLECTOR: Leo Wiener. SOURCE: *Mitteilungen zur judischen Volkskunde* 9, 1902, no. 2, pp. 104–7. TALE TYPE: 325. COMMENTS: A common method of introducing a hero who is in some way strange is to begin with an episode such as we have here. A childless couple goes to a wonder rebbe and asks him to pray for the birth of a child. The rebbe tells them they can't have both riches *and* a child, and must make a choice. The implication is that they should be satisfied with their fate. Cf. V.A. 69:8, where the hero is a bear, and our no. 36, "The Snake Bridegroom."

29. TELLER: Yankl Mikantshik, a night watchman, Kiev, U.S.S.R., 1940. SOURCE: V.A. 154:2. TALE TYPE: 757. COMMENTS: See the Talmudic story about Solomon's banishment and three years of wandering in far-off lands in *Gittin* 68a–b. Y.-L. Peretz's *Der arendar* (The Innkeeper) is a literary rendering of a variant of this tale published in *Mitteilungen* 9 (1902) p. 108.

30. TELLER: Ite Kuperman, n.p., n.d. SOURCE: V.A. 154:27, abridged. TALE TYPE: cf. 403 (I, IIc, III, IVa, c, d); cf. also 510 (IId, IIIb), 709, 712 (Ib) as well as 506 (IVc). COMMENTS: The teller rambled on occasionally, and some rough edges have been smoothed out in this translation.

31. SOURCE: V.A. 57:5. TALE TYPE: 1164. COMMENTS: Cf. Cahan (1938), no. 23, p. 133.

32. TELLER: Khave Rubin, Smargon (Smorgonie), Poland, n.d. COLLECTOR: Y.-L. Cahan. SOURCE: C.A. 35. TALE TYPE: 923. COMMENTS: There are several Yiddish variants—all told by women storytellers—with culturally specific markers that support its designation as a Yiddish oicotype of the tale. See Alan Dundes, *Cinderella: A Case Book,* New York, 1983.

33. TELLER: Noyekh Kubel (called by the nickname *Noyekh Riz,* "Noah the Giant"), Warsaw, Poland, n.d. COLLECTOR: Shmuel Lehman, who began recording storytellers in 1902, was a tireless folklore collector until his death, in 1942, in the Warsaw Ghetto. One of the most faithful of recorders, Lehman was a master at capturing subtle oral styles. SOURCE: Vanvild (1923), no. 5, pp. 72–75, abridged. TALE TYPE: 950 and 1525. COMMENTS: For a structural analysis of several Yiddish variants of this popular tale, see B. Weinreich (1954).

34. TELLER/COLLECTOR: A. Y. Kon, n.p., n.d. SOURCE: V.A. 154:8. TALE TYPE: 610. COMMENTS: In variants of this tale other tellers (see V.A. 154:16) have included the motif of the Jewish community being threatened if the princess is not cured, a common motif in Yiddish tales (for which, see V.A. 154:32, 33a, 26:14).

35. SOURCE: V.A. 57:3. TALE TYPE: cf. 461, episode, IIIff. COMMENTS: The final episode, in which the envious brother tries in vain to imitate his poor brother, has parallels among our tale no. 41, "The Hunchbacks and the Dancing Demons," and V.A. 154:17.

36. TELLER: Rivke Dizhur, n.p., n.d. COLLECTOR: Sorke Kuperman. SOURCE: V.A. 154:14. TALE TYPE: cf.311 (Ia, II, IIIa, IV, V). COMMENTS: See comments to no. 28, "The Sorcerer's Apprentice," regarding unusual heroes. For an English translation of a Yiddish variant in which the hero is a bear, see "The Bear Bridegroom," in B. Weinreich (1957) pp. 288–94.

37. SOURCE: V.A. 154:9. COMMENTS:

This story sounds like a "modern" rather than a traditional fairy tale. The Slavic name of the hero and the lack of any culturally specific markers (except perhaps the focus on learning and the hero's opening a textile shop) points to a teller's adapting a tale heard from a Slavic neighbor.

38. TELLER: Nyome Pikover, Grodne (Grodno), Poland, 1927. COLLECTOR: Berl Verblinski, Grodne. SOURCE: C.A. 27:12, abridged. TALE TYPE: 675 (I, IIa, IIIa, b, IV, V); cf. 571 (III). COMMENTS: In the unabridged original the hero is brought to task at the end for having married out of the fold.

39. TELLER: Moyshe Zlotkevitsh, Bialestok (Bialystok), Poland, 13 years old, son of a beggar woman. COLLECTOR: Berl Verblinski, 1929. SOURCE: *Yidisher folklor* (1954), vol. I, pp. 13–14. TALE TYPE: a combination of 530, 850 (II), and 506. COMMENTS: Culturally specific motifs in this tale include the description of the "helpers" (a rabbi and the mysterious man—a mystic? a *lamed-vovnik?*), and the specification that the kings were Polish and German, and not just "any" kings.

40. TELLER: Ruvn Kravitski, 45 years old, father of collector, Yedvabne (Jedwabne), Poland, 1928. COLLECTOR: A. Kravitski, Yedvabne, who reported that he heard this tale from others as well, "mostly soldiers." SOURCE: V.A. 32:17. TALE TYPE: 400. COMMENTS: This culturally specific variant of an international tale type contains some magical elements from the Cabalistic sphere. It also incorporates Jewish motifs from the traditional Purim story—specifically where the hero gets drunk and boasts of his wife's beauty. The reference to the hero's thirteenth birthday (his *barmitsve*) is another such motif.

41. TELLER/COLLECTOR: A. Y. Kohn, 1940, U.S.S.R. SOURCE: V.A. 154:7. TALE TYPE: 503. COMMENTS: The failure of imitations is a favorite folktale theme. Cf. no. 59, "A Passover Tale."

42. TELLER: Khinye Lifshits, 57 years old, Krementshug (Kremenchug), U.S.S.R., 1940. COLLECTOR: S. Verite. SOURCE: V.A. 154:19. TALE TYPE: cf. 501, 510, and 506 (IVb).

43. TELLER: Yitskhok Vayner (b. 1846), Podbrodz (Podbrodzie), Poland, 1926. COLLECTOR: Arn and Khaye Eyngeldin. SOURCE: V.A. 30:34. COMMENTS: On the simplest level this seems to be the perfect male counterpart to the Yiddish Cinderella tale. Whereas the loveliness of a Cinderella dazzles (as in no. 32, "How Much Do You Love Me?"), in this story it is the learning of the young man that dazzles, and he ends up marrying the daughter of a prestigious rabbi. The number of cultural markers is striking; and

unlike most Cinderella tales, this one ends with the hero being reunited with his dead parents. But this is no ordinary "fairy tale." This story is reminiscent of tales spun by Reb Nakhmen of Bratslav, the Hasidic master storyteller. It is full of biblical and Cabalistic-mystical symbolism, and Messianic allusions. With a knowledge of the culture's mystical "subtexts," it can be read as an allegory. (See the introduction to this section.)

44. TELLER: Sholem Troyanovski, 62 years old, Yevpatorye (Yevpatorya), Crimea, U.S.S.R.—a shoemaker, a former longshoreman, and a member of a collective farm in Peretsfeld, Crimea. The collectors note that "he is not highly literate. He uses a great many Russian words in his daily life." COLLECTORS: Y. Tshernyak and Shike Troyanovski (son of the teller). SOURCE: V.A. 154:16, abridged. TALE TYPE: 570. COMMENTS: Troyanovski in this tale, as in others of his in the YIVO archives (V.A. 154:18 and 154:20), likes to end with revolution and overthrow of *anciens régimes,* adding his own twist to an otherwise fairly formulaic telling of a fairy tale.

45. TELLER/COLLECTOR: Noyekh Fishman, Torne (Tarnów), Poland, 1930. SOURCE: V.A. 26:8. TALE TYPE: This tale has certain parallels to types 313 and 400 (IIIa), but appears to be a well-devel-

oped tale, with many culturally specific motifs that do not fit the above tale types. See Schwartzbaum (1968), p. 86, note 46, and p. 459, addendum to note 46. COMMENTS: Ashmodai is the chief demon, the King of Demons in Jewish demonology. The marriage of Ashmodai's daughter to a mortal reflects the medieval belief in "the need of . . . spirits to find completion in the body of man," and the final rabbinical court scene deals with moral and legal problems raised by this belief (see Trachtenberg [1939], pp. 51–52). In East European Jewish folk tradition, the Land of the Demons is not unlike an ordinary *shtetl,* hence *kheyder*-demons, like *kheyder*-boys, must attend school. This tale is thought to have had a long history in Jewish oral as well as literary traditions. See, e.g., Gaster, "An Ancient Fairy Tale Translated from the Hebrew" in *Folklore,* London, vol. XLII, pp. 156–78; Gaster (1971), vol. II. pp. 908–42; Pipe (1968), pp. 35–36 and 56–67. An-ski's satiric Yiddish poem *Der ashmeday* (Petersburg, 1905) and Moyshe Broderzon's poem *Sikhas kholin* (Moscow, 1917, illustrated by El Lissitzky) are two of several modern Yiddish literary treatments of the tale.

46. SOURCE: V.A. 154:20. TALE TYPE: 563 (Ia, b, d, IIc, d).

47. TELLER: Peshe-Rive Sher, 64 years old, Kozlovitsh (Kozlovich/Ko-

zlovshch), U.S.S.R., n.d.; heard from her mother. COLLECTOR: Y.-L. Cahan, 1928. SOURCE: Cahan (1931), no. 10, pp. 42–47; Cahan (1940), no. 21, pp. 78–83. TALE TYPE: cf. 531. COMMENTS: There are no culturally specific markers, except perhaps the name of the witch, *Bobe Ha,* and this is most likely a recently learned tale from Slavic neighbors, among whom there exist variants with a witch named Baba Yaga.

48. TELLER: Shoshe Halkon, Grodne (Grodno), Poland, 1928; an excellent narrator who used colloquial language, idioms, asides, and rhetorical questions. COLLECTOR: Berl Verblinski. SOURCE: V.A. 33:8. TALE TYPE: cf. 1313.

49. TELLER: Shoshe Halkon, Grodne (Grodno), Poland, 1929. COLLECTOR: Berl Verblinski, Grodne. SOURCE: V.A. 28:4.

50. TELLER: Sonye Naymark (b. ca. 1835; nicknamed *Sonye di khakhome,* "Sonye the Wise"), Mohilev province. COLLECTOR: A. Litwin. SOURCE: Litwin (1917), vol. III, pp. 1–4, abridged. COMMENTS: In the unabridged original, the teller concluded with an explicit summation: "The tale was created, of course, so that people like Berl would learn from Borekh's anguish that it was unwise to light the samovar or smoke cigars on the Sabbath." Note that in this modern tale, hell consists in repeating *ad infinitum* the impious acts that got you there in the first place.

51. SOURCE: V.A. 27:2. COMMENTS: This is an example of the many tales read in the Talmud which circulated orally in the nineteenth and twentieth centuries in Eastern Europe. The prototype of this tale is found in the Babylonian Talmud, tractate *Shabbat* 150b. See also Gaster (1924), no. 17, p. 210; and Gaster (1934) no. 8, p. 13.

52. TELLER: Yehoshua Yafe, n.d. COLLECTOR: Toyvye Yafe. SOURCE: V.A. 69:1. TALE TYPE: cf. 545.

53. TELLER/COLLECTOR: Sheyne Kitanik, n.p., n.d. SOURCE: V.A. 167:7. COMMENTS: See An-ski (1925) pp. 101–54 and Dov Noy (1966) on the blood libel.

54. TELLER: Meri Balkon, Grodne (Grodno), Poland. COLLECTOR: Berl Verblinski. SOURCE: V.A. 26:31. COMMENTS: Focusing on another kind of slander, this Passover tale is not connected with the infamous blood libel, but rather with alleged cheating. The happy ending with Yankl made king is unusual. Most often in Yiddish tales the hero ends up viceroy to a king, not a king himself.

55. SOURCE: V.A. 27:1. TALE TYPE: 938A and 938B. COMMENTS: Elijah the Prophet is one of the most beloved characters in Yiddish folktales. A detailed analysis of sixty Yiddish Elijah stories, where his varied disguises and roles are

delineated, can be found in B. Weinreich (1957). This particular tale has a long history both as a literary tale, going back to the Midrashic tradition (*Ruth Zutta, Yalkut Ruth* 607), and in oral tradition as well. (Cf. Ginzberg [1913], pp. 56ff., and Gaster [1934], pp. 292–94.) Peretz used this tale as a model for his artistic retelling *Di zibn gute yor* (Liptzin [1947], pp. 120–27). This type of tale was also popular in Poland among the non-Jewish population.

56. TELLER: A. Akives, 55 years old, Litin (Lityn), Poland, 1936. COLLECTOR: Musye Mayzls. TALE TYPE: cf. 930 (II, III, IV). COMMENTS: See tale no. 64, "Upon Me."

57. TELLER: Yehoyshua Yafe, Sharkoyshtshine (Szarkowszczyzna), Poland, 1926. COLLECTOR: Toyvye Yafe. SOURCE: V.A. 30:1. COMMENTS: Midrashic variants appear in *Hibbur Yafe* (Ferrara, 1557; Amsterdam, 1745). See English translations in Bin Gorion (1976) pp. 658–59; Gaster (1924), no. 368, p. 137. Our version ends with the hero living happily ever after, while the version in Bin Gorion ends with a Biblical reference—"For He shall pay a man according to his works" (Job 34:11)—typical of printed ethical tales. The collector of our tale titled it with a rhyming Yiddish proverb: *Got git dem tsadek skhar loyt zayn tsar* (God

rewards the pious man according to his grief). Though the teller apparently knew the tale from oral tradition, the collector seems also to have read it, stating that it is "from a midrash." Note, too, that the older, written variant has the charitable man giving money "for the redemption of captives" and for orphans, while our version has him giving money specifically to help a poor bride and, more generally, to charity. Modern oral versions will often delete outdated motifs.

58. TELLER: G. Aporets, Bialestok (Bialystok), Poland, 1929. COLLECTOR: Berl Verblinski. SOURCE: V.A. 33:13. TALE TYPE: 832. COMMENTS: This is the kind of tale that very likely was used as a parable by preachers.

59. TELLER: Khinye Lifshits, 57 years old, Krementshug (Kremenchug), U.S.S.R., 1940. COLLECTOR: S. Verite. SOURCE: V.A. 154:28. TALE TYPE: cf. 834*. COMMENTS: Compare this tale with our tale no. 41, "The Hunchbacks and the Dancing Demons," and others in which success is not achieved through imitation.

60. TELLER: Benyomin Pikover, 54 years old, Grodne (Grodno), Poland. COLLECTOR: Berl Verblinski. SOURCE: V.A. 33:10. COMMENTS: Two typically Jewish tale types and motifs are combined here: first, a Jewish community threatened with annihilation is rescued (note that

in magical/fairy tales it is an individual who is saved from danger) through the intervention of a spiritual type of hero. He is a silent, retiring, "unlikely" sort of a hero, a *lamedvovnik* who frequently lives in the quiet outskirts of a city or in a forest. He is the antithesis of the physically active hero of the fairy tale; through prayer, piety and fasting he achieves what folktale heroes achieve through actions. Combined with the first motif is a second one in which the Jewish hero helps uncover a plot to overthrow a king. As in the Book of Esther, recounted every Purim, such tales usually end with the noose put around the wicked minister's head, and not the innocent man's. This novella-tale probably had as its source one of the Yiddish chapbooks that were so popular in the nineteenth and twentieth centuries. It is interesting to note that Gaster discovered a story about the annual sacrifice of a Jewish child by Christians (Gaster [1924], no. 346[9], p. 127).

61. TELLER: Anon., from Kviv (Klwow), Poland, 1906. COLLECTOR: Shmuel Lehman. SOURCE: Prilutski and Lehman (1933), no. 11, pp. 154–57. TALE TYPE: cf. 555.

62. TELLER: Mendl Berkhon, Sharkheyshtshine (Szarkowszczyzna), Poland, 1926. COLLECTOR: Pinkes Khidekl. SOURCE: V.A. 30:17. COMMENTS: The main characters

are not historic figures, but simply a pious couple, and the setting can comfortably be construed as twentieth-century Eastern Europe. This tale has also had a long literary history where the protagonists were historic figures. In the *Yalkut Shimeoni*, possibly the earliest printed source (earliest known edition: Salonica, 1521), this tale is told about the Tanna, R. Meir, and his pious, learned wife, Beruriah, born in the first quarter of the second century. See also Gaster (1924) p. 87, and story 147, p. 217. A Yiddish variant is also found in the morality book, *Simkhes hanefesh* (earliest known edition, 1707), with a happy ending.

63. TELLER: Tsivye Fridman, 50 years old, Yedvabne (Jedwabne), Poland, 1927. COLLECTOR: A. Kravyetski. SOURCE: V.A. 32:88. TALE TYPE: cf. 933. COMMENTS: Other Jewish variants to this tale are listed in Schwartzbaum (1968), pp. 28–29. Christians tell this as a legend about Pope Gregory (see Aarne and Thompson [1928], p. 140.)

64. TELLER: Brokhe *di tshulotshnitse* (Brokhe the stocking-maker), Roslov (Roslavl), U.S.S.R., 1928. COLLECTOR: A. Tshernyak. SOURCE: V.A. 167:3. TALE TYPE: 837. COMMENTS: Here is a close variant of this international tale type, and in view of the teller's bilingual (Russian-Yiddish) rendering of the tale, it would not be

surprising if she had learned this from a Russian neighbor. This tale and no. 56, "Set a Trap for Another" demonstrate the proverb, *"Ver es grobt a grub far yenem, falt in im aleyn arayn"* (Dig a pit for another and fall into it yourself). This one belongs to the genre of tales that explicitly illustrate a proverb. See B. Weinreich (1964) for a study of the Yiddish proverb.

65. TELLER: Anon., from Warsaw, Poland, n.d. COLLECTOR: Y.-L. Cahan. SOURCE: Cahan (1957), no. 40, pp. 55–56. TALE TYPE: cf. 880. COMMENTS: Such ballads are a popular narrative form for the themes of unrequited love and fidelity in marriage.

66. TELLER/COLLECTOR: Anon., from Rige (Riga), Latvia, n.d. SOURCE: Cahan (1938), no. 25, pp. 134–36.

67. COLLECTOR: Z. Okun (Shneyer), n.p., n.d. SOURCE: Shneyer (1939), pp. 26–27.

68. TELLER/COLLECTOR: Yekhiel Shapiro, n.p., n.d. SOURCE: V.A. 136:11. COMMENTS: Jews who lived in villages far from a congregation are frequently depicted in folklore and literature as unlearned boors. Visitors to such out-of-the-way villages were generally most welcome and treated hospitably.

69. COLLECTOR: Z. Okun (Shneyer), n.p., n.d. SOURCE: Shneyer (1939), pp. 23–25.

70. TELLER: Bas Shava (no surname recorded), Korets (Korzec), Poland,

n.d. COLLECTOR: Meyer Tshidner, who heard it from a 16-year-old *yeshive* student, who had heard it from the teller listed above. SOURCE: V.A. 26:5. COMMENTS: Other examples of narratives about treasures appear in Part 7 of this book.

71. TELLER: Khaye Tverski, 50 years old, of a rabbinic family, Shipkov (Szybkow), Poland. COLLECTOR: Y.-L. Cahan, 1930. SOURCE: Cahan (1931), no. 17, pp. 85–88; Cahan (1940), no. 28, pp. 119–22. TALE TYPE: 875. COMMENTS: This tale, along with "Hang the Moon on My Palace Roof," "The Bishop and Moshke," and "Why the Head Turns Gray before the Beard" (nos. 27, 75, and 101) are all about clever riddle-solvers—a very popular motif among East European Jews.

72. TELLER/COLLECTOR: Mikhl Zaydelov, Kamenets-Podolsk (Kamenets-Podolski), U.S.S.R., n.d. SOURCE: V.A. 159:14.

73. TELLER: Borekh Godlin, a bookbinder, born in Dubrovne (Dubrovno), U.S.S.R. COLLECTOR: Sh. Beylin, 1886. SOURCE: V.A. 159:30.

74. TELLER: Gitl Rokhes, Grodne (Grodno), Poland, 1927. COLLECTOR: Berl Verblinski, Grodne. SOURCE: C.A. 26:37. COMMENTS: The name Khaim Yankl became a generic term for a hapless fellow, a *shlimazl*.

75. SOURCE: V.A. 28:13. TALE TYPE: 922. COMMENTS: This particular

tale type has been studied more fully than many others. See Anderson (1921 and 1923) for his pioneering comparative analyses of its Jewish and Slavic variants. Anderson had collected as many as twenty-four Jewish variants of this tale (fourteen in Yiddish) from secondary-school students in Minsk between 1918 and 1920. Applying the historic-geographic method of analysis, he concluded that the international tale type (Aarne-Thompson) 922 was originally a Jewish tale that had spread from the Near East to Europe. See also Schwartzbaum (1968), pp. 115–16, and Thompson (1946), pp. 161ff. Many oral variants of this popular tale have been noted from the seventeenth-century *Mayse-bukh* onward. Note, however, that the *Mayse-bukh* version appears to be much closer to a German folktale rendition than to the modern oral Yiddish variants of the tale. Therefore this particular variant may have been an adaptation from the folklore of Gentile neighbors who had at an earlier period adapted it from a Jewish model and changed it to suit their culture. Other present-day Yiddish tales may likewise bear the imprimatur of the Jews' long, diverse, multicultural experience. See Gaster (1934), no. 227, pp. 571–76.

76. COLLECTOR: S. Verite, n.p., n.d. SOURCE: V.A. 159:9. TALE TYPE: 1696.

77. COLLECTOR: S. Verite, n.p., n.d. SOURCE: V.A. 159:9. TALE TYPE: 1685. COMMENTS: Similar stories are told about Khoyzek, another such numbskull: see Joseph Margoshes (1929), pp. 57–61, and Ignaz Bernstein (1908), s.v. *khoyzek*.

78. TELLER: A pupil in a *talmed-toyre* (a tuition-free traditional Jewish elementary school maintained by the community for poor children) in Korets (Korzec), Poland, n.d. COLLECTOR: Meyer Tshidner. SOURCE: V.A. 26:4.

79. TELLER: Tsvi Moyshe (no surname recorded), Podbrodz (Podbrodzie), Poland, n.d. COLLECTOR: Khaim Lunyevski. SOURCE: V.A. 30:22. TALE TYPE: 785A. COMMENTS: See Schwartzbaum (1968), pp. 56 and 452; also Blum-Dobkin (1977), Holdes (1960), and Epshteyn (1938).

80. TELLER: Anon., from Loytsk, Poland, n.d. SOURCE: Cahan (1938), no. 16, p. 200. COMMENTS: Schwartzbaum (1968), p. 181, traces the tale to Talmudic-Midrashic sources. In one Yiddish variant (Segel, 1904), Elijah the Prophet has the role that Hershele plays in this version; see B. Weinreich (1957), pp. 279–80, for an English translation.

81. TELLER: Anon., from Kolonye Kamenevke, U.S.S.R., ca. 1932. COLLECTOR: T. S. Kantor, 1937, Kalinindorf, U.S.S.R. SOURCE: V.A. 163. COMMENTS: Numerous Yiddish chapbooks were devoted to Khelm tales, which circulated

widely, both orally and in written form in the nineteenth and twentieth centuries. Indeed, these well-loved Yiddish tales have also been collected and retold in more modern Hebrew, Polish, English, and German collections, as well as in American Yiddish primers. But these Yiddish tales have a longer history than the last two centuries. Paucker (1973) traces the earliest Yiddish version of the stories about the Schildberg fools to an Amsterdam edition, ca. 1700, which he found to be a reworking of P. P. Filtschut's 1650 German edition. The German literary versions of this cycle of tales in turn became material for new literary editions in Hebrew and Yiddish. See Vaynig (1929); Schwartzbaum (1968), p. 537, s.v. *Helm,* especially pp. 189ff.

82. TELLER: Anon., from Kolonye Kamenevke, U.S.S.R., ca. 1932. COLLECTOR: T. S. Kantor, 1937, Kalinindorf, U.S.S.R. SOURCE: V.A. 163.

83. TELLER: Anon., from Kolonye Kamenevke, U.S.S.R., ca. 1932. COLLECTOR: T. S. Kantor, 1937, Kalinindorf, U.S.S.R. SOURCE: V.A. 163.

84. TELLER: Anon., from Kolonye Kamenevke, U.S.S.R., ca. 1932. COLLECTOR: T. S. Kantor, 1937, Kalinindorf, U.S.S.R. SOURCE: V.A. 163. TALE TYPE: 1326.

85. COLLECTOR: I. Olsvanger. SOURCE: Olsvanger (1931), no. 348, pp. 231–32. TALE TYPE: cf. 1335A.

COMMENTS: Prilutski (1917), vol. II, p. 191, records a Yiddish variant in which, amusingly, the moon is captured in a barrel of borsht.

86. TELLER: Anon., from Lublin, Poland, n.d. COLLECTOR: N. Prilutski. SOURCE: Prilutski (1917), vol. II, pp. 192–93.

87. TELLER: Anon., from Lublin, Poland, n.d. COLLECTOR: N. Prilutski. SOURCE: Prilutski (1917), vol. II, pp. 197–98. TALE TYPE: 1243.

88. TELLER: Anon., from Kolonye Kamenevke, U.S.S.R., ca. 1932. COLLECTOR: T. S. Kantor, 1937, Kalinindorf, U.S.S.R. SOURCE: V.A. 163. TALE TYPE: 1281.

89. TELLER: Anon., from Kolonye Kamenevke, U.S.S.R., ca. 1932. COLLECTOR: T. S. Kantor, 1937, Kalinindorf, U.S.S.R. SOURCE: V.A. 163.

90. TELLER: Anon., from Galicia (southern Poland), n.d. COLLECTOR: Benyomin Volf Segel (pen name of B. V. Shiper). SOURCE: Segel (1892), p. 29.

91. COLLECTOR: Y.-Kh. Ravnitski, n.d. SOURCE: Ravnitski (1932), no. 400, pp. 199–200.

92. COLLECTOR: I. Olsvanger, n.d. SOURCE: Olsvanger (1947), p. 117.

93. TELLER: A member of the Ozet collective farm, Stalindorf, U.S.S.R., 1937. COLLECTOR: A student in the *Kalinindorfer pedshul* (Kalinindorf School for Teachers), U.S.S.R. SOURCE: V.A. 163:11. TALE TYPE: 1200.

94. TELLER: Moyshe Kador, Warsaw, Poland, n.d. COLLECTOR: Shmuel Lehman. SOURCE: Prilutski and Lehman (1933), no. 6, pp. 382–84.

95. TELLER: Moyshe Gross, father of collector, Kolemey (Kolomyja), Poland, n.d. COLLECTOR: Naftoli Gross, who writes that his father often told Froyim Greydinger stories to the children at bedtime. SOURCE: Gross (1955), pp. 9 and 196–97. TALE TYPE: 1548. COMMENTS: Froyim's last name is sometimes given as Greydiger. Schwartzbaum (1968), pp. 176–77, discusses variants of this tale.

96. TELLER: B. Brukelman, who heard it in the *yeshive* of Novograd-Vilenske (Novograd-Volynski), U.S.S.R. COLLECTOR: A. Litwin. SOURCE: *Yidisher folklor,* vol. I, p. 17.

97. TELLER: Moyshe Sifit, Warsaw, Poland, n.d. COLLECTOR: Shmuel Lehman. SOURCE: Vanvild (1923), p. 75. TALE TYPE: cf. 1540. COMMENTS: This is an example of a tale that has been adapted to fit different heroes and settings. In one Yiddish variant (e.g., C.A. 26:29) the protagonist is a demobilized soldier who returns home after twenty-five years of serving Czar Nicolas I; in another (Cahan 1938, p. 202) the wag Froyim Greydinger teaches a lesson to a stingy villager.

98. TELLER: Pinkhes Bukhman, a 30-year-old worker, heard this tale from his father, who heard it from the local prankster (called a *kopoytser*—lit., "head treasure") in Komarne (Komarno), Poland, n.d. COLLECTOR: Y.-L. Cahan. SOURCE: Cahan (1931), no. 19, pp. 93–94; Cahan (1940), no. 30, pp. 127–28. TALE TYPE: 1287. COMMENTS: This tale is a comment on the "second-class citizenship" of women and points up their dissatisfaction with it. It is fascinating that the teller of this international tale type made it culturally specific by centering it around the motif of the prayer quorum.

99. TELLER/COLLECTOR: Khaim Sheskin, Grodne (Grodno), Poland, n.d. To this day Sheskin continues collecting Yiddish folklore and mailing his collections to YIVO. Sheskin, who now lives in New York, has possibly the longest continuous history of dedicated folklore collecting for YIVO. SOURCE: Cahan (1938), no. 13, p. 199.

100. TELLER: Anon., from Dunilovitsh (Dunilowicze), Poland, n.d. SOURCE: Cahan (1938), no. 5, p. 197.

101. TELLER: Rokhl Rabin (b. 1901), Orinyen (Orinin), U.S.S.R. COLLECTOR: Y.-L. Cahan. SOURCE: Cahan (1931), no. 23, pp. 120–24; Cahan (1940), no. 34, pp. 151–54.

102. TELLER: Peshe Rive Sher (b. 1864), Kozlovitsh (Kozlovich/Kozlovshch), U.S.S.R., heard her mother tell the tale, n.d.

COLLECTOR: Y.-L. Cahan. SOURCE: Cahan (1931), no. 14, pp. 64–66; Cahan (1940), no. 25, pp. 99–101.

103. COLLECTOR: I. Olsvanger, n.d. SOURCE: Olsvanger (1931), no. 364, p. 259. COMMENTS: Like tale no. 98, "The Ten Women," this story also points to women's dissatisfaction with their limited role in the religious sphere. It ends on a somewhat more optimistic note: women keep hoping that this will change with *Skotsl*'s return.

104. TELLER: Moyshe Zimnik, Belz (Balti/Beltsy), Rumania, who heard it from his grandfather, n.d. COLLECTOR: Y.-L. Cahan. SOURCE: Cahan (1931), no. 29, pp. 148–51; Cahan (1940), no. 40, pp. 178–81. TALE TYPE: 151 and 1159.

105. TELLER: Mikhoel Filrayz, Warsaw, Poland, n.d. COLLECTOR: Shmuel Lehman. SOURCE: Prilutski and Lehman (1933), no. 1, pp. 355–60.

106. TELLER: V. Ayzenberg, who heard this tale in Eastern Europe before 1920, mailed it to Litwin from New York. COLLECTOR: A. Litwin. SOURCE: L.A. 86a:6.

107. TELLER: Toyvye Brand, 18 or 20 years old, Torne (Tarnow), Poland, 1930. COLLECTOR: Noyekh Falman. SOURCE: V.A. 26:6. COMMENTS: The rebbe in this tale is most likely Rebbe Elimeylekh of Lizhensk (d. 1787).

108. TELLER: Sh. Horenshteyn, Yanushpol (Ivanopol), U.S.S.R., n.d.

COLLECTOR: Shmuel Rubinshteyn. SOURCE: Rubinshteyn (1938), pp. 106–108. COMMENTS: See Ben-Amos and Mintz (1970) and Mintz (1968) for additional legends about the Baal Shem Tov in English translation.

109. TELLER: Azriel Klaynor, a Hasid of the Stolin Rebbe, Horkhov (Horochow), Poland, 1928. COLLECTOR: B. Oksman, Poland. SOURCE: V.A. 32:37. COMMENTS: Rebbe Yisroel (1868–1923), the son of R. Asher of Stolin, became rebbe at the age of four.

110. TELLER/COLLECTOR: R. Gavriyel, Warsaw, Poland, n.d. SOURCE: V.A. 32:40. COMMENTS: The hero of this legend is probably R. Yankev Yoysef (d. 1791) of Ostrovets (Ostrowiec), Poland.

111. COLLECTOR: A. Rekhtman, member of An-ski Expedition. SOURCE: Rekhtman (1958), pp. 259–61. COMMENTS: Shneyer Zalmen (1745–1813) of Lyadi (Lyady), U.S.S.R., was the founder of Habad Hasidism, Habad being an acronym for *khokhme* (wisdom), *bine* (understanding), and *daas* (knowledge). See tale no. 175, "The Bridge Hobgoblin," for another story about this rebbe.

112. TELLER: E. Zilberman, Ostrov (Ostrów), Poland, 1929. SOURCE: V.A. 32:66.

113. TELLER/COLLECTOR: Sh. Fuks, n.p., 1926. SOURCE: V.A. 32:4. COMMENTS: Rebbe Yitskhok Ayzik of Kaliv (d. 1821) was a disciple

of R. Shmelke of Nikolsburg, Czechoslovakia.

114. TELLER: Moyshe Zilbershteyn, Mekarev (Makarov/Makorovo), U.S.S.R., ca. 1900. COLLECTOR: M. Tolpin, Ostre (Ostrog), Poland, who mailed it to YIVO in 1928. SOURCE: V.A. 32:48. COMMENTS: If the collector first heard the tale at the turn of the century, then the hero of this legend is probably Rebbe Nokhem of Mekarev (d. 1852), who lived during the reign of Czar Nicolas I (1825–1855). Eighteen is considered a lucky number in Jewish lore, because the letters *khes* and *yud* which spell the Hebrew word for life, *khay,* have the numerical value of eighteen (see *gematriye* in Glossary).

115. SOURCE: V.A. 28:9a.

116. TELLER/COLLECTOR: K. Volf, Tomeshev (Tomaszów), Poland, n.d. SOURCE: V.A. 32:10. COMMENTS: The hero of this legend is probably Rebbe Yisroel Shmuel of Tomeshev (d. 1869).

117. TELLER/COLLECTOR: Nosn Mark, Redevits (Radauti), Rumania, n.d. SOURCE: V.A. 32:51. COMMENTS: Reb Shmelke (d. 1778) of Nikolsburg, Czechoslovakia.

118. SOURCE: V.A. 32:3. COMMENTS: The anonymous collector noted at the bottom of the manuscript, "I tell this story because it reminds me of Yehoash's '*A yonkiper maysele.*'"

119. TELLER: Azriel Klayner, a Stolin Hasid, Horkhov (Horochów), Po-

land, 1928. COLLECTOR: B. Oksman, Rozhishtsh (Rozyszcze), Poland. SOURCE: V.A. 32:37 (2). COMMENTS: R. Yisroel Perlov (d. 1922), hero of this legend, was the son of the Rebbe of Karlin. (See the introduction to Part 6 regarding the local gentile population's belief in the wonder-working abilities of Hasidic rebbes.) A similar tale was told about the founder of Hasidism, the Baal Shem Tov. (See "The Besht's Prayer Produces Rain" in Ben-Amos and Mintz, *In Praise of the Baal Shem Tov* [1970], pp. 35–36.

120. TELLER/COLLECTOR: Nosn Mark, Redevits (Radauti), Rumania, n.d. SOURCE: V.A. 32:78.

121. TELLER/COLLECTOR: Sh. Morovitsh, Gorzhkovits (Gorzkowice), Poland, 1927. SOURCE: V.A. 32:42. COMMENTS: The Rebbe of Khentshin referred to is probably R. Khayim Shmuel of Khentshin (d. 1916).

122. TELLER: Brokhe *di tshulotshnitse* (Brokhe the stocking-maker), Roslov (Roslavl), U.S.S.R., 1928. COLLECTOR: J. Tshernyak. SOURCE: V.A. 154:3.

123. TELLER/COLLECTOR: M. Hoyzknekht, n.p., n.d. SOURCE: V.A. 32:38.

124. TELLER: E. Zilberman, Ostrov (Ostrów), Poland, 1929. SOURCE: V.A. 32:81. COMMENTS: Reb Henekh was the founder of the Alexander Hasidic dynasty in Poland.

125. TELLER/COLLECTOR: Anon., from

Warsaw, Poland, n.d. SOURCE: V.A. 32:9a. COMMENTS: The rebbe in this legend is probably R. Yekhezkl Taub of Kuzmir (d. 1856).

126. COLLECTOR: Nosn Mark, Redevits (Radauti), Rumania, n.d. SOURCE: V.A. 32:50. COMMENTS: Rebbe Avrom HaMalekh, "The Angel," was the son of Dov Ber of Mezritsh and grandson of the Baal Shem Tov.

127. TELLER: M. Kosavski, Kaminke (Kamionka), Poland, 1927. COLLECTOR: M. Barshavski. SOURCE: V.A. 32:8. COMMENTS: The letters of the Jewish alphabet that spell the word *shabes* (sabbath) have a total numerical value of 702 (*shin* = 300, *beys* = 2, *sov* = 400); hence the "702" candles in this Cabalistic legend. (See *gematriye* in Glossary.)

128. COLLECTOR: B. Oksman, who heard it from his father, in Rozhishtsh (Rozyszcze), Poland, 1928. SOURCE: V.A. 32:37 (3). COMMENTS: The *rebbe* of this legend is probably R. Mordkhe of Nizkhizh (Niesuchojeze), Poland (d. 1880).

129. TELLER/COLLECTOR: Hersh Elavski, Koyl (Kolo), Poland, 1929. SOURCE: V.A. 32:67. COMMENTS: Older variants of this tale can be found in Bin Gorion (1967), vol. II, story 160, and vol. III, p. 1513; cf. Gaster (1924), story 138, and Schwartzbaum (1968), p. 291. Folktale collectors often note the freedom with which storytellers change the names of the heroes of a legend. The teller of this story, which is a version of a Talmudic legend (*Kethuboth* 77b), replaced the original hero—(Rabbi Joshua Ben Levi, who lived in the first half of the third century) with the twelfth-century Hebrew poet and philosopher Judah Halevi. In the Yiddish variant (in V.A. 30:20), which is told like a wonder tale, the hero is simply "a man named Joshua," in a nonspecific setting. The number of narratives about Biblical and post-Biblical scholars and leaders in the YIVO archives as well as in the published collections of Yiddish folktales of the twentieth century were small. The reason for the paucity may well be that the collectors understood literally their instructions not to write down any stories which informants might have read in written sources. These included chapbooks and the various compendia of tales in Hebrew or the Yiddish vernacular. If the collector was aware of a written source, even if the teller knew the story only as an oral legend, the collector would be apt to exclude it. Another possibility is that this was mainly a written genre, rather than one favored by oral narrators. Finally, the paucity of these tales may, of course, result from the loss during World War II of the archival folders that contained such tales.

130. TELLER: Grunye Royznberg, Sharkoyshtshine (Szarkowszczyzna),

Poland, 1927. COLLECTOR: Toy-vye Yofe. SOURCE: V.A. 32:20. COMMENTS: This is an oral variant of a Talmudic legend (*Hullin* 60a) with a long tradition in printed Yiddish sources (e.g. the six-teenth-century *Mayse-bukh*). See Gaster (1934), story 57; cf. Gaster (1924), story 9, and his sources on p. 187.

131. TELLER: Toyvye Brand, 20 years old, Torne (Tarnów), Poland, 1930. COLLECTOR: N. Falman. SOURCE: V.A. 26:9.

132. TELLER: Anon., from Brod (Brody), Poland, n.d. SOURCE: Cahan (1938), no. 5, pp. 140–41. COMMENTS: Abraham Ibn Ezra (1089–1164), was a Biblical com-mentator, poet, grammarian, phi-losopher, astronomer, and physician.

133. SOURCE: V.A. 27:3. COMMENTS: This tale is a close retelling of a Talmudic tale (*Shabbat* 89a); cf. the Midrash quoted by Tosafot. Louis Ginzberg (1909–1938) vol. III, p. 118, gives an English trans-lation of the Talmudic tale, and in vol. VI, p. 49, n. 257, he pro-vides other explanations, as given in various midrashic tales, for why the Scriptures speak of "the Torah of Moses."

134. COLLECTOR: Anon., from Hru-beshoyv (Hrubieszów), Poland, n.d. SOURCE: V.A. 32:62. COMMENTS: Jonathan Eybeschuetz (1690/95–1764), the *Baal ha Urim ve Tummim,* an eighteenth-century Talmudist and Cabalist, was one

of the greatest preachers of his time and one of the giants of the Talmud.

135. TELLER/COLLECTOR: Moyshe Klaynman, Preshberg (Pressburg/Bratislava), Czechoslovakia, 1926. SOURCE: V.A. 32:41. COMMENTS: Distinguished religious scholars were often called by the titles of their major works. The *Ksav-soyfer (Ketav Sofer),* is Abraham Samuel Benjamin Schreiber (1815–1871), rabbi and head of a *yeshive* in Preshberg, and the oldest son of the *Khsam-soyfer (Hatam Sofer),* Moses Schreiber.

136. TELLER/COLLECTOR: Yerakhmiel Shteygman, Lomzhe (Lomza), Po-land, n.d. SOURCE: V.A. 32:75. COMMENTS: Talmudic scholar, Rabbi Akiba Eger of Preshberg (Pressburg/Bratislava), Czechoslo-vakia (d. 1758), was the author of *Mishnat de Rabbi Akiba.*

137. TELLER/COLLECTOR: Anon., from Redevits (Radauti), Rumania, n.d. SOURCE: V.A. 32:18. COMMENTS: Rabbi Isaiah Horowitz (1565?–1630) author of *Shenei Luhot ha-Berit* (Two Tablets of the Cove-nant), was a rabbi, Cabalist, and communal leader. The name She-lah is taken from the first letters of each word in the title of his major work. Cf. Bin Gorion (1976), vol. II, story 315, p. 891.

138. TELLER/COLLECTOR: Reb Khaim Brisker, Hrubeshoyv (Hrubi-eszów), Poland, 1927. SOURCE: V.A. 32:59. TALE TYPE: 1639*. COMMENTS: This legend and the

many variants of it reflect the distress of the wives and children of scholars who were poor breadwinners. In Lehman's variant (Prilutski and Lehman [1933], pp. 165–68) Elijah the Prophet advises the wife to induce her husband to start a practical business, stop his interminable studies and apply himself to his familial responsibilities.

139. TELLER: M. Shmid, who heard it in Eastern Europe sometime before 1920, mailed to Litvin from Youngstown, Ohio, n.d. COLLECTOR: A. Litwin. SOURCE: V.A. 86a:7.

140. TELLER: Anon., from Myor (Miory), Poland, n.d. COLLECTOR: Shmuel Zanvl Pipe. SOURCE: Pipe (1941), no. 37, p. 164; also Pipe (1946), no. 10, p. 296.

141. TELLER: From Konstantin (Konstantynów), Poland, n.d. COLLECTOR: Shmuel Zanvl Pipe. SOURCE: Pipe (1941), no. 70, pp. 175–76; also Pipe (1946), no. 25, p. 298.

142. TELLER: N. Gelfand, n.p., 1921. COLLECTOR: A. Litwin. SOURCE: V.A. 86a:10. COMMENTS: 1) Czar Nicholas I reigned in Russia from 1825 to 1855, a time when minorities were severely oppressed. Under the dreaded "cantonist" legislation (1827–1856), a quota of Jewish boys between the ages of twelve and twenty-five were forced to serve for twenty-five years in the army. It was the gov-

ernment's hope that the military life would alienate Jewish cantonists from their own people and religion. Russian Jewish communities had special officers, dubbed *khapers,* who seized male children —some as young as eight or ten—who were then incarcerated in a communal building and handed over to the military authorities to fill the cantonist quota. 2) The *Eyn yankev* is a bilingual Yiddish-Hebrew edition of Jacob ben Solomon ibn Habib's (1445?–1516) *Ein Ya'akov.* It is a collection of all the *agodes* (legends) from the Babylonian Talmud and a few from the Jerusalem Talmud, together with various commentaries. Conceived as a popular work and designed to educate the general public to the religious life and faith, it has appeared in over one hundred editions.

143. TELLER: Anon., from Pshiskhe (Przysucha), Poland, 1909. COLLECTOR: Shmuel Lehman. SOURCE: Prilutski and Lehman (1933), no. 19, p. 169.

144. TELLER/COLLECTOR: Moyshe Dovid Berzhan, Poland, 1928. SOURCE: V.A. 32:14. COMMENTS: A variant of this tale, in which Reb Israel Salanter is the hero, is given in Dawidowicz (1967), pp. 173–74. Cf. our tale no. 118, "Reb Khaim Urbakh Rocks a Cradle on Yom Kippur."

145. COLLECTOR: I. Olsvanger, n.d.

SOURCE: Olsvanger (1931), no. 79, pp. 45–46.

146. TELLER/COLLECTOR: Anon., from Loytsk, Poland, n.d. SOURCE: Cahan (1938), no. 28, p. 205.

147. TELLER/COLLECTOR: Anon., from Sonik (Sanok), Poland, n.d. SOURCE: Cahan (1938), no. 8, p. 143.

148. TELLER/COLLECTOR: Anon., from Sukhodol (Suchodol), Poland, n.d. SOURCE: Cahan (1938), no. 75, p. 170.

149. TELLER/COLLECTOR: Sh. An-ski, ca. 1912, An-Ski Ethnographic Expedition. SOURCE: An-ski (1925), pp. 248–49; Rekhtman (1958), pp. 55–56.

150. TELLER/COLLECTOR: Anon., from Ignaline (Ignalino), Poland, n.d. SOURCE: Cahan (1938) no. 55, pp. 161–62, abridged.

151. TELLER/COLLECTOR: Anon., from Visoke (Wysokie Litewskie), Poland, n.d. SOURCE: Cahan (1938), no. 127, pp. 190–91.

152. TELLER/COLLECTOR: Anon., from Ostre (Ostróg), Poland, n.d. SOURCE: Cahan (1938), no. 77, p. 171.

153. TELLER: Alter Zilberman, born in Motele (Motol), Poland; mailed to Litwin in 1926 from Long Branch, N.J. COLLECTOR: A. Litwin. SOURCE: V.A. 86a:3.

154. TELLER: Brokhe *di tshulotshnitse* (Brokhe the stocking-maker), Roslov (Roslavl), U.S.S.R., 1928. COLLECTOR: J. Tshernyak. SOURCE: V.A. 154:2.

155. TELLER/COLLECTOR: Anon., from Berzhan (Brzezany), Poland, n.d. SOURCE: Cahan (1938), no. 66, pp. 165–66.

156. TELLER/COLLECTOR: Anon., from Cracow, Poland, n.d. SOURCE: Cahan (1938), no. 36, pp. 152–53. COMMENTS: Rema is an acronym for Rabbi Moses ben Israel Isserles (1525?–1572), one of the great authorities and codifiers of Jewish law. Called the "Maimonides of Polish Jewry," R. Isserles wrote on *halakha,* philosophy, Cabala, homiletics, and science. He is perhaps best known for his work *Ha-Mappah,* which contains explanations and supplements to Caro's *Shulkhan Arukh,* giving the specific customs of Ashkenaz.

157. TELLER/COLLECTOR: Sh. An-ski, ca. 1912, An-ski Ethnographic Expedition. SOURCE: An-ski (1925), pp. 249–51; Rekhtman (1958), pp. 58–59.

158. TELLER: The story appears in actor Joseph Buloff's memoirs; he heard it from the wife of his *kheyder* teacher, in Vilna, Poland, ca. 1920. SOURCE: Buloff (1986), pp. 159–60, abridged. COMMENTS: The golem legend in Jewish folklore goes back to Rabbinic times, when Rabbi Raba, for example, is said to have created a homunculus who was like a man in all but the ability to speak. In Eastern Europe there were many legends about the making of *goylomim* by both famous and lesser-known

rabbis and mystics. One of the most popular Polish Jewish legends was about the golem of Khelm (Chelm), Poland, created by the Cabalist Rabbi Elijah of Khelm in the sixteenth century. When the Khelm golem ran amok, like the Prague golem before it, it was returned to dust by removing from its forehead the piece of parchment containing God's name. See Scholem (1965), pp. 203–4.

159. TELLER: Ben Schneider (b. 1888); Lutsk (Luck), Poland; heard it in Berlin after World War II. COLLECTOR: Barbara Kirshenblatt-Gimblett. SOURCE: Kirshenblatt-Gimblett (1972b), pp. 135–36.

160. TELLER/COLLECTOR: Anon., from Sukhodol (Suchodol), Poland, n.d. SOURCE: Cahan (1938), no. 76, p. 171.

161. TELLER/COLLECTOR: Anon., from Visoke (Wysokie Litewskie), Poland, n.d. SOURCE: Cahan (1940), no. 129, pp. 191–92.

162. TELLER/COLLECTOR: Anon., from Sukhodol (Suchodol), Poland, n.d. SOURCE: Cahan (1938), no. 80, pp. 172–73.

163. TELLER/COLLECTOR: Anon., from Gorlits (Gorlice), Poland, n.d. SOURCE: Cahan (1938), no. 25, p. 149.

164. TELLER/COLLECTOR: Anon., from Rige (Riga), Latvia, n.d. SOURCE: Cahan (1938), no. 68, p. 166.

165. TELLER/COLLECTOR: Anon., from Shebershin (Szczebrzeszyn), Po-land, n.d. SOURCE: Cahan (1938), no. 20, p. 147. COMMENTS: See Bernard Weinryb, The Beginnings of East European Jewry in Legend and Historiography (Leiden, 1962), for legends concerning the arrival of Jews in Eastern Europe.

166. TELLER/COLLECTOR: Anon., from Yas (Jasi/Jassy), Rumania, n.d. SOURCE: Cahan (1938), no. 137, p. 153.

167. TELLER/COLLECTOR: Anon., from Lodz, Poland, n.d. SOURCE: Cahan (1938), no. 106, p. 183.

168. COLLECTOR: Avrom Rekhtman, 1912–1914. SOURCE: Rekhtman (1958), pp. 275–77.

169. TELLER/COLLECTOR: Anon., from Berditshev (Berdichev), U.S.S.R.; he claimed to have seen this tale in the *Pinkes* (Book of Records) of Sharigrad, n.d. SOURCE: Cahan (1938), no. 2, pp. 138–39.

170. TELLER/COLLECTOR: Anon., from Hrubeshoyv (Hrubieszów), Poland, n.d. SOURCE: Cahan (1938), no. 32, p. 151.

171. TELLER/COLLECTOR: Anon., from Sonik (Sanok), Poland, n.d. SOURCE: Cahan (1938), no. 87, pp. 175–76.

172. TELLER/COLLECTOR: Anon., from Visoke (Wysokie Litewskie), Poland, n.d. SOURCE: Cahan (1938), no. 97, p. 180.

173. TELLER/COLLECTOR: Anon., from Ruzhan (Rozan), Poland, n.d. SOURCE: Cahan (1938), no. 100, p. 98.

174. TELLER: Sonye Naymark (b. ca.

1835), known as *Sonye di Khak-home* (Sonia the Wise), Mohilev province. SOURCE: Litwin (1917), no. 7, vol. III, pp. 1–3.

175. TELLER: H. Yaffe, n.p., n.d. COLLECTOR: M. Weinreich. SOURCE: M. Weinreich (1926), pp. 235–36. COMMENTS: See note to tale no. 111, "The Rebbe's Melody."

176. TELLER/COLLECTOR: Anon., from Hrubeshoyv (Hrubieszow), Poland, n.d. SOURCE: Cahan (1938), no. 88, p. 176. COMMENTS: According to tradition, on the seventh day of the holiday of Succos, everyone's fate for the coming year is irrevocably sealed. Willow twigs *(heshaynes)* are traditionally carried during processions around the synagogue on this day.

177. TELLER/COLLECTOR: Anon., from Lodz, Poland, n.d. SOURCE: Cahan (1938), no. 101, pp. 181–82. COMMENTS: The collector notes that "the *zmore* is an ancient creature in human form that goes at night to suck milk from the breast of its victim. Since it is female, its chosen victims are men."

178. TELLER: Velvl Godl (b. ca. 1853), witnessed this event in 1865. COLLECTOR: A. Litwin. SOURCE: Litwin (1917), vol. IV, pp. 1–9.

Notes

(Works listed in the bibliography are cited by author and date of publication. Refer to bibliography for full publication information.)

Introduction

1. See Zinberg (1975) vol. 8, which is devoted to this literature.

2. The earliest printed edition appeared in Basle in 1602, compiled by Jacob ben Abraham of Mezritsh, Lithuania (now Miedzyrzec, Poland). See Jakob Meitlis (1933) *Das Ma'assehbuch, seine Entstehung und Quellengeschichte,* Berlin.

3. The An-ski expedition's precious collections are stored in several libraries in Leningrad, but unfortunately, scholars in the U.S.S.R. have not published them nor made them available to folklorists from other countries. Little is known of the fate of the tales and other folklore forms collected by the "Historic-Ethno-graphic Societies in Memory of An-ski" that sprang up in East European towns and cities after An-ski's death in 1920. We do know, however, that the Historic-Ethnographic Society he founded in Vilna shortly before he died named YIVO as the official heir to its materials, and that they were transferred in 1938. Some of these have turned up in YIVO's Vilna Ethnographic Commission Archive in New York. See Eleanor Gordon-Mlotok, ed. (1980) *S. An-ski, His Life and Works,* catalog, YIVO, New York, vol. 9, pp. 113–19.

4. "Ankete numer 2: Folksmayses," in *Yedies fun YIVO,* no. 22, July 29, 1927.

5. Szajkovski (1976) *YIVO and Its Founders,* catalog, YIVO, New York, p. 13, items 203–7.

6. "Ankete numer 2: Folkmayses," in *Yedies fun YIVO,* no. 22, July 29, 1927.

7. Cahan, who started gathering Yiddish folklore as early as 1896, was a member of a distinguished circle of collectors in Warsaw, headed by classic Yiddish writer Y.-L. Peretz. When Cahan emigrated to the United States in 1904, he continued gathering material from East European immigrants in this country, and later emerged as mentor to YIVO's folklorists in Vilna, Poland.

8. Later, when the YIVO *aspirantur* (an advanced program of study) was established in Vilna in 1935, Cahan enabled Pipe to attend. Upon completion of the course, Pipe became an associate of YIVO. He published a number of important studies and collections and would undoubtedly have attained eminence had he not died at the hands of the Nazis at the age of thirty-six.

9. A. Litwin (1917), vol. 3, "Sonye di Khakhome," pp. 1–20.

10. YIVO Archive, V.A. 154:150.

11. A. Litwin (1917), vol. 3, p. 1 of "Sonye di Khakhome." See her story "The *Balshem* and the Dibbuk."

12. The Vilna Archive includes collections created by the YIVO Ethnographic Commission, as well as those received from the Jewish Section of the Minsk Institute for Belorussian Culture and from various Jewish ethnographic societies throughout Eastern Europe. The Cahan and Litwin Archives at YIVO, though much smaller than the Vilna Archives, were also good sources of Yiddish folktales and legends. Litwin's collection from the 1920s consists of both handwritten tales readers sent him and newspaper clippings of his columns *"Fun zeydns vinkl"* ("From Grandpa's Corner") and *"Fun altn kheyder"* ("From the Old *Kheyder*"), in which he published legends, short local traditions (memorats), and humorous anecdotes. Some of the tales in this volume are from these two archives. I also utilized some fifteen sources of Yiddish oral folktales collected by eminent folklorists such as An-ski, Lehman, Olsvanger, Ravnitski, Pipe, Prilutski, and Wiener. Here I found material to complement the existing body of tales selected from the archival sources.

Part One

Epigraph: Yekhiel Shtern (1950), pp. 95–96, paraphrased.

Part Two

Epigraph: Benyomin Yankev Bialostotzky (1962), p. 164, paraphrased.

Part Three

Epigraph: Frieda Waletsky, *Yidisher folklor* (1954), vol. 1, p. 56. She may well have been referring to tale no. 36, "The Snake Bridegroom."

1. Adin Steinsalz, *Beggars and Prayers: The Tales of Rabbi Nachman of Bratslav.* New York: Basic Books, 1985, p. xvii.

2. Max Weinreich, "Yiddish, Knaanic, Slavic: The Basic Relations" in *For Roman Jakobson.* The Hague: Mouton, 1956, p. 628.

3. Jacob Shatzky, "Mitskevitsh un di yidishe folks-mayse" in *YIVO bleter* (1934) vol. 6, p. 186.

Part Four

Epigraph: Max Grunwald, "Märchen u. Sagen . . ." *Mitteilungen der Gesellschaft für jüdische Volkskunde* (1898), vol. 5, no. 1, p. 1.

1. Sholem Rabinovitsh (Sholom Aleichem), 1955, *The Great Fair: Scenes From My Childhood,* Noonday Press, New York, 1955, p. 184. This is Tamara Kahana's translation of her grandfather's childhood memoirs, originally titled *Funem yarid: lebnsbashraybungen.*

Part Five

Epigraph: Benyomin Yankev Bialostotzky (1962) p. 166, paraphrased.

1. Yehoshua-Khone Ravnitski (1932), pp. vii–viii.
2. Barbara Kirshenblatt-Gimblett (1974), p. 298; and Ezekiel Lifschutz (1952), pp. 43–83.
3. In a class on Yiddish folklore at U.C.L.A. in 1948, Dr. Max Weinreich offered as a possible explanation for Khelm's status as archetypal Jewish town of fools the fact that the first story of the creation of a golem in Eastern Europe was set in Khelm. In addition to Khelm, there were other towns of fools: the Galician town of Linsk, for example, played the same role in Congress Poland.
4. Toby Blum-Dobkin (1977) offers a structural analysis of this genre.
5. Other regions had their favorite local wags. Perhaps less well known are the following pranksters who appear in Yiddish folktales: Mordkhe Rokover, Shayke Fayfer, Shmerl Snitkever, Yosl Marshelik, Shloyme Loydmirer, and Leybele Gotsvunder. See A. Holdes (1960), pp. 6–7.
6. Meir Noy (1968) speaks of three types of cante fables. In the first, a tune is bought by a naïve fellow, as in our examples; the second focuses on the origin of a famous melody, as in our nonhumorous "The Rebbe's Melody" (no. 111) and "The Dibbuk Melody of Tolne" (no. 168); the third is about a person who wants an opportunity to sing, as in "The Clever Little Tailor" (no. 104). Cante fables have been collected in Byelorussia, Rumania, and eastern Galicia.

Part Six

Epigraphs: Moyshe Meylman, Berestetshka, Poland, 1925, YIVO Archive, V.A. 32:11; Zborowski and Herzog (1952), p. 91.

1. For more information on Hasidic legends as they appear in America, see Jerome Mintz (1968).
2. See L. Holomshtok (1930) for the work of a Soviet scholar who describes many of the Hasidic tales as a form of social protest against various authority figures (e.g., tax-collectors, local squires, landlords, anti-Semitic priests).

3. An-ski (1925), vol. 5, p. 264.

4. According to An-ski, the typical Jewish hero of post-Biblical legend is not a brave warrior, as in other cultures, but rather a scholar. See An-ski (1925) vol. 15, pp. 33ff.

5. Hayyim Schauss, *The Lifetime of a Jew.* Cincinnati: Union of Hebrew Congregations, 1950, p. 106.

6. Abraham Joshua Heschel, (1950), pp. 88–89.

7. Hayyim Schauss, *The Lifetime of a Jew,* p. 106.

8. Most of the items are in Yiddish and were collected in Eastern Europe. See Pipe (1942).

Part Seven

Epigraphs: Naftoli Gross (1955) p. 9, paraphrased; Zborowski and Herzog (1952), p. 91, paraphrased.

Bibliography

Aarne, Antti and Stith Thompson. 1961. *The Types of the Folktale,* 2nd ed. Folklore Fellows Communications no. 184, Helsinki.

Abramovitsh, Hirsh. 1931. "A litvish shtetl." In *Af khurves fun milkhomes un mehumes,* ed. Moyshe Shalit, Farlag gegnt-komitet "Yekopo," Vilna.

Anderson, Walter. 1921. "Der Schwank von Kaiser und Abt bei den Minsker Juden." In *Acta et commentationes Universitatis Dorpatensis,* vol. 1, no. 4.

——— 1923. *Kaiser und Abt.* Folklore Fellows Communications no. 42, Helsinki.

An-ski, Shloyme (pen name of Shloyme-Zanvl Rappoport). 1915. *Dos yidishe etnografishe program,* L. J. Shternberg, ed., part 1: *Der mentsh.* Di yidishe etnografishe ekspeditsye inem nomen fun Baron Herts Ginzburg, St. Petersburg.

——— 1925. *Folklor un etnografye: Gezamlte shriftn,* vol. 15. Farlag An-ski, Vilna–Warsaw–New York.

Bastomski, Shloyme. 1925–26. *Yidishe folks-mayses un legendes,* vol. 1: *Legendes vegn Besht*; vol. 2: *R. Yoysef dela Reyna.* Farlag di naye yidishe folkshul, Vilna.

——— 1928–31. *Amol iz geven . . . : yidishe folks-mayses.* Farlag di naye yidishe folkshul, Vilna.

——— 1938. *Mayselekh vegn Motke Khabad.* Vilna.

Ben-Amos, Dan. 1967. *Narrative Forms in the Haggadah: Structural Analysis.* Ph.D. diss., Indiana University Microfilms no. 67-15064.

——— 1976a. *Folklore Genres.* University of Texas Press, Austin.

——— 1976b. "Talmudic Tall Tales." In *Folklore Today: A Festschrift for Richard M. Dorson,* Degh, Glassie, and Oinas, eds., Indiana University Press, Bloomington, pp. 25–43.

Ben-Amos, Dan, and Jerome R. Mintz. 1970. *In Praise of the Baal Shem Tov: Shivhei ha-Besht.* Indiana University Press, Bloomington.

Ben Yehezkel, Mordecai. 1961. *Sippur Ha-Maasiyot.* Dvir Ltd., Tel Aviv.

Berger, Abraham. 1938. "The Literature of Jewish Folklore." *Journal of Jewish Bibiography* 1(1):12–20; 1(2):40–49.

Bergman, J. 1919. *Die Legenden der Juden.* Schwetshcke & Sohn, Berlin.

Bernshtein, Ignaz. 1908. *Shprikhverter un redensarten,* 2nd rev. ed. Yoysef Fisher, Warsaw.

Bialostotzky, Benyomin Yankev. 1962. *Di mesholim fun dubner maged.* CYCO, New York.

Bin Gorion, [Berdyczewsky], Micha Joseph. 1976. *Mimekor Yisrael: Classical Jewish Folktales.* Ed., Emanuel Bin Gorion, Indiana University Press, Bloomington.

Blum-Dobkin, Toby. 1977. *Yiddish Folktales about Jesters: A Problem in Structural Analysis and Genre Definition.* Working Papers in Yiddish and East European Jewish Studies, No. 22, YIVO, New York.

Bribram, Gershon. 1965. *Fourteen Jewish Folktales from Hungary.* Israel Folktale Archive Series, no. 10, Haifa.

Buber, Martin. 1947–48. *Tales of the Hasidim.* Schocken Books, New York.

Buloff, Joseph. 1986. "Fun altn markplats." In *Di goldene keyt,* vol. 18, pp. 159–60.

Cahan, Yehude-Leyb. 1928. "Yidishe folksmayses." In *Pinkes* (YIVO, New York), 1(1):65–128, 321–64.

1929. "Yidishe folksmayses." In *Pinkes* (YIVO, New York), 2(1):35–56.

1931. *Yidishe folks-mayses.* YIVO, Vilna.

1938. *Yidisher folklor: Filologishe shriftn fun YIVO* no. 5, YIVO, Vilna.

1940. *Yidishe folks-mayses.* YIVO Filologishe sektsye, Vilna.

1952. "Vegn yidishe folksmayses," in *Shtudyes vegn Yidisher folksshafung.* Ed., Max Weinreich, YIVO, New York, pp. 53–57.

1957. *Yidishe folkslider mit melodyes.* Ed., Max Weinreich, YIVO, New York.

Dan, Joseph. 1968. "Research Techniques for Hasidic Tales." In *Fourth World Congress of Jewish Studies,* World Union of Jewish Studies, Jerusalem, vol. 2, pp. 53–57.

Dawidowicz, Lucy S., ed. 1967. *The Golden Tradition: Jewish Life and Thought in Eastern Europe.* Holt, Rinehart, and Winston, New York.

Epshteyn, Nekhama. 1938. "Notes on Jokes and Humorous Stories." In *Yidisher folklor: Filologishe shriftn fun YIVO* no. 5, ed., Y.-L. Cahan, pp. 319–21.

Etnografishe Komisye. 1931. *Vos iz azoyns yidishe etnografye? Hantbikhl far zamler.* Organizatsye fun der yidisher visnshaft. no. 6, YIVO, Vilna.

Fus, Dvora. 1969. *Seven Bags of Gold: Seven Yiddish Folktales from Lithuania.* Israel Folktale Archive Series, no. 25, Haifa.

Gaster, Moses. 1924. *The Exempla of the Rabbis.* Asia Publishing Company, London and Leipzig.

1934. *Ma'aseh Book.* Jewish Publication Society, Philadelphia.

1971. *Studies and Texts in Folklore, Magic, Medieval Romance, Hebrew Apocrypha, and Samaritan Archaeology.* Ktav, New York.

Ginzberg, Louis. 1909–38. *The Legends of the Jews,* 7 vols. Jewish Publication Society, Philadelphia.

1937. "Jewish Folklore: East and West." In *Independence, Convergence, and Borrowing.* Harvard University Press, Boston, pp. 89–107.

Goebel, Franz M. 1932. *Jüdische Motive in Märchenhaften Erzählungsgut.* Ph.D. diss., Greifswald Universitat, Gleiwitz.

Gross, Naftoli. 1955. *Mayselekh un mesholim.* Aber Press, New York.

Grunwald, Max. 1952. "Zikhroynes un briv: kapitlekh fun an oytobiografye." *YIVO-bleter,* vol. 36, 241–51.

Gutter, Malka. 1969. *Honor Your Mother: Twelve Folktales from Buczacz.* Israel Folktale Archive Series, no. 23, Haifa.

Hechel, Edna. 1983. "A Bibliography of Dov Noy's Writings in Folkloristics and Talmudic-Midrashic Literatures." In *Folklore Center Research Studies: Studies in Aggadic and Jewish Folklore,* I. Ben-Ami and Joseph Dan, eds., Jerusalem.

Heschel, Abraham Joshua. 1950. *The Earth Is the Lord's: The Inner World of the Jew in Eastern Europe.* Henry Schuman, New York.

Holdes, A. 1960. *Mayses, vitsn un shpitselekh fun Hershele Ostropolyer.* Farlag Yidishbukh, Warsaw.

Holomshtok, L. 1930. "Der yidisher lebnshteyger in 18tn yorhundert." *Tsaytshrift* no. 4, 85–120.

Jason, Heda. 1970. "The Russian Criticism of the 'Finnish School' in Folktale Scholarship." *Norveg,* no. 14, 285–94.

Kipnis, Menahem. 1930. *Khelemer mayses.* Farlag Sh. Tsuker, Warsaw.

Kirshenblatt-Gimblett, Barbara. 1972a. "Problemen fun der yidisher folklorterminologye." *Yidishe shprakh,* no. 31, 42–48.

1972b. *Traditional Storytelling in the Toronto Jewish Community.* Ph.D. diss., Indiana University Microfilms no. 73-2724.

1974. "The Concept and the Varieties of Storytelling Performance in East European Jewish Culture." In *Explorations in the Ethnography of Speaking,* Bauman and Sherzer, eds., Cambridge University Press, New York, pp. 282–308.

1975. "A Parable in Context: A Social Interactional Analysis of Storytelling Performance." In *Folklore: Performance and Communication,* Ben-Amos and Goldstein, eds., Mouton, The Hague, pp. 283–308.

1986. "Reading List: Jewish Folklore and Ethnology: Towards an Intellectual History." In *Jewish Folklore and Ethnology Newsletter,* 6(1–2): 19–23.

Lehman, Shmuel. 1923. "Ganovim un gneyve." In *Bay undz yidn,* M. Vanvild, ed., Graubard, Warsaw, pp. 43–91.

1933a. "Elyohu hanovi in der folks-fantazye: mayses un legendes." In *Arkhiv far yidisher shprakh-visnshaft, literatur-forshung un etnologye,* Noyekh Prilutski and Shmuel Lehman, eds., Nayer Farlag, Warsaw, pp. 115–78.

1933b. "Folksmayselekh un anekdotn mit nigunim." In *Arkhiv far yidisher shprakh-visnshaft, literatur-forshung un etnologye,* Noyekh Prilutski and Shmuel Lehman, eds., Nayer Farlag, Warsaw, pp. 355–432.

Lifschutz, Ezekiel. 1952. "Merrymakers and Jesters Among Jews." *YIVO Annual of Jewish Social Science* vol. 7, pp. 43–83.

Liptzin, Sol. 1947. *Peretz.* YIVO, New York.

Litwin, A. (pen name of Shmuel Hurwitz). 1916–17. *Yidishe neshomes* (vol. 3, *Lite;* vol. 4, *Galitsye*). Folksbildung Publishers, New York.

Lüthi, Max. 1982. *The European Folktale.* Institute for the Study of Human Issues, Philadelphia.

Margoshes, Joseph. 1929. "Mayselekh vegn Khoyzekh." *Pinkes,* (YIVO, New York) vol. 2, 57–61.

Mark, Yudl. 1951. "Vos azoyns iz yidisher folklor?" *Yidisher kemfer,* April 20, pp. 61–74; May 18, pp. 9–15.

Meitlis, Jakob. 1933. *Das Ma'assebuch: seine Entstehung und Quellengeschichte.* Buchhandlung Rubin Mass, Berlin.

Menes, Abraham. 1955. *Fun undzer oytser: Elyohu hanovi–agodes un folks-mayses.* CYCO, New York.

Mintz, Jerome R. 1968. *Legends of the Hasidim: An Introduction to Hasidic Culture and Oral Tradition in the New World.* University of Chicago Press, Chicago.

Mitteilungen zur jüdischen Volkskunde. 1898–1929. (Title varies: *Mitteilungen der Gesellschaft für jüdische Volkskunde* [1898–1904]; *Jahrbuch für jüdische Volkskunde* [1923–29]).

Mlotek, Eleanor Gordon. 1978. "Soviet-Yiddish Folklore Scholarship." *Musica Judaica* 2(1): 73–90.

Noy (Neuman), Dov. 1954. "Motif-Index of Talmudic-Midrashic Literature." Ph.D. diss., Indiana University Microfilms no. 8792.

    1955. *Taktsir hamivtah letipusey hama'asiyot ulemotivey hasifrut ha'ammamit.* Jerusalem.

    1959. *Ma'asiyot Am be-Yidish.* Jerusalem.

    1966. "Blood Libels in the Folktales of the Heterogeneous Communities of Israel." *Mahanayim* no. 110, 32–51.

    1972. "Folklore." Entry in *Encyclopaedia Judaica,* Keter, Jerusalem. vol. 7, pp. 1374–1410.

    1976. *The Jewish Animal Tale of Oral Tradition.* Israeli Folktale Archive Series, no. 29, Haifa.

    1980. "Eighty Years of Jewish Folkloristics: Achievements and Tasks." In *Studies in Jewish Folklore,* Frank Talmage, ed., Association for Jewish Studies, Cambridge, Mass., pp. 1–12.

Noy, Meir. 1968. *East European Jewish Cante Fables.* Israel Folktale Archive Series, no. 20, Haifa.

Olsvanger, Immanuel. 1931. *Rosinkess mit mandlen,* 2nd ed. Schweitzer Gesellschaft für Volkskunde, Basle.

    1947. *Royte pomerantsen.* Schocken Books, New York.

1949. *L'chayim! Jewish Wit and Humor.* Schocken Books, New York.

Patai, Raphael. 1946. "Problems and Tasks of Jewish Folklore and Ethnography." *Journal of American Folklore,* vol. 59, 25–39.

Patai, R. F., F. L. Utley, and D. Noy, eds. 1960. *Studies in Biblical and Jewish Folklore.* Indiana University Press, Bloomington.

Paucker, Arnold. 1973. "Di yidishe nuskhoes fun shildberg bukh." *YIVO bleter,* vol. 44, 59–77.

Pipe, Shmuel Zanvl. 1941. *"Napolyon in yidishn folklor."* In *Yidn in Frankraykh,* Elias Tcherikower, ed., YIVO, New York, vol. 1, pp. 153–89.

1968. *Twelve Folktales from Sanok.* Israel Folktale Archive Series, no. 15, Haifa.

Prilutski (Prylucki), Noyakh, ed. 1912–17. *Zamlbikher far yidishn folklor, filologye un kultur-geshikhte.* Vols. 1 and 2, Nayer Farlag, Warsaw.

Prilutski, Noyekh and Shmuel Lehman, eds. 1926–33. *Arkhiv far yidisher shprakhvisnshaft, literatur-forshung un etnologye.* Nayer Farlag, Warsaw.

Propp, Vladimir. 1968. *Morphology of the Folktale,* 2nd ed. University of Texas Press, Austin.

Rappoport, Angelo Solomon. 1937. *The Folklore of the Jews.* Soncino Press, London.

Ravnitski (Rawnizky), Yehoshua-Khone. 1922. *Yidishe vitsn.* Moriya, Berlin.

Rekhtman, Avrom. 1958. *Yidishe Etnografye un folklor: Memuarn fun der An-ski expeditsye.* YIVO, Buenos Aires.

Roskies, David. 1975. *The Genres of Yiddish Popular Literature: 1790–1860.* Working Papers in Yiddish and East European Jewish Studies, no. 8, YIVO, N.Y.

Rubinshteyn, Shmuel. 1937. *Shriftn fun a yidishn folklorist.* Yoyvl-komitet, Vilna.

Scholem, Gershom Gerhard. 1941. *Major Trends in Jewish Mysticism.* Schocken, Jerusalem.

1965. *On the Kabbalah and Its Symbolism.* Schocken Books, New York.

Schwartzbaum, Haim. 1968. *Studies in Jewish and World Folklore.* Walter de Gruyter, Berlin.

Segel, Benyomin Volf. 1892. "Abderiten von Heute unter den Juden." *Am Urquell* 3(1):28ff.

1893. "Materialy do etnografii Zydow." In *Zbior wiadomosci do antropologii krajowej.* (Akademia Umiejetnosci, Cracow, Komisja antropologii i prehistorii), vol. 17, pp. 261–332.

1904. "Eliah der Prophet: Eine Studie zur jüdischen Volks und Sagenkunde." In *Ost und West,* Berlin, pp. 677ff.

Shatzky, Jacob. 1938. "Y.-L. Cahan (1881–1937)." In *Yorbukh fun Amopteyl fun YIVO,* vol. 1, pp. 9–38. 1941. "Shmuel Lehman." *YIVO-bleter* vol. 18, pp. 80–83.

Shneyer, Zalman. 1939. *Antireligyeze mayses un vertlekh.* Farlag Der Emes, Moscow.

Shtern, Yekhiel. 1950. *Kheyder un besmedresh.* YIVO, New York.

Sider, Fishl. 1968. *Seven Folktales from Boryslaw.* Israel Folktale Archive Series, no. 19, Haifa.

Slotnick, Susan. 1976. *The Contributions of the Soviet Yiddish Folklorists.* Working Papers in Yiddish and East European Jewish Studies, no. 20, YIVO, New York.

Soifer, Paul. 1978. *Soviet Jewish Folkloristics and Ethnography: An Institutional History, 1918–1948.* Working Papers in Yiddish and East European Jewish Studies, no. 30, YIVO, New York.

Sydow, C. W. von. 1948. "Kategorien der Prosa-Volksdichtung." In *Selected Papers on Folklore,* Rosenkilde and Bagger, Copenhagen, pp. 60–88.

Thompson, Stith. 1946. *The Folktale.* Holt, Rinehart, and Winston, New York.

1955–58. *Motif-Index of Folk Literature,* 2nd ed. Indiana University Press, Bloomington.

Trachtenberg, Joshua. 1939. *Jewish Magic and Superstition: A Study in Folk Religion.* Jewish Publication Society, Philadelphia.

Vanvild, M. (pen name of Moses Joseph Dickstein), ed. 1923. *Bay undz yidn.* Graubard, Warsaw.

Weinreich, Beatrice Silverman. 1954. "Four Yiddish Variants of the Master-Thief Tale." In *The Field of Yiddish,* vol. 1, Linguistic Circle of New York, New York, pp. 199–213.

1957. "The Prophet Elijah in Modern Yiddish Folktales." M.A. thesis, Columbia University, New York.

1965. "Genres and Types of Yiddish Folktales about the Prophet Elijah." In *The Field of Yiddish,* vol. 2, Mouton, The Hague, pp. 202–31.

1978. "Formal Problems in the Study of the Yiddish Proverb." *YIVO Annual of Jewish Social Science,* vol. 17, pp. 1–20.

Weinreich, Max. 1926. "Lantukh, di geshikhte fun a heymishn nit gutn." In *Shriftn fun YIVO.* vol. 1, YIVO, Vilna.

1952. Epilogue to Y.-L. Cahan, *Shtudyes vegn Yidisher folksshafung.* YIVO, New York, pp. 352–66.

1980. *History of the Yiddish Language.* Shlomo Noble, trans., YIVO/University of Chicago Press, Chicago.

Weinreich, Uriel and Beatrice. 1959. *Yiddish Language and Folklore: A Selective Bibliography for Research.* Mouton, The Hague.

Wiener, Leo. 1899. *The History of Yiddish Literature in the 19th Century.* New York.

1902. "Märchen und Schwänke." In *Mitteilungen der Gesellschaft für Jüdische Volkskunde,* no. 10, pp. 98–121.

Zborowski, M., and E. Herzog. 1952. *Life Is with People: The Jewish Little-Town of Eastern Europe.* Schocken Books, New York.

Zfatman, Sarah. 1985. *Yiddish Narrative Prose from Its Beginnings to "Shivhei ha-Besht": An Annotated Bibliography.* Hebrew University, Jerusalem.

Zinberg, Israel. 1932. "Vegn vanderndike motivn in yidishn folklor." *YIVO bleter* vol. 3, pp. 330–36.

———. 1975. *A History of Jewish Literature: Old Yiddish Literature from Its Origins to the Haskalah Period.* Vol. 7, Bernard Martin, trans., Hebrew Union College and Ktav, Cleveland and London.

BEATRICE SILVERMAN WEINREICH (editor), a research associate in folklore at the YIVO Institute for Jewish Research in New York, has published numerous articles in academic journals on Yiddish culture and folklore, as well as a basic bibliography for research in that field. She has co-edited the journal *Yidisher folklor* and has contributed to the *Language and Culture Atlas of Ashkenazic Jewry,* the first volume of which is forthcoming. Currently, she is preparing a collection of Yiddish folktales in their original language.

LEONARD WOLF (translator) is a fiction writer, dramatist, poet, biographer, and one of our foremost translators of Yiddish. His most recent books include *The False Messiah,* a novel; *The Family Mashber,* a translation from the Yiddish; and *Bluebeard: The Life and Crimes of Gilles de Rais.* He is a Professor Emeritus of English and Creative Writing at San Francisco State University, and is presently translator-in-residence at the YIVO Institute.

THE PANTHEON FAIRY TALE AND FOLKLORE LIBRARY

African Folktales, selected and retold by Roger D. Abrahams

Afro-American Folktales, selected and retold by Roger D. Abrahams

America in Legend, by Richard M. Dorson

American Indian Myths and Legends, selected and edited
by Richard Erdoes and Alfonso Ortiz

Arab Folktales, translated and edited by Inea Bushnaq

Chinese Fairy Tales and Fantasies, translated and edited by Moss Roberts

The Complete Grimm's Fairy Tales, introduced by Padraic Colum

Eighty Fairy Tales, by Hans Christian Andersen

An Encyclopedia of Fairies, by Katharine Briggs

Favorite Folktales from Around the World, edited by Jane Yolen

Folktales from India, edited by A. K. Ramanujan

Folk-Tales of the British Isles, edited by Kevin Crossley-Holland

French Folktales, by Henri Pourrat, selected by C. G. Bjurström,
and translated by Royall Tyler

Gods and Heroes, by Gustav Schwab

Irish Folktales, edited by Henry Glassie

Italian Folktales, selected and retold by Italo Calvino

Japanese Folktales, selected, edited, and translated by Royall Tyler

The Norse Myths, introduced and retold by Kevin Crossley-Holland

Northern Tales, selected and edited by Howard Norman

Norwegian Folk Tales, collected by Peter Christen Asbjørnsen and Jørgen Moe

The Old Wives' Fairy Tale Book, edited by Angela Carter

Russian Fairy Tales, collected by Aleksandr Afanas'ev

The Victorian Fairy Tale Book, edited by Michael Patrick Hearn

Yiddish Folktales, edited by Beatrice Silverman Weinreich,
translated by Leonard Wolf